W. Friend — What
one 130's Adrienne
work on production.
i.e. our
schedule,

Call Jerry in New
York's offer on
employee benefits

LAND RUSH

Other books by Mark Stevens:

The Big Eight

Model

Like No Other Store in the World: The Inside Story
of Bloomingdale's

MARK
STEVENS

LAND

RUSH

McGRAW-HILL BOOK COMPANY

New York   St. Louis   San Francisco
Hamburg   Mexico   Toronto

1 2 3 4 5 6 7 8 9 D O C D O C 8 7 6 5 4

ISBN 0-07-061273-0

LIBRARY OF CONGRESS CATALOGING IN PUBLICATION DATA

Stevens, Mark, 1947–
Land rush.
1. Real estate business.   I. Title.
HD1375.S743 1984   333.33   83-24924
ISBN 0-07-061273-0

Book design by Virginia Soulé

To C, H and JB

Contents

Introduction

There have always been people of the land. Through the centuries—while the fashions favored investments in jewels, precious metals, and corporate securities—real estate visionaries quietly amassed raw acreage, abandoned farms, vast woodlands, deserted islands, antebellum mansions. This preference for terra firma, often passed from one generation to the next, rewarded the faithful with long-term appreciation and a rock hard asset base that proved resilient to even the most jarring economic crises. Save for occasional, generally short-term declines in their portfolios' market value, the landed families maintained their wealth and used the borrowing power this provided to acquire more mansions, more acreage, more barren farmlands often from others forced to sell (at distress prices) to cover losses on more vulnerable investments.

Franklin Delano Roosevelt, whose considerable business acumen is often overshadowed by his political skills, observed that "real estate is about the safest investment in the world."

Andrew Carnegie had similar praise for real estate, noting that "ninety percent of all millionaires became so through owning real estate."

Respect for real estate's power as a wealth-producing asset spread to the middle class only with the meteoric rise in post World War II residential property values. As the equity in their suburban splits doubled, tripled, and quadrupled in the decade between John Kennedy's assassination and Ronald Reagan's inauguration, millions of Americans were swept along in a "land rush," for the first time buying and selling real property much as they traded stocks and bonds. Many have profited handsomely, turning $100,000 investments into $250,000, $500,000, $1 million or more. Local merchants, doctors, stockbrokers, smitten by land fever, have reinvested their gains in shopping centers, apartment buildings, housing developments, swelling the ranks of real estate entrepreneurs well beyond the once exclusive fraternity of landed families.

But this widespread participation obscures the fact that a coterie of investors, brokers, and developers at the center of the land rush still manipulate the market, control the choicest properties, and measure their profits in the hundreds of millions—in the billions of dollars. Some, with deep roots in real estate, constructed the very foundation on which the land rush is built; others have moved in after the fact, shrewdly capitalizing on the growing infatuation with real property. In spite of their widely disparate methods and backgrounds, all exhibit a strikingly similar determination to dominate a key segment of the real estate market, to serve as catalysts (rather than passive investors) in the creation of wealth and the escalation of property values, and to bring to real estate a meticulously constructed business strategy that assures a competitive advantage over the bit players who rely on luck and inflation to fuel their relatively meager profits.

Land Rush focuses on these central powers both in residential and commercial real estate. Tracing the emergence of the sophisticated brokerage from the creation of the stock exchange for real estate more than a half century ago to the recent sale of Ronald Reagan's Pacific Palisades home, *Land Rush* observes the super brokers at work in the enclaves of wealth and power from Greenwich, Connecticut, to Beverly Hills. We learn how they use celebrity sales (singer Kenny Rogers' purchase of the most expensive residential property in the United States) to build a glamorous image that is fundamental to their powerful and highly profitable property marketing systems. And we see how major financial services institutions, insurance companies, and Wall Street investment houses are committing enormous resources to establishing and securing positions in the residential brokerage business, forcing independent brokers, now an endangered species, to battle for survival.

On the commercial side, *Land Rush* peers into the secretive world of the urban developer, revealing the newest major forces in American real estate and following the international odyssey of a landed family that may well be the wealthiest in the world. By observing the behind-the-scenes evolution of their grandest deals—including the largest commercial lease in history—we learn how these last of the laissez-faire capitalists earn and risk hundreds of millions on high-risk ventures; how they force multinational giants to bid for their services; and how, as a famed property consultant put it, "they are born to real estate the way Mozart was born to music."

Land Rush is a story of land and of money; of business minds and corporate strategies; of failure of conflict and of extraordinary success. But it is also a glimpse into how real estate's most dominant forces structure deals, negotiate sales, secure brokerage listings, assemble properties, arrange financing, attract joint ventures, and create ingenious marketing networks that give property liquidity and ever-greater value. This, the author believes, will offer invaluable lessons in real estate brokerage, development, and investing. There are no greater models for success than those who have written the rules.

I

RESIDENTIAL REAL ESTATE

1

Previews: Launching the Stock Market for Real Estate

Owning a home is still the American dream. Previews goes one step beyond. It sells dream houses.

Merv Griffin

It is a lovely jewel of a place, set high on the southern slope of the Santa Monica Mountains. The kind of secluded setting that makes the upper Riviera section of Pacific Palisades so dear to the old moneyed Californians who run the banks and the insurance companies and who regard Beverly Hills as a teeming ghetto for the nouveau riche.

Built for Nancy and Ronald Reagan in 1957, the home reflects the couple's California state of mind: touches of redwood, Palos Verdes fieldstone, and an airy floor plan that flows toward the octagonal pool, the bougainvillea, and the view. And what a view. By day and night there is a sweeping panorama of the Queen's Necklace, a coastal archipelago composed of Santa Monica Bay, Los Angeles Airport, and Palos Verdes.

Soon after assuming the presidency, Reagan decided

that the White House and his Santa Barbara ranch were home enough even for the First Family and that the time had come to turn a handsome profit on the Pacific Palisades contemporary twenty-three years after it was built for him as an all-electric GE showcase. Reagan's long-time friend and business adviser Justin Dart, chairman of Dart Industries, agreed to oversee the transaction and turned first to the Brentwood, California office of Coldwell Banker, the nation's largest* real estate brokers.

But Coldwell's resident manager in charge of the office, suggested that a third party be called in to give the home wider exposure and hopefully to speed the sale. When Dart agreed, a national realty marketing firm headquartered in a woodsy corporate park 3,000 miles from the San Andreas fault was called in.

"I was invited to meet with the Reagans to discuss the marketing of their home," says Bruce Wennerstrom, the highly regarded chief executive of Greenwich, Connecticut-based Previews, Inc. A dashing patrician whose blond-haired, blue-eyed good looks are reminiscent of the "thank you, Paine Webber" man, Wennerstrom moves peripatetically about his spacious office—its tasteful appointments obscured by a crazy-quilt blanket of property brochures, magazines, video tapes, contracts, appraisals, blueprints, renderings, brokerage agreements, and a collection of mildewed styrofoam coffee cups. "Although I rarely meet with buyers or sellers—our field people and local brokers share that responsibility—this was the president of the United States calling."

He caught the first wide-body to Los Angeles. Flying over the nation's heartland, Wennerstrom mused about the strange psychology of the land rush. That tiny pocket of affluence amounting to only a speck of the United States land mass accounted for a disproportionate share of real estate dollar transactions and for a lopsided percentage of his firm's commissions.

Premier real estate in the United States has soared in

* For combined commercial and residential real estate.

value, not because of its intrinsic worth, but because so many dollars are chasing so few properties. While vast stretches of magnificent woodlands are ignored at $500 an acre, the rich outbid each other for million-dollar Southampton lots just wide enough for beach bungalows. A property's size and its inherent beauty may not be as important as its place in the social hierarchy.

"It's a matter of fashion," Wennerstrom says. "All the rich want to live in the same few places. So once a community gets on the itinerary of the well-to-do—once it becomes fashionable to live, winter or summer there—then its real estate transcends standard valuation formulas. It becomes greater than the sum of its parts. Its lofty price is a reflection of the fact that there simply is not enough to go around. Not in that tiny enclave where all the big spenders are competing for a strip of earth."

Upon his arrival in California, Nancy and Ronald escorted Wennerstrom on a tour of their house, showing off the place much like any other well-to-do couple putting their pride and joy on the market—boasting about the spacious rooms, the sunny atrium, the comfortable master bedroom complete with stone fireplace. This was to be expected. Affluent sellers typically think their homes to be the standard of style and beauty. It is the broker's job to bring them down to earth tactfully, pointing out that nothing, after all, is perfect and here's where the hidden faults lie. But there wasn't much to dislike about the Reagan house. Previews' president—whose eyes like computer scans instantly calculate property values—thought it attractive, in fine condition, and easy to sell. He liked the expansive living room (33 feet by 20½ feet) with its traces of fieldstone and conversation corner of bleached redwood, the elegant den overlooking the pool and the ocean, and the roomy, well-equipped kitchen. Yes, he considered it an easy sale.

That's until the Reagans excused themselves and handed him over to their business advisers. One version of what went on within the inner sanctum goes like this: No sooner had the heavy oak door shut behind the First Couple than the advisers buttonholed the visiting broker, asking how much the house was worth. When they were told "$1.1 million," they demanded that this be doubled to reflect the property's status as a former residence of the First Family. Informed that this was wildly over market value, they nevertheless held their ground, agreeing only to a slightly reduced asking price of $1.9 million.

What the president's advisers refused to accept is that the Pacific Palisades home, for all its handsome appointments, is not world class. Comfortable, airy and well-situated though it is, the house is also rather characterless—Ozzie & Harriet's archetypal suburban American gothic blown up to 5,000 square feet. It lacks the exclusive features—the rolling horse pastures, the dune-scaped beachfront, or the medieval timbers—that liberate the truly pedigreed properties from the bounds of comparable value and make them worthy of multimillion-dollar price tags. That a living president of the United States called it home doesn't qualify.

The property languished on the market, failing to attract a single legitimate bid for the asking price. The only offer that purported to pay the $1.9 million price was regarded by the broker as a publicity stunt. The would-be buyer— who timed his bid with the distribution of press releases promoting himself and his business interests—offered only $300,000 up front and then a moratorium on additional payments for seven years. The offer was rejected out of hand.

Although the brokers received a half dozen serious bids, all were substantially below the asking price. The market's appraisal of the property—the only one that ultimately matters in real estate—was far closer to Previews' estimate than the President's. A year after putting the property up for sale, Reagan's advisers conceded that they would have to downscale their aspirations to reflect economic realities. Humbled by the free market mechanism that is at the heart of his administration's fiscal programs, Reagan agreed to accept an offer of $1.1 million.

Why is Previews called on to sell presidential properties? Why is its name linked with many of the world's extraordi-

nary real estate transactions? Why is it at the heart of the
land rush?

First, it is not what it appears to be. In spite of its
resemblance to a real estate brokerage firm, in spite of the
fact that its key executives are real estate brokers, in spite
of the fact that it is licensed to sell real estate in forty-
three states, Previews is not so much a brokerage firm as
an international marketing organization whose principal
product happens to be real estate. This is what distinguishes
it from the local and national brokers it is often compared
to and what gives it an integral role in the land rush. The
company is built on an ingenious system that elevates it
above the competition for local brokerage, makes it privy
to thousands of the most sought-after listings, and motivates
the brokerage community to work, albeit grudgingly, for its
benefit. Although Previews wins many prestigious listings,
such as the Reagan property, on the strength of its glamorous image, its real forte is in the marketing of extravagant
properties that need exposure beyond their local market.

To understand how this works, we must grasp the firm's
founding principles. Previews traces its roots back a half
century to a fraternity of young Wall Street executives and
real estate brokers who were united by a common conviction
that big money could be made by creating a stock exchange
for real estate. They believed that property, like securities,
would increase in value in direct proportion to its liquidity
and that people would invest in land, as they did in stocks,
providing they were assured of finding a buyer when the
time came to sell.

With this in mind, the youthful entrepreneurs set out
to create a real estate market mechanism and incorporated
their company's founding concept in its advertising slogan
"Buy Real Estate Like You Buy Stocks."

John Colquin Tysen, an early Previews executive who
became the firm's president in the 1950s, explained the idea
behind the new venture this way:

If it weren't for the New York Stock Exchange, how
would a man in Westport who wants to sell a hundred

shares of something even know there's a woman in Duluth who wants to buy them? The securities market was never liquid until some of the boys downtown got together and said "Look chums, let's get together for a few hours each day and see who's got what and who wants what." That's the kind of service we try to provide in real estate. Let's say a savvy broker in Duluth is approached by a woman who's planning to move to Westport and wants something in French Provincial there. The broker can do one of three things.

He can tell her to go away and find a Westport broker, or he can ask his secretary who sent in that brochure about a Westport French Provincial they threw away several months back, or he can call Previews and we'll mail him information about a whole batch of French Provincials—in Westport and a lot of other places.*

But there was more to the Previews' concept. Yes, the firm would be a clearinghouse for real estate, but one with a technological twist. The entrepreneurial visionary most responsible for Previews founding, Henderson Talbot, had the brainstorm of uniting buyers and sellers through a video hookup much the way stock investors were linked by ticker tape.

An experienced broker with the New York real estate firm of Douglas L. Elliman, Talbot believed he'd hit on an ideal way to circumvent the dual obstacles of time and distance that often impede the sale of major properties. Rather than asking prospective buyers to sacrifice a few days' work (and many thousands of dollars) flying off to inspect available mansions in Newport, Palm Beach, or Southampton, Talbot decided to bring the mansions to the buyers, so to speak. Clearly a pioneer in the use of technology as a marketing tool, his "better idea" was to dispatch film crews to shoot

* E. J. Kahn, Jr., in *The New Yorker* © 1956. Reprinted by permission.

motion pictures of the properties, later screening them for prospective buyers in the comfort and convenience of Previews' New York offices. If all went as planned, sellers would request that their properties be filmed, buyers would flock to the screenings, and Previews would earn commissions on the resulting transactions.

Fingers crossed, the founders christened their fledgling venture the "See-It-First-Bureau" and opened for business in 1933. The results were disappointing. Two major flaws nearly sent the young firm into bankruptcy. First, the prospect of being coddled like millionaires in Previews' elegant offices appealed to many whose net worth was several zeros from the six figures then required to buy a major property. Talbot discovered that an alarming number of his early prospects hadn't the means to purchase a bungalow, much less a Southampton estate. They simply liked the idea of posing rich—of waltzing up to Previews' screening room for a dash of attentive service and a rare glimpse of how the other half lives.

"An occasional deadbeat must be accepted as part of the business but if they're swarming all over like locusts, you're in trouble," Wennerstrom says, recalling the company's early days.

> Wasting half your time catering to impostors leaves precious little time to make any money. So my predecessors established procedures to weed out the deadbeats— procedures we use to this day. Most important is to screen prospects at the outset. When someone calls us to request an inspection of a celebrity's home, we confirm that the caller is a qualified buyer before taking him out to see the place. Prominent people are usually listed in something on the order of Debrett's Peerage or Standard & Poor's Register of Corporate Executives. We check these volumes carefully. Of course, impostors still manage to wriggle through the screening, but a little homework on the broker's part can reduce the incidence of this. Previews' early management discovered

this: Reference checks kept most of the pretenders out
of the company's screening room.

But "See-It-First-Bureau's" most damaging problem
was that it allowed legitimate clients to tap the firm's services for too small a fee. Initial terms called for property
owners to pay an upfront charge of fifty dollars for listing
with the video clearinghouse and 4 percent of the sales price
if the property was sold. The retainer proved wholly inadequate, falling far short of the costs incurred in shooting
and presenting Previews films.

There was also a psychological impediment. The get-
what-you-pay-for skepticism of the super rich holds that any
service valued at fifty dollars could hardly succeed at the
formidable task of marketing baronial mansions. Saddled
with this less than auspicious image and burdened by costs
that dwarfed its fifty-dollar retainer, the company, now renamed Previews, lost a quarter of a million dollars in its
first seven years of operations. It didn't help that some of
its biggest sales were made to the bureau's own executives
who were so mesmerized by the films of lavish homes that
they bought the properties themselves. These in-house deals
did little to relieve the company's fiscal woes.

But a turning point came with Tysen's appointment as
sales manager in May of 1940. A few days later, a client
stopped by his office to inquire about the fee for marketing
a $75,000 home.

"Fif—," Tysen began, and then paused. His nebulous
thoughts about the company's plight had suddenly jelled:
Perhaps the reason Previews had been in the red all along
was that its retainers were too skimpy, and perhaps clients
would not balk at a fee amounting to 1 percent of the asking
price, to be applied against the commissions they would pay
in the event of a sale.

Tysen boldly told his visitor that the initial charge would
be seven hundred and fifty dollars. The man agreed
to it unhesitatingly, and Tysen asked him in an offhand

manner what his reaction would have been if the answer had been fifty dollars. "I'd have thought you were either crazy or crooked," the man replied. "If you took so little and did a lot of work, you ought to have your heads examined for underpaying yourselves. And if you took the fifty and did nothing, you'd be guilty of fraud."*

Previews' management quickly adopted Tysen's ad-lib pricing policy, finding, to their utter delight, that the reaction of the guinea pig client was the rule rather than the exception. Respect for Previews' service clearly rose in tandem with the size of its retainer—listing activity soared and the corporate bank account grew exponentially. The latter was crucial to the company's long-term success. For the first time there was a pool of working capital available for marketing programs. Management put the money to good use, producing slick brochures of listed properties and distributing them to a wide network of well-connected brokers.

Gradually, Previews executives were forced to admit that their cherished motion pictures had to be cast aside in favor of a more aggressive approach. To breathe life into the clearinghouse concept, they had to extend its reach beyond the screening room, bringing properties to prospective buyers' homes and offices via direct mail brochures. Tysen recognized that the novelty of video brokerage was less important than achieving the widest possible market coverage and, in turn, the greatest liquidity. This epiphany gave birth to the company's motto "the broader the exposure, the easier the sale."

Fortunately, market forces started working in sync with management's revamped strategy. As the Previews name became associated with "unique" properties—through its aggressive mailings and steadily increasing sales—and as word of its track record buzzed through the brokerage grapevine, a growing number of once skeptical brokers started calling on the New York marketing organization to

* Ibid.

help sell those listings that needed exposure beyond the local market. Previews, in turn, started developing both the all-important element of self-confidence and the subtle negotiating skills that are the hallmarks of successful brokers. In one case, Previews' suggestion for a coin toss sealed one of the major property transactions of the day.

> Previews arranged another harmonious union of dweller and dwelling in 1947 when Gerard B. Lambert, of Princeton, the author and yachtsman member of the Listerine family, informed the firm one morning that he would like to sell, for $275,000, a five-hundred-acre estate he owned in Virginia. Real estate men often toil for years to find a buyer with serious interest in a place like that, but only a couple of hours after Lambert had sought Previews' assistance, a broker in Norwalk coincidentally called the company to say that a client of his—a West Virginian industrialist named Frank Christopher—was looking for a large estate in Virginia. Before the day was out, the two principals had been in touch with each other. The sale of the estate was all but completed when a hitch—of a sort for which Previews hardly felt responsible—developed over the disposition of a Gilbert Stuart portrait of George Washington that was hanging in the house; Lambert wanted to keep it so badly that he was unimpressed when Christopher offered to toss in an extra twenty-five thousand for it, and Christopher was dubious about taking the place without it. The impasse was finally resolved by the two art lovers flipping a coin. Christopher won, Lambert got the additional twenty-five thousand, George Washington remained in Virginia, and Previews, as its commission on this last-minute windfall, got a *pourboire* of $800.*

Previews sailed through the 1940s, building its marketing network, improving its balance sheet, and showing the world that here indeed was a firm worthy of a lofty position

* Ibid.

in the real estate hierarchy. Its one major blunder during the period was a potentially disastrous diversification into manufacturing. Shortly after World War II, Previews launched a subsidiary, Precision Built Homes, to make and sell cheap prefabricated houses. Intoxicated by the industrial growth of post-war America and fired by its growing confidence in real estate marketing, Previews suffered an early case of the "empire fever" that two decades later would turn many of the nation's corporations into conglomerates. Suffice it to say that Previews got carried away with itself, venturing far afield of the property marketing system it had labored to perfect. It paid dearly for the mistake, writing off more than $200,000 in losses before folding the poorly conceived subsidiary. But there was a silver lining. Management never again strayed from its basic course of business, and this discipline has served the company well.

The modern Previews* —hands down the most successful marketer of luxury homes—is a hybrid of its early concepts and strategies. Still very much the "stock exchange for real estate," it lists more than 400 properties annually, marketing 75 percent of them. Over the years, the firm has refined its marketing tactics, bringing ever greater sophistication to the clearinghouse approach and to the effort to give expensive properties the characteristics of negotiable currency.

Today, two superbly designed and photographed magazines are at the heart of Previews' operations. They serve, much like the floor of the New York Stock Exchange, as a central forum for listing and trading properties. The flagship publication—the annual "Guide to the World's Fine Real Estate"—is essentially a sales catalogue. Luxury properties are presented in artfully photographed four-color advertisements each with about 200 words of copy highlighting the home's "country club ambience," its "Frank Lloyd Wright traditions," or its "27-acre grounds including a brick-walled

* Now, along with Coldwell Banker, Previews is a subsidiary of Sears Roebuck, the retailer turned financial services giant that also owns Allstate Insurance and Dean Witter.

courtyard with patterned walkways, two ponds and a lighted equestrian ring, which is larger than official size." About 80 percent of the ads are Previews listings with the balance placed by independent brokers seeking to tap into Previews' network of home buyers and property investors.

Previews' highly segmented distribution plan gets the "Guide" into the right hands. Paid subscriptions, at the $15 cover price, go to 3,000 upscale realtors and 6,000 affluent individuals with a history of making substantial real estate purchases. Newsstand copies, often prominently displayed alongside such coffee table magazines as *Architectural Digest* and *Interiors*, are sold in the clubby hotel smoke shops of New York's St. Regis, Boston's Ritz Carlton, and Los Angeles' Beverly Wilshire. Complimentary circulation is mailed to chief executives of the Fortune 1000, trust officers of major banks, airline VIP lounges, and assorted oases of the affluent, including plastic surgeons' waiting rooms and art galleries.

By disguising the "Guide" as a magazine, Previews makes its sales material welcome in the homes and offices of the professional and managerial elite. Simply bulk mailing thousands of catalogs to prominent people is not a significant accomplishment. Lists of wealthy individuals, from CEOs to widowed heiresses, are widely available from mail order houses for forty dollars per thousand names. Competing real estate firms can easily blanket the same audience Previews calls its own and can claim to be on equal footing with the Greenwich-based market leader. But they are omitting, intentionally or otherwise, an important point: The great bulk of commercial mail addressed to the Paleys, the Fords, and the Carsons is immediately filed in the wastebasket. Because there is a direct correlation between a person's net worth and the volume of his junk mail—those at the top of the socioeconomic pyramid are subject to a blizzard of the stuff. Most is sifted, screened, and discarded by secretaries, assistants, and housekeepers.

But the strength of Previews' "Guide" is that it makes its way through the selection process and on to the VIP's desk. It succeeds because it has won a place, along with Neiman Marcus's Christmas catalog and Sotheby Parke Bernet's auction letter, in the magazine racks of the rich. By spending lavishly to create the slick appeal of a sophisticated magazine in the tradition of *Town & Country,* and by taking a low-key, soft-sell approach that is more like a securities prospectus than a traditional mail order catalog, Previews has created a marketing tool that slips subliminally into the lifestyle of the target audience. Once through the inner sanctum, the "Guide" makes for enchanted browsing, tempting the well-endowed to add a Vail chalet or a Back Bay townhouse to their portfolio of properties. Among the "Guide's" noted readers, past and present, are Leonard Bernstein, Gerald Ford, Mike Wallace, Jimmy Stewart, Bing Crosby, the Duke of Windsor, Dean Martin, Julie Andrews—all of whom have purchased or listed properties through Previews.

Previews' sister publication, *Homes International,* is a similarly upscale mix of attractive photographs and evocative copy. Published monthly, it is carried as an in-flight magazine by sixteen of the world's major airlines. Here again, the distribution strategy is ingenious. By making the publication available to a captive audience of first-class travelers, *Homes International* introduces Previews services—and its collection of attractive properties—to an ever wider universe of prospects. Like a stockbroker cold calling sales leads, the magazine generates new business and steadily expands the firm's client base.

Homes International is a direct response sales mechanism. Should a reader see something he likes, he'll find in each ad a broker's name and a phone number to call for further information. At the back of the magazine, there are response cards that can be mailed to arrange for personal inspections of any properties in the book.

"But some people can't wait to move through ordinary channels," Wennerstrom notes. "In those first-class airline cabins, you'll find a high concentration of decision makers—I mean people used to running companies or entire industries. If they want to launch a new product or close a manufacturing plant, they pick up the phone and have it done. And if they find themselves enamored of one of our properties, they do much the same. They call and order it. That's exactly how we sold La Cuesta de Camellia to John DeLorean."

The DeLorean episode reveals just how effectively *Homes International* can serve as a catalyst for million-dollar impulse sales. By reaching the hard-to-reach when they are most vulnerable to commercial solicitations—locked as they are in air-tight cabins hurtling through the upper atmosphere at 37,000 feet—it preys on an audience momentarily isolated from the diversions of the office or the film studio.

It was on a TWA flight from New York to the west coast that DeLorean, then divisional vice president in charge of General Motors' Pontiac division, was skimming through the latest edition of *Homes International.* As the 727 made its final approach to the Los Angeles airport, DeLorean, anticipating the landing, was about to replace the magazine in the seat pouch when he found his eyes drawn to the photographs of a stunning adobe ranch house surrounded by brilliant citrus groves on the grounds of San Diego's exclusive Pauma Valley Country Club. The 7,000-square-foot La Cuesta de Camellia, then owned by oil man W. R. Sudenfaden, was tastefully appointed with marble baths, peaked beamed ceilings, skylights, and an aviary wall.

"On the basis of the photographs alone, DeLorean knew that he had to have La Cuesta and that anything later than immediately would be too late," Wennerstrom says. "Suddenly, his pressing business appointments in Los Angeles took a back seat to buying the property that had so completely captivated him. Word has it that minutes after the jet's wheels screeched along the runway, he was on the phone with our local office making arrangements to see La Cuesta. Speaking in the no-nonsense style that characterizes the man, he made it clear that he was going to buy it. And he did. The deal was closed soon after for $975,000."

The year was 1972. DeLorean, then virtually unknown

outside of the auto industry, went on to achieve fame and subsequent notoriety as the precocious vice president of General Motors' massive North American car and truck division, as the rebel who walked away from a half-million-dollar salary and the post position in the race to become GM's next president, as the flamboyant entrepreneur who thrilled the world with the introduction of his own stainless steel dream machine, and as the controversial defendant in a drug smuggling case. In his darkest hour—with his auto manufacturing venture in liquidation and his legal bills mounting faster than his inventory of unsold sports cars—DeLorean asked Previews to sell a now substantially shrunken La Cuesta for more than four times his purchase price. "Only 48 of the original 208 acres were still part of the estate when Mr. DeLorean asked us to remarket it," says Jim Retz, Previews' Los Angeles Vice President. "He'd previously sold off the rest for use as citrus orchards. But the reduction in gross acreage did not interfere in any way with the property's appreciation. That's because in luxury real estate, mass is not the prime consideration; that belongs to the property's major structural features and its location.

La Cuesta's major appeal was always its privacy and seclusion. The sale of the orchards—all of which were outlying lands removed from the main residence—did not detract from this. The home was still encircled by an ample buffer of private property."

The realtors also recognized that La Cuesta, unlike the Reagans' Pacific Palisades home, enjoyed a unique selling point that made it impervious to the restraints of "comparable value" that ordinarily limit a property's market value. La Cuesta is the largest estate situated on the grounds of a private country club anywhere in the United States. Because of this distinction, it could appreciate to the extent of the next wealthy, seclusion-loving buyer's determination to own it.

So when Previews' initial attempt to remarket La Cuesta failed to produce an acceptable deal, the company reversed the traditional remedy for hard-to-sell properties. "We raised

the price from $4 million to $5.25 million," Retz explains.
"Why? Because we knew that the original price had no bearing on the property's difficulties—it was simply a matter
of finding the right buyer. In the meantime, we wanted to
reflect in the asking price improvements Mr. DeLorean had
made in the ranch house and the landscaping during the
first eight months the property was on the market. In addition, there was a general escalation of real estate values
in the area, and we had every right to build that into La
Cuesta."

Retz crystallizes Previews' strategy for marketing
unique homes this way:

> When you have something special, something no one
> else has, you don't panic. You don't slash prices just
> because the place doesn't sell as quickly as you'd like.
> Unique properties often need time to find a buyer. To
> succeed at this end of the real estate business, you need
> patience and the nerve to stand by the properties you
> believe in. If you have access to an international network
> of buyers and investors, you'll find another prominent
> person willing to pay for privacy and seclusion in an
> extraordinary setting and who'll snatch up the property
> the way Mr. DeLorean did. That's the kind of clients
> we have.

Yes and no. Tales of famous people falling wildly in
love with million-dollar properties—of dashing pellmell from
first-class cabins to pay phones to stake their claims—are
grist for Previews' publicity mill, but they can paint a dis-
torted picture of the company. At first glance, the national
marketing firm that traces its roots back to the "See-It-First-
Bureau" appears to live a charmed life, casually matching
moneyed buyers with the world's most desirable homes. But
were it only that simple. Previews' rose-colored self-portrait
omits a rather unattractive blemish. That is, many of its
listings have characteristics that make them difficult to sell.
Few are gobbled up anywhere near as quickly as DeLorean's

purchase of La Cuesta; some take more than a year to sell
and others never move at all. Many have stubbornly resisted
heroic efforts by the local brokers. Were this not the case,
Previews would not be hired. Brokers and owners alike turn
to the "stock exchange for real estate" primarily when their
properties are too costly or exotic for the local market to
absorb, or when there is reason to believe they will fetch
significantly higher prices if exposed to a wider network
of prospective buyers.

Previews' involvement is often contingent on these factors because the firm charges a substantial premium over
local brokerage rates. In most cases, working with Previews
costs a property owner 11 percent of the sales price. Of
this, 6 percent is Previews' marketing fee and 5 percent
goes to the local broker responsible for the sale. For the
largest transactions, Previews' and the local brokers' fees
drop to 3 percent and 2.5 percent respectively after the first
$2.5 million in sales price.

On a $2 million property, hiring Previews costs the
owner an additional $100,000 over a 6 percent local broker-
age rate. What's more, Previews demands an exclusive
three-year contract and a third of its commission up-front
as a nonrefundable payment for promotional costs. Brokers
recommend Previews, and sellers gladly pay the fee, but
usually when they know or have learned the hard way that
their assets need exposure beyond the city line.

Take a breath-taking contemporary on thirty acres of
Arizona's celebrity-packed Paradise Valley. The desert mansion has everything anyone could ever design into a dream
house—and more. But the "more" is the problem. While
most of Arizona's premier homes are designed in harmony
with the environment—blending like cactus into the rugged
terrain—this 23,000-square-foot behemoth, complete with an
indoor ice-skating rink, rises from the sands like an out-of-
place Taj Mahal. It is ornate, ostentatious, and totally out
of sync with the Arizona lifestyle.

Most of the world's extraordinary residences are built
as the fulfillment of personal dreams. In most cases, this

enhances the property's position as an investment asset.
When a shipping magnate erects a colossal surfside villa
overlooking the Pacific, his fondness for a waterfront mansion will be shared by others in his socioeconomic class. To
live in grand style at the water's edge has near universal
appeal. The house will likely gain in value over the years
and will resell easily over and over again. But this is not
the case when a residence is designed to conform to a personal quirk or idiosyncracy. Regardless of its location or
cost, this compromises the property's value as negotiable
currency. Limited appeal transforms the residence from a
highly liquid asset (remember all of those dollars chasing
a handful of prestige properties) to a work of art appealing
only to those with a similar aesthetic vision.

Sometimes the features the wealthy build into their
homes border on the eccentric—and beyond.

> One Previews representative imperturbably inspected
> the tower room of a Greenwich, Connecticut mansion
> and later reported that it contained a mechanical horse
> and a motion picture projection outfit. It seems that
> the former owner, during his declining days, had been
> forced to give up his favorite sport of riding to the
> hounds in Virginia. Not to be frustrated by age and
> aches, the indomitable old man had ridden his mechani-
> cal horse in the tower room while the movie projector
> unreeled before him a panorama of the Virginia country-
> side he loved so much.*

Adds Charles Seilheimer, a one-time Previews executive and
former president of arch competitor Sotheby Parke Bernet
International Realty, "Don't think of a wealthy person's
home as shelter or anything quite so functional. Look at
this." He spreads across his desk a beautifully photographed
brochure of Cliffside, a La Jolla, California, beach complex

---

* Richard Throelsen, in *Saturday Evening Post*, March 7, 1953.

composed of two detached living units—one jutting from a
rocky cliff and the other nestled on the craggy shore below—
both joined by an elevator cut through a wall of stone.

"Here we have one man's statement of the ultimate
lifestyle," Seilheimer explains. "The home is a reflection of
his personal vision. He's saying this is how life should be
lived: half the time at the heights and half at the shore.
That's fine as long as he lives there, but what happens when
he tires of the place? He'll want it sold and all the development costs recovered plus an additional amount for appreciation. He views it as an asset that can be traded for cash
or other properties. The challenge is to find another wealthy
and discriminating person with identical tastes—one who
fancies taking an elevator through a wall of rock and who
has $2,950,000 to pay for the experience. It is hard to get
one man to pay for another's vision. But sellers don't understand that."

John Colquin Tysen, a former Previews president, explained the problem of turning dream properties into liquid
assets by saying: "It's not easy to convince someone who
has put a hundred thousand dollars' worth of imported
panelling in his living room or spent a hundred and fifty
thousand on his wife's bath that this sort of thing doesn't
necessarily contribute real value. It simply reflects his individual taste and his only hope of recovering even part of
what he's splurged on his home is to find somebody somewhere whose tastes are similar."*

Reading between the lines of Previews' 1981–1982
"Guide"—the one with the Reagan pool patio on the cover
(recall the public relations mileage of a presidential sale)—
we can identify impediments to sales in virtually every listing, some of which relate to the original owner's vision and
others to circumstances beyond his control:

• Bluebird Cottage in Tryall Golf and Beach Club, Sandy
  Bay, Jamaica. A charming villa with high-peaked roofs

* E. J. Kahn, Jr., in *The New Yorker*, © 1956. Reprinted by permission.

and expansive windows looking out on the sea, this 10-
room $300,000 island residence sits in a dreamy tropical
setting thick with banana trees and lazy palms.

The problem is that the wealthy, always sensitive to
social unrest, have come to view Jamaica as a turbulent
island, boiling with racial hatred and prone to violence. Certainly not the choice location for a major property investment. For Bluebird Cottage, Previews must find a buyer
willing to take a contrarian position, acting on the belief
that law and order will ultimately prevail and will protect
property rights. This relates directly to the concept of the
stock exchange for real estate. The Big Board functions in
a similar way. When the once-mighty International Harvester found itself near bankruptcy, Harvester's specialists
on the floor of the New York Stock Exchange received orders
from speculators around the world willing to take positions
in the slumping security. Few of the takers were from Wall
Street's major institutions—the bank trust departments and
pension funds had bailed out of Harvester months before.
But by reaching out to the wider universe of buyers, the
NYSE attracted traders willing to buy devalued stocks with
long-shot appeal. Some add these out-of-favor securities to
their portfolios because they see underlying assets whose
value exceed the per share price; others believe the firm
to be fundamentally stronger than the current price would
suggest; and some simply cannot resist a speculative fling.
Previews' international marketing system attracts buyers to properties for much the same reasons. That is, they
see the strengths as well as the flaws. The bottom line is
that "the broader the exposure, the easier the sale" is a
truism for marketing real estate because it diminishes the
importance of property flaws. Previews' slogan could, in fact,
be changed to "the broader the exposure, the less damaging
the flaws." As a property comes to the attention of a wider
range of national, cultural and socioeconomic segments, the
fact that it is considered risky, tasteless or remote in the
local market becomes less important to the sales effort.
Somewhere, someone is bound to like it that way.

"Our international sales network enables us to sell some truly extravagant properties sight unseen," says Bruce Wennerstrom. "It happened that way with Sturgeon Valley Ranch. A 1,058-acre wilderness spread in Vanderbilt, Michigan, it seemed like one of our most difficult listings. Nothing against Michigan but in real estate, location is still the most crucial factor and this was a rather remote spot. It's part of that huge land mass that's so often ignored by so many wealthy celebrities and industrialists. Nevertheless we accepted the listing because we believed it was an attractive home and worth the price. A hard sell but worth the price.

"And our hunch was confirmed. As it happened, a German-born, Swiss-based industrialist visiting New York saw a copy of the brochure we'd produced on the ranch and found himself enchanted with the place."

Bob Riley, an executive with Previews' Chicago office, remembers it well.

> He made an appointment to fly out to Michigan to see the property, but then was forced to cancel at the last minute when his wife took ill. Before he returned to Switzerland, I rushed him a hastily prepared album of photographs of the house—pictures that were not included in the brochure. He liked what he saw so much that he made an offer of $1.2 million, in cash, without ever having seen the place in person.

> I'd say the clincher was a photograph of a trout stream that runs along the property. The gentleman prided himself on being an avid fisherman back in Switzerland and he wanted to be able to indulge this passion when he was in the states.

But the sale was by no means concluded. Incredibly, Sturgeon Valley's owner rejected the offer, noting that it fell $50,000 short of the asking price. Intoxicated by his own subjective appraisal of the property's value, he was determined to hold out for the full $1.25 million. It added up to a broker's nightmare. A bid within 10 percent of the asking price is considered excellent; this was only 4 percent off the mark, and all in cash.

"No matter how long they've been in the works, no matter that the most complex issues have been cleared away, property transactions boil down to that last bit of bargaining where the buyer and the seller decide they're going to hold their ground," says Sally Siano, owner of a successful brokerage firm in Bedford, New York's gentleman's horse country about forty miles and two centuries from the World Trade Center. "It's purely emotional and often irrational. I mean to bicker about $25,000 on a million-dollar residence, and to risk losing a deal because of it, doesn't make one a shrewd negotiator. If the property is worth $975,000, it is surely worth a million.

"Still, this is where people get hung up—even those with the means to buy a 50-room house set on 100 acres. In fact, the incidence of petty bickering is probably greater with grand properties than with suburban tract houses. In a residential development, value is quite easy to determine because all the homes are basically the same and recent sales can be used as a pricing yardstick. If one house has a finished basement and the other doesn't, you give or take a few thousand dollars. There's little guesswork involved. But pricing unique properties is far more difficult. Because there are no comparables, the only price is that which the buyer will pay and the owner will accept.

"This is where the broker can use his skills to bring off a deal. Like a mediator, you have to get the parties in a transaction to budge from their positions, to inch toward each other, to realize that what they really want is not the extra $25,000 but instead to strike a fair deal."

Previews' executives, also believers in the "inch and budge" technique, failed to get either party in the Sturgeon Valley negotiations to extend as much as a big toe toward each other. The seller's price remained at $1.25 million firm; the prospective buyer held fast at $1.2 million.

"Faced with that kind of intransigence on both sides, we feared the deal would collapse," Riley recalls. "But we pressed the ranch owner to reconsider, to recognize that a cash bid so close to the asking price was too good to turn down. That if he didn't want to risk losing the best deal we thought would come along, he'd be wise to accept.

"Fortunately, he saw the wisdom of our position and agreed to take the bid. A deal was struck for $1.2 million. But it was only a verbal commitment. Our next challenge was to get the papers signed before the buyer returned to Switzerland. We didn't have much time. The offer was accepted on a Monday and he was scheduled to depart for Europe that Thursday.

"I'm from the strike-while-the-iron's-hot school of brokerage. When I see an opportunity, I seize it. So I booked two first-class airline tickets, asked the owner to fly with me to New York and brought along the necessary paperwork for both parties to sign. We took off on Tuesday morning, met at the buyer's Manhattan apartment for breakfast, went to his lawyer's for lunch and had the final negotiations complete and the papers signed in time to catch the TWA commuter back to Chicago."

Looking behind the logistics of Previews' Zurich to New York to Michigan relay—beyond the broker's marketing efforts—we can isolate an underlying factor that gave impetus to the deal: Luxury property has emerged as a preeminent form of international currency. Swiss gold traders, Wall Street investment bankers, London rock stars and Jidda oil princes view prized parcels of earth—especially those in the safe, stable, "last capitalist will die there" United States— as secure havens for francs, marks and pounds. They know that in a tumultuous world jarred by sociopolitical crises, tomorrow's headlines can reduce paper money to just so much scrap in a wheelbarrow.

"The German gentleman who bought Sturgeon Valley had just sold a major industrial company in Europe," Riley notes, "and was looking for ways to invest the proceeds. He made it clear that U.S. property purchases were at the top of his shopping list. Certainly, Sturgeon Valley was more of an investment than an indulgence. Although he liked trout

fishing, he didn't have to spend a million two, to gain access
to a stream."

Sally Siano, a gifted saleswoman who appoints her offices with fresh cut roses and strains of Vivaldi and who
refuses to list pedestrian properties for fear they will dilute
her prestige image—puts it this way:

> Luxury properties are greater than the sum of their
> parts. They should be marketed not as heaps of timber,
> glass and fieldstone but as investment assets. More than
> anything else, the wealthy covet material assets that
> appreciate over the years. It's the only way to protect
> their fortunes from inflation and from the other ravages
> of an unsettled world. Brokers can profit handsomely
> by reserving for these clients properties that are likely
> to meet the acid test of long-term appreciation.

Previews' integrated marketing communications system is
designed to give properties of this sort the widest possible
exposure and to match active prospects with local brokers
who in turn negotiate the buy and sell transactions. Each
step in the sales process reinforces the other.

Assume a potential buyer is attracted to a property advertised in *Homes International* and calls any one of Previews' regional offices for an appointment to inspect the
place. The lead is promptly relayed to an independent broker
assigned to handle the listing in the local market. Previews
rarely handles a sale single-handedly, preferring instead to
combine its marketing skills with the hometown broker's
knowledge of the community.

The terms of Previews' local broker relationships depend on where the listing originates. When a broker refers
a listing to Previews, he is designated the "controlling broker" and gains exclusive rights to represent the property.
All sales leads generated through Previews' publications or
related promotions are directed to the controlling broker,
who has sole authority to show the property. Should the
property be sold at any time during the term of Previews'

contract with the owner, the controlling broker can collect the 5 percent brokerage commission if he makes the sale himself or he may co-broke with another realtor.

About half of Previews' listings come to the company directly from property owners. In these cases, the competition among local brokers is wide open. Although Previews often appoints a "servicing broker" to act as a community liaison for that listing, any realtor can show the property, can make the sale and can earn the local brokerage commission. In the event that another broker makes the sale, the servicing broker is paid an override of up to 1 percent (which comes out of Previews' 6 percent).

> When you recommend Previews and the owner uses our services, Previews makes every effort to help you make the sale. With the owner's consent, we make you the exclusive local sales representative (called the controlling broker) to whom we send all our buyers and through whom all other brokers must work. Should an owner come to Previews directly, we may elect to appoint a servicing broker on a non-exclusive basis. The servicing broker is protected by an override of up to one percent, paid out of our fee, in the event he does not make the sale, and another broker does.*

Active brokers can keep abreast of Previews' listings by requesting copies of the "Guide" and Previews brochures. By doing so, the broker expands his property inventory and is in a position to offer clients a wider range of listings. What's more, brokers who perform well for Previews are selected as servicing brokers. Although Previews does not designate exclusive affiliates in any of its markets, the company's regional executives closely monitor local broker performance, giving the best leads to the hottest producers. The servicing broker is the first to get the listing, is generally the first to advertise it locally and is the first in line for

---

* "How Brokers Make More Money Through Previews."

Previews-generated sales leads for that property. He enjoys
a clear advantage in closing sales and may earn a commission
even if another broker makes the sale: the 1 percent override
on Previews' average $1.3 million transaction comes to
$13,000.

Still, skeptics among the nation's brokers say that this
is not enough. Not at 1 percent, a co-broke 2.5 percent or
even the full 5 percent. Not good enough because . . . because they just don't trust this thing called Previews. This
entity garrisoned in a corporate park in snobby Greenwich,
Connecticut. This marketing octopus with its arms winding
through local communities, wrapping around the wealthiest
citizens. This nebulous presence with its slick magazines
in the slick smoke shops of slick hotels and its publisher-
turned-real-estate-marketer president with his Madison Avenue tactics and his way of remaining aloof from local realtors, while turning their efforts in his favor.

The truth is that real estate brokerage is a highly competitive, intensely jealous collage of profit-worshipping zealots
who circle the wagons only when the government threatens
to disturb the protected commission system. On a day-to-
day basis, there is no brokerage community per se, but instead a mob of competitors fighting among themselves to
list and sell a limited number of properties. Even brokers
who profit from the Previews connection have a love/hate
relationship with the firm. The reasons for this are as varied
as the personalities involved, but all related to the competitive nature of real estate brokerage. Add to this the fact
that successful real estate brokers are born optimists, convinced that they can sell anything to anyone. To succeed
they must think this way; must convince themselves that
the property doesn't exist that they cannot market. For other
brokers to claim superiority is not only an insult but also
a threat to the realtor's positive thinking. He resents it.

This antagonism is not new to Previews. Dark suspicions
about the firm's operations date back to its earliest days.

Previews operated at a loss throughout the thirties,
partly because a great many real estate brokers, feeling

that the enterprise was out to invade their bailiwicks and rob them of business, declined to cooperate with it. As time went on, however, a considerable number of them became tolerant of—or even pleased with—its operations, though quite a few brokers are to this day leery of the organization; every member of the Real Estate Board of Greenwich, for example, has pledged never to give the company any information about his Greenwich listings. Previews has stoutly maintained all along that such embargoes are woefully shortsighted, and that it not only does not compete with local brokers but actually furthers their businesses, since it urges its clients to sell through the men who are in a position to handle on-the-spot details.*

Although draconian embargoes are a thing of the past, Previews' executives still spend a considerable amount of time trying to convince local brokers to refer listings to them. Wennerstrom's spiel on this subject goes like this:

Brokers should be aware that we are not competing with them. We're a marketing organization whose role in the real estate business is to assist local brokers in developing buyers for properties they cannot sell through the local market.**

Previews' concerns about its standing vis-à-vis local brokers is reflected in a booklet it has published, "How Brokers Make More Money Through Previews." The messages are both direct and subliminal. The cover illustration, that of a mansion perched perilously on a partially eroded cliff, is a symbolic expression of Previews expertise in selling flawed properties. Judging by the picture, there is a clear danger that a hurricane would send the house sliding down the muddy banks. How to get buyers to invest in so vulnerable a property? Brokers can't miss the message.

* E. J. Kahn, Jr., in *The New Yorker*, © 1956. Reprinted by permission.
** *Linger's Real Estate*, July 1980.

We won't compete with you for the easy sales; we'll just help you make the tough ones—the cliff hangers.

The text tries to reassure brokers of Previews' intentions and to convince them that they will profit in partnership with the national marketer.

Our business is helping brokers to sell properties. . . . Over the years, the great bulk of Previews' listings has been the result of recommendations from brokers who know that Previews' broad market coverage and planned promotional campaigns sell real estate.

Brokers everywhere recommend Previews, because Previews helps them to sell the larger properties and reach out-of-area buyers. Brokers welcome the special sales and promotional work and the broad market coverage Previews provides. Most of all, they welcome the opportunity to make more money. . . .

Because Previews is paid to do special sales work for the owner, we can spend the time and money necessary to find buyers for out-of-the-ordinary properties, time and money that otherwise would have to be expended by the broker.

Previews' points, all well taken, have convinced thousands of brokers to work with the company since its inception. The holdouts, determined though they may be to remain that way, make for a vocal minority. The fact is that Previews successfully markets homes that might otherwise go unsold—reason enough for most brokers to cast aside personal considerations and to work with the firm. It is also reason enough for others to imitate and compete with the Previews system. Previews' annual revenues make a tempting target for aggressive entrepreneurs seeking to claim a share of land rush profits.

One challenger, the Confederation of International Real Estate, seeks to best Previews by offering property owners similar marketing services at lower commissions. Launched by a Briton, Johnathon Coltman-Rogers (chairman of the board), and run in the United States by Americans, the Confederation is essentially an international referral system for carriage trade brokers. The outfit is based on a promising idea: to unite the nation's most sophisticated brokers in an exclusive and potentially profitable fraternity. The move is designed to capitalize on the recent emergence of elite local brokers who have come to prominence by employing an arsenal of sophisticated marketing techniques once exclusive to Previews. Although they are true believers in "the broader the exposure, the easier the sale" philosophy, these independents prefer to keep even those listings that require national exposure in-house. Instead of referring leads to Previews, they buy advertising space in national publications such as *Town & Country* and the *New York Times* Sunday magazine, conduct highly targeted direct mail campaigns, and produce slick, newsstand quality brochures of their own.

"There was a time when Previews was the only sophisticated real estate marketer," says Confederation president Robert H. Kelsey. "But no longer. Today, the elite independents do everything Previews does—and many do it all quite a bit better.

"What these brokers lack, however, is an international identity and a formal mechanism for worldwide referrals. That's what the Confederation provides. It joins together the top drawer brokers in a business network that enables them to share information, leads and listings. Because the Confederation itself does not charge fees, our brokers can offer property owners the broad exposure and state-of-the-art marketing services of a Previews, but at an average 6 percent local brokerage commission versus Previews' 11 percent marketing/brokerage fee. In effect, our members can offer sophisticated real estate marketing at a discount."

The Confederation (which is in desperate need of a name that sounds less like a municipal employees union and more like the prestigious service it is designed to be) has borrowed unabashedly from the Previews formula. The basic sales tool is none other than a glossy magazine, *Great Estates*, filled with the now-familiar photos of horse farms, plantations and beachfront villas. Any similarity to *Homes International* is more than coincidence. Kelsey founded *Homes International* in 1970 and published it for four years before selling out to Previews in 1974.

"But there is a major difference between *Homes International* and *Great Estates* and that's in the way they are distributed," says Palm Beach broker Steve Cutter, a vice president and part owner of the Confederation. "*Great Estates* is distributed only by Confederation members to mailing lists of local property owners.* These are very select mailings. In Palm Beach, for example, we limit our distribution to the top 1,000 homes, all of which are prime waterfront properties. Here, the water line is also the money line and that's where we want the magazine to go. This kind of pinpoint circulation is made possible because local Confederation members know their markets best and have full control over the distribution.

"Equally important, only Confederation members can advertise in *Great Estates*, so their listings alone come to the readers' attention. If a local Palm Beach reader is attracted to an ad for a Manhattan townhouse, he'll likely call Douglas Elliman–Gibbons Ives, our New York City Confederation member, and a broker there will make the sale. Conversely, when Douglas Elliman distributes their copies of *Great Estates*, a Park Avenue surgeon may see our ad for a Palm Beach home and buy from us."

Should the surgeon contact Douglas Elliman directly, the Manhattan broker would be entitled to a fee (20 percent of the gross commission if a sale is made) for referring the listing to Cutter. The Confederation's membership rules require that this referral commission be paid to the introducing broker within thirty days of the selling broker's collection of the full commission.

"This is one of the great strengths of the Confedera-

* Limited newsstand sales were added in January 1983.

tion," Cutter says. "By distributing *Great Estates*, the members help each other and themselves simultaneously.

"The Confederation's other great strength is in the uniformly high caliber of our member brokers. This is important because if a client asks for my assistance in finding a property in New York, Beverly Hills, or even in France, I can refer him to a Confederation affiliate with full confidence that the broker I'm recommending operates according to similar quality standards we practice at Cutter Real Estate. And we get that 20 percent referral commission if a sale is made. It's a wonderful arrangement."

Cutter, one of the founding members of the Confederation, is not exactly an impartial observer. His involvement with the organization began when Coltman-Rogers, publisher of a European real estate magazine, the *International Property Catalogue*, visited Cutter's office to pitch advertising space.

"For years, I'd dreamed of starting an international referral network limited only to high-quality brokers experienced in selling luxury properties," Cutter says, recalling his first meeting with the British entrepreneur. "But for one reason or another I never did anything about it. Then, sitting across the table from Johnathon, it suddenly hit me that he was just the fellow to make that dream a reality. I believed he, a spirited young man with wide contacts throughout the real estate community, could bring the right parties together in a loose-knit sales network.

"Johnathon seemed taken by the idea and he left my office with the pledge to give it serious consideration. But he did more than that. Six months later I received an application to join his newly launched Confederation of International Real Estate. I was delighted that he'd gotten the idea off the ground and I wanted to be part of it.

"With this in mind, my associate Ben Johnson and I flew to England to meet with Johnathon. We negotiated for more than a week, shuttling between his London apartment and his medieval castle in the English countryside.

"When the talking stopped, Ben and I had bought into

the Confederation. That was in mid-1979. Five months later Bob Kelsey joined us and soon after that we launched our first promotion to attract broker members.

"The response was overwhelming. More than 5,000 brokers applied for membership. From this pool of candidates we had the luxury of selecting what we considered to be the top 75. We purposely kept the organization small at the start but we're now continuing with the selection process, attracting new applicants and separating the wheat from the chaff until we have 250 members. That's if we can find that many brokers capable of meeting our standards."

Translate "standards" to mean a propensity for selling properties priced substantially above the local market average. The Confederation's screening process is designed to identify those brokers who are blessed with the reputation and the connections for successfully marketing luxury listings.

The realtor's track record is the key criterion. Applicants are required to break down their gross sales figures into units of property value, revealing the number of homes sold in the following price ranges:

$250,000 to $500,000

$500,000 to $750,000

$750,000 to $1 million

$1 million plus

"We also look at the applicant's average sales price and compare it to the community average," says Ben Johnson. "If the numbers indicate that the broker substantially outperforms the other brokers in his market, then in all likelihood we have that one tenth of one percent of all brokers who can effectively market luxury homes. At Cutter, for example, our average transaction is $700,000. That's well above the $400,000 Palm Beach average. We don't expect applicants in less affluent markets to match our figures— just to be significantly above the local average, whatever that may be. That's the best test of a broker's mettle.

Confederation of International Real Estate

Company: Telephone:

Address:

                                      Telex:

Number of associates:*   Number of Offices: Year of establishment:

Number of residential sales per year: $200,000 U.S.:
                                            $250,000—500,000:
                                            $500,000—1,000,000:
                                            $1,000,000+:

Sales volume of residential division: $

Specific market area in which you specialize:

Languages spoken within your oganization:

Bank references:

Geographic areas to or from which you send or receive business:

Signed: Date

Name (in block letters)
Position in Company

U.S.A., Canada applicants only Professional designations held by firm: Positions held in local, state, national, levels of national association of realtors:	
Membership in other professional organizations:	(on reverse)
Please return this form to:	Confederation of International Real Estate 316 Royal Palm Way Palm Beach Florida 33480, USA Tel. (305) 655-3973

(continued)

Other firms you wish invited to join the confederation:	
Membership in other professional organizations:	

* *The original chart included translations into French, Spanish, and German.*

"But we don't base our membership decisions on statistics alone. Once we identify a qualified prospect, we make an appointment to meet with the principals—to observe their management first hand. Remember, the Confederation prides itself on maintaining a prestigious referral network. All of our brokers must feel comfortable sending clients to one another. They must be absolutely certain that their customers will receive extraordinary service. That's why we started this organization."

Perhaps, but there's another motive at work here—the profit motive. While Cutter and Johnson cite chapter and verse on "the network of trust and confidence," they stand to earn a handsome profit from the Confederation's services.

To partake of the brokerage network's fraternal spirit, members must pay a $3,000 initiation fee, annual dues of $1,000 and roughly $1,000 a page for advertisements in *Great Estates*. With a full roster of members, this will generate projected initiation fees of $750,000 and annual revenues of more than $1 million. This booty will flow directly to the founders. A mutual aid society, it is not.

"Heavens yes, we want to make money on this," Cutter admits when questioned about the Confederation's finances. "Although we're still in the red, we expect to cross the break-even point at 125 members and move solidly in the black by the mid-1980's."

The Confederation's principals may be its major beneficiaries. The founding concept—that of a discount alternative
to Previews' marketing system—is fundamentally weak.

"When I have a tough property to sell, I give it to Previews, not to the Confederation," says Sally Siano, herself
a Confederation member. "I look at the Confederation as
a sorority of top brokers rather than a marketing force. I
don't expect to make money from this affiliation—just
friends. Previews may cost the seller a more substantial
fee but they offer so much more in terms of name, connections and international exposure."

Brokers with Siano's half-hearted commitment to the
Confederation cannot be relied on to play the kind of team
ball that networking demands. Most damaging, they may
be remiss in distributing copies of *Great Estates*, thus de-
priving the system of its key promotional tool. As it is designed, the referral network works well only if every member blankets his market with copies of the publication.

Aware of this weak link, Confederation executives try
to build enthusiasm by hyping the members with visions
of spectacular sales. Note this excerpt from the Confederation's July 1982 newsletter:

What are you doing with your copies of the summer
issue of *Great Estates* magazine? Every office received
at least 25 complimentary copies and some have ordered
quantities of as many as 600, 800, 1,200 and 1,500 at
$1.00 apiece. Initial reports are that *Great Estates* is
turning into a money-saving gold mine for the offices
using it. One report comes from a Confederation office
that was going head-to-head with the local Coldwell
Banker office for two of the most expensive listings in
the area; the broker reports getting both of them and
feeling that in both cases *Great Estates* was the main
reason.

Another reports over $21,000 in commissions directly
attributable to advertising in *Great Estates*. An office
sending out 300 copies of *Great Estates* to the most

expensive homes in the area received a $2,000,000 listing because "the owner" was so impressed with the Confederation office's contacts in luxury real estate.

More impressed, it seems, than some of the Confederation's own members.

"I don't have much faith in *Great Estates,*" Siano says, "and I can tell from some of the meetings I've been to that others share my view. The magazine is definitely a lightweight. I don't advertise in it because its circulation is too small to be of any consequence. In fact, I rarely distribute my copies. That makes the magazine a paper tiger, don't you think?"

Feature for feature, the Confederation stacks up poorly against Previews. Brokers mesmerized by the Confederation's promises of local market exclusivity and the ability to offer clients a low-commission alternative to Previews are blind to a crucial point: that the Confederation is to Previews as a lover is to a spouse. The latter picks up where the former leaves off. While the Confederation simply maintains a mechanism for informal broker referrals, Previews' elaborate marketing/communications system can generate fresh and original approaches for the sale of hard-to-sell properties.

Previews succeeds where others fail because it has learned to view real estate problems as opportunities in disguise. Perhaps its greatest talent is in transforming the sales impediments in most of its listings into bankable assets. Because its expertise has always been tilted toward difficult properties, it has learned to repackage and present these inpediments in a way that appeals to at least one tiny market segment or special interest group. It relies on wide exposure, yes, but on intelligent, often ingeniously planned, exposure.

Crucial to this is the creative design of direct mail campaigns. Previews identifies those segments most likely to be attracted to a property's dominant feature—the same feature viewed by the wider market as a flaw. Consider Previews' handling of a California home, blessed (or cursed) with a 20-car garage. To the typical well-to-do house hunter, this vehicular warehouse was an eyesore that made the place look semicommercial. But Previews' marketing strategy was not geared to the "typical" buyer. Taking its "problem as an opportunity in disguise" approach, Previews set its sights exclusively on wealthy auto enthusiasts.

"Rather than trying to camouflage the garage, we touted it as a key selling point," Wennerstrom explains. "We knew that classic car collectors often have to store their treasures in a hodge podge of garages scattered hither and yon. Certainly, the ability to house the '57 T-Bird, the gull-wing Mercedes and the rest of the valued collection in the backyard would appeal to them the way a mass of stables delights horse breeders. The challenge is to reach that ever so tiny group of auto enthusiasts with the means to buy an extravagant home. That takes a bit of detective work.

"For this assignment, we asked E. L. Polk—an outfit that develops mailing lists based on automobile registrations—for the names of Ferrari, Rolls-Royce, and Mercedes owners in Texas and California. Our experience over the years has revealed that if you take a close look at any group of luxury product owners you'll find that some are fanatics, absolutely obsessed with collecting every painting, porcelain or, in this case, exotic automobile they can get their hands on. When you have a 20-car garage, these are the people you have to reach. In direct mail, you do it by identifying some characteristics, like the ownership of a $50,000 or a $100,000 car, and mail to those who fit the mold. If you're on target, the right buyer turns up. In any case, at least you know you are tapping the most promising pool of prospects."

Sometimes, Previews' talent for identifying target groups is positively sublime.

. . . Previews listed a summer camp on the Maine coast. The owners, who had operated the place for many years, wanted to start a new life. Local efforts to sell the camp proved unavailing. But an engraved and personally

signed Previews letter to the family of every known
visitor to the camp did flush out of the bushes a wealthy
businessman with a sentimental yearning for his days
there . . .

"Then there was the classic case several years ago of
the twenty-three room palais on the French Riviera—
la Villa Aujourd'hui—entrusted to Previews' hands.
Taking a chance on the then-budding amour between
the Riviera and Hollywood, Previews decided to zero
in on fifty movie moguls in its marketing campaign.
One of them—the late Jack Warner—could not resist
and bought the place for cash.*

These cases illustrate that Previews' most important
contribution to the marketing of real estate is its recognition
that good brokerage demands more than good salesmanship.
From its earliest days, Previews has employed the once-ob-
scure marketing strategy, segmentation, that is now widely
used by consumer goods marketers to sell beer, toothpaste,
and laundry detergent. Segmentation views the market, not
as a homogeneous mass, but instead as clusters of individuals united by common tastes and standards. While the hard
core of the beer market, the six-pack-a-day crowd, sticks
with the middle of the road brews—Bud and Miller—compar-
atively small but highly profitable segments prefer imported
lite beer, dark beer, German beer, Dutch beer, Mexican beer,
Chinese beer, weekend beer, American beer with Bavarian
names, all natural beer, Austrian beer, French beer, Japa-
nese beer, beer brewed with spring water, and beer brewed
in the Rockies.

By focusing for many years only on stereotypical Bud-
gulping steel workers, by failing to produce alternative products that would draw more discriminating consumers into
the market, the big brewers artificially limited their sales
potential. Similarly, by viewing the real estate market as
homogeneous, or by identifying prospective buyers on the

* *Esquire,* November 1979.

basis of income alone, brokers overlooked the small, but extremely important, segments with a penchant for 20-car garages and indoor ice skating rinks. By mastering the art and science of segmentation, Previews has taken real estate brokerage beyond the limited potential of the "dinner at the country club, day on the golf course" salesmanship to a sophisticated business discipline that simultaneously reduces brokerage risks and maximizes its profits. And by creating a stronger market for luxury properties—by turning brick and mortar into liquid assets through the stock exchange for real estate—it has been a true catalyst in the land rush.

The bottom line is that Previews fills a gaping void in the real estate market. For the local independent to treat the national marketer as an unwanted intruder is small-minded and counterproductive. Instead, savvy realtors will want to pursue a double-edged strategy, welcoming Previews as a sophisticated ally in the sale of difficult properties while at the same time denying it access to those listings that can move for top dollar in the local market. This balanced approach all but assures the broker of incremental sales without diluting his commission base.

The fear that property sellers will leap-frog local realtors, jumping directly into Previews contracts, is a phobia. The disparity in commissions is too great to justify a wholesale defection. Few owners will pay the 4, 5 or 6 percent premium over going commission rates unless they are convinced that their properties need extraordinary exposure. Enlightened brokers will see this as a plus. Rather than fighting Previews, they will build an identity as a Previews affiliate, thus prompting sellers to stop at their offices in search of Previews' assistance. This enables the local broker to refer the listing to Previews and to gain controlling broker status in the process.

Says a Beverly Hills broker who asked to remain anonymous: "When a property appears to be a real stubborn case—the kind that is unlikely to respond to standard sales efforts—I'm pleased to refer it to Previews. This way they assume the marketing costs, which are apt to be enormous, and I have the chance to collect an especially high-margin commission.

"Not more than a month ago, a young woman—whose garish pink leather jumpsuit I shall never forget—walked into my office to ask if I would arrange to have Previews sell her home. It seemed as if they'd sold her sister's Connecticut home to a rock musician for twice as much as anyone in Westport thought it was worth. Now, she wanted a repeat performance.

"What she needed was a miracle. Her house was situated on a perfectly lovely and quite valuable piece of property but, my word, what a hideous structure it was. I wouldn't even know how to advertise it. It looked like a combination Swiss Chalet and Chinese pagoda.

"I'd worked with Previews maybe a dozen times during my 19 years in real estate brokerage and I knew from experience that they'd have the best chance of selling the godawful thing. Success in this very difficult and demanding business comes only if you analyze every transaction from a business rather than an emotional standpoint. That means putting aside petty concerns about who gets credit for what. You analyze the property and its potential market, determine who is in the best position to negotiate a favorable deal, and if all signs indicate third-party involvement, enlist their aid in accomplishing the overriding objective of turning the listing into a sale."

Insecure brokers often hold on to properties they know they can't sell under the rationale that they make for good listing tools. A solid glass house, were there such a thing, would not sell in hometown U.S.A., but the hometown broker, who manages to gain the listing for it, would likely hold on to the property. By advertising the fishbowl residence he draws curiosity seekers, who, the theory goes, can be directed to more salable listings. The glass house is viewed as a traffic builder.

Similarly, luxury properties are often used as a PR device. Take the broker, in a solidly middle class community, whose average listing is $100,000. Assume the wealthiest person in town dies and the broker, through his friend the estate executor, gains the listing for the deceased's $1 million Victorian mansion. Well, that's a quantum leap from the broker's standard assortment of smallish capes and clapboards. Even though he has little chance of selling the mansion in the local community, he is reluctant to give it up. His fantasy is that his sudden association with a major property will serve as a magnet, bringing more of the town's better listings.

"Perhaps, but I don't believe in carrying an inventory of unmarketable homes," Siano says. "A broker succeeds by marketing properties, period. Build a reputation for that and you'll have all the business you can handle."

A skilled marketer in her own right—typical of the new breed of sophisticated independents—Siano stretches the parameters of "hard-to-sell," closing many difficult sales without third-party assistance.

"I never hold on to a listing simply because I think the property will bolster my image. But I have learned in recent years that I can handle myself more of the properties I once thought were too great a challenge for local brokers. I do it by placing my own national advertising and producing my own brochures, sometimes charging owners—much like Previews—2 percent of the standard commission up front. This retainer is vitally important: it enables me to commit to a costly promotional campaign without the fear of winding up in the minus column should the property go unsold.

"Getting clients to go along with this is a matter of education. Demonstrate to them what the retainer will buy—show them the difference between a typical grainy newspaper ad and a superbly produced brochure—and in most cases they'll be willing to pay.

"If you consider the fact that most owners of luxury homes are business people, you recognize that they will react positively to dollars and cents proposals. Convince them that the investment in a brokerage retainer will return a yield equal to or better than their Exxon shares and they won't hesitate to write out a check."

Clearly, Siano has borrowed a page from Previews. The

"stock exchange for real estate" has always positioned its up-front fee as a hedge against market risk. Instinctively, Previews executives have known how to talk to their clients in the language they understand best. Credit this for much of the firm's success in carving out a lucrative practice at the pinnacle of real estate brokerage.

"Brokers and owners with hard-to-sell properties approach Previews with the wistful air of a fabled prince with the glass slipper—somewhere, they hope, there will be a Cinderella to fit it. When the property owner blanches at the prospect of paying Previews a flat fee in advance for promotional purposes, the firm's representatives suavely remind him that the monthly carrying cost of his unwanted property will amount to approximately 1 percent of its value. This, in the vernacular of the trade, is often what is known as the clincher."*

Will cost 1% a month to carry.

---

* Richard Thruelson, in *Saturday Evening Post*, March 7, 1953.

2

Sotheby's International Realty: of Castles and Kings and Rock Star Retreats

To say that most of our clients do their own financing is an understatement, a good many own their own banks.

Charles H. Seilheimer, Jr.
Former president of Sotheby Parke Bernet
International Realty

If Previews sells dreams, its closest competitor in worldwide property marketing, Sotheby Parke Bernet International Realty, sells a fairy tale. A tale of kings and queens, of castles and balls, of coachmen and ladies-in-waiting. A tale of make-believe in which nuclear age man holds forth behind castle walls, protected from the modern day vulgarities of recession, Big Macs, urban guerrillas, steel workers, Miller Lite, plastic bananas, prefabricated condominiums, and Hamburger Helper. A tale in which native Americans grown rich making micro-chips and Broadway musicals glide back through the centuries to live in the manner of the Earl of Surrey.

Sotheby's markets real estate on a most unusual premise: that it will create for its clients the privileges and treasures of another age. To do so, the firm draws on its stately image to list and market a kingdom of glorious properties, many extraordinary relics of British and American history.

Consider Sotheby's 1982 listing for Hever Castle, a thirteenth-century fortress once home to Anne Boleyn, Henry VIII's unfortunate wife who failed to produce a male heir to the throne of England. The castle's genealogy dates back through seven centuries. To learn how this formidable property came to market and how Sotheby obtained the listing, we have to trace its rather complicated history. Named for a Norman family that had settled in the Parish of Hever in or about A.D. 1200, the property then consisted of a fortified farmhouse and yard, surrounded by a moat and approached by a wooden drawbridge.

"It remained in the Hever family until 1399 when it was purchased by Sir Stephen Scrope from Sir John de Cobham, whose grandmother Joan was coheir of William de Hever and inherited the Castle in 1360. When Sir Stephen died in 1408, his widow, Millicent, took as her second husband Sir John Fastolf (later characterized as Falstaff by Shakespeare). Sir John and Lady Fastolf occupied Hever until 1423 when it was conveyed to Sir Roger Fiennes. Succeeding members of the Fiennes family lived at Hever until 1462 when it was sold to Sir Geoffrey Bullen, who had been Lord Mayor of London in 1459. From Sir Geoffrey, Hever passed to his eldest son William and from William to his eldest son Thomas. Sir Thomas Bullen married Lady Elizabeth Howard, the eldest daughter of Thomas Howard, Earl of Surrey and second Duke of Norfolk. His eldest daughter, Mary, became lady-in-waiting to Queen Catherine of Aragon and soon caught the eye of Henry VIII himself. Henry's amorous advances to Mary ceased after a period of time, leaving him the opportunity to devote his attention to her younger sister Anne. And so it was to Hever that Henry would ride out with an escort of cavalry to court Anne. By January of 1533, she was expecting his child, and in that same month Henry and Anne were secretly married.

"Anne was crowned Queen in Westminster Abbey on June 1, 1533, and their daughter Elizabeth was born on September 7. But by 1536 Anne had still not produced the necessary male heir to the throne, so Henry lost his patience and had her arrested and committed to the Tower of London on a charge of High Treason for adultery. Her trial followed on the fifteenth of May and her own uncle, the Duke of Norfolk, condemned her to death. Her father, Sir Thomas, continued to live at Hever until his death in 1538. The Crown then took possession of Hever and, in 1540, Henry granted it to his recently divorced fourth wife, Anne of Cleves, who lived there until her death in 1557. It was then regranted by Mary Tudor to Sir Edward Waldegrave as compensation for his having allowed Mass to be said in a house where Mary was living during the reign of Edward VI.

"And so, Hever Castle, having changed hands several times, gradually slipped out of the public gaze until 1903 when it was purchased by the American millionaire, William Waldorf Astor, who was impelled by a passion for history. What William Waldorf Astor purchased in 1903 was in reality a very modest, but ancient, residence, although in Tudor England it had been considered one of the most exquisite examples of English architecture of the period.

"At once, many problems faced Mr. Astor. He was primarily attracted by Hever's historical associations and by its beauty, but he also wished to live in twentieth-century comfort and to entertain his friends. His greatest desire was to preserve Hever intact; to enlarge the castle would destroy its perfect proportions. With his architect, Frank L. Pearson, the difficulty of enlargement was overcome by leaving the castle just as it was and building alongside it a Tudor-style village composed of haphazard cottages in such a way that, far from being dwarfed, the Castle would still be the main feature which dominated the scene.

"It has been estimated that William Waldorf Astor spent over $10 million to create 'a perfect jewel of a small castle.' Beginning in 1903 and continuing for a period of four years, more than 1,000 workmen toiled to convert the Castle to

Mr. Astor's modern requirements. In December 1904, Sir
Douglas Fox and partners began work on the thirty-five-
acre lake which was completed in nineteen months by 800
men with six steam diggers and seven miles of railway.
By the shores of this new lake a huge loggia with a colon-
naded piazza was built. The central feature is a fountain
with figures carved by the sculptor W. S. Frith. Behind this
piazza, an Italian garden, complete with pergola, Roman
bath, grottoes and marble pavements, was laid out in a design which accommodated the statuary and sculpture which
Mr. Astor had collected during his service as American Minis-
ter in Rome some fifteen years before. In the immediate
precincts of the Castle and just across the inner moat, simple
gardens and flower beds were planned, typical of those which
might have existed in the time of Henry VIII and Anne
Boleyn. These included a maze planted with more than 1,000
yew trees and other topiary work such as a unique set of
chessmen. All this was surrounded by an outer moat, beyond
which all manner of walks, avenues and gardens were
formed."*

Astor, a native New Yorker, great grandson of fur
trader, oil tycoon, and one-time ambassador to Rome John
Jacob Astor, was a dedicated Anglophile possessed of a lifelong fantasy to live as an English nobleman. Shortly after
purchasing Hever Castle, he became a British subject and
was named First Viscount Astor—a little fringe benefit that
often comes along with English property. Content with his
life in England and his restructured castle, W. W. remained
in the United Kingdom for the rest of his life. His son, christened John Jacob in honor of the child's illustrious ancestor,
became a prominent British businessman and politician, serving both as Chairman of *The London Times* and a member
of Parliament. John Jacob inherited Hever in 1956. But this
marked the end of an era. When it came time for John Jacob's
eldest son Gavin to take title to the property, the realities

---

* Copyright © 1982 by Sotheby Parke Bernet Inc. Excerpts reprinted
by permission.

of mid-twentieth-century economics were taking the fun out of owning a medieval fortress. To help defray the mounting costs of maintaining a small city complete with a staff of sixty estate managers and caretakers, Gavin turned Hever into a living museum, opening its doors to the public for two days a week. In the ensuing years (beginning in 1963), more than 3 million visitors paid admission to tour the grounds.

The next major change of title—the one that ultimately led to Sotheby's being granted the listing—came in 1974 when Gavin put the castle in trust for his eldest son, J. J. He would be the last of the Astors to own Hever. When it came time to exercise his prerogatives, J. J.—known in British society as Johnnie—decided to sell.

"He doesn't have much of a taste for living in a castle," says Virginia Haynes, a former Sotheby's publicity director. "He grew up there, you know, and I assume he simply preferred a change. Besides which, he is now based in Paris where he's active in the real estate business."

Word has it that "Johnnie's" distaste of the Castle relates to its station as a semipublic facility. The idea of having tourists Polaroid their way through his childhood home is not Mr. Astor's notion of living well. Little did William Waldorf know when he constructed his grand estate that its enormous scale would force future generations to turn it into a museum to pay the bills, or that they would someday remove it from the family corpus.

"Johnnie instructed the trustees to sell the property," Haynes adds, "with proceeds of the sale going into the trust fund established for him by his father."

The trustees promptly turned to Sotheby's International Realty to market the property. Like the castle itself, the firm is steeped in British history. Although it is the newest entrant in the world of multinational property marketing, having sold its first mansion in 1976, it draws through osmosis the aristocratic blood of its noble parent, Sotheby's, a venerable British auction house. Sotheby's traces its pedigree to 1744 when Samuel Baker, a London bookseller, opened a small auction firm to specialize in the sale of rare books. His business a success, the auctioneer expanded his services to include appraising and auctioning paintings, porcelain, sculpture, coins, stamps, and gems. Because it could be relied upon to provide accurate appraisals of valuable assets, many of which were family heirlooms, and because it guarded the privacy of its patrons, Sotheby's earned a place in the social hierarchy as a confidante to Britain's ruling class. When death, divorce, marriage, or business reversals prompted changes in a family's holdings, Sotheby's was called on to buy, sell, and evaluate its most precious assets. Generation after generation of Havermeyers, Smythes, and Churchills turned to Sotheby's much as they did to their barristers, chartered accountants, and bankers.

The firm's success was due, in great measure, to its abiding respect for tradition. Over the years, Sotheby's steadfastly resisted change, clinging to the fundamental business practices forged by its founder: a scholarly approach to the auction business, an emphasis on classic art collections, and a low-keyed salesmanship that relied more on word-of-mouth than splashy promotions.

Sotheby's transplanted this basically European concept to the United States with the 1960 opening of its New York branch. Never mind that the colonies were home to a newly minted class of well-to-do that regarded resistance to fashion as a stodgy affectation, terribly Old World. Sotheby's remained loyal to its charter. To the surprise of many who thought the firm out of its element in the United States, Sotheby's prospered in its new market.

Impressed by the unalterable Sotheby's standards and enamored of its venerable name, wealthy Americans began entrusting the firm to auction their most precious assets. Quickly, Sotheby's was in the enviable position of handling some of the nation's most prominent collections.

The 1964 acquisition of New York's Parke Bernet helped immeasurably. Founded in 1934 by Hiram Haney Parke and Otto Bernet—two former executives of an old, established auction house called the American Art Association—Parke

& Bernet Galleries set numerous records over the years including sales of the "Cartier–Liz Taylor" diamond for $1,050,000 and the Edgar William and Bernice Chrysler Barbisch art collection for $20.3 million. The acquisition was, as Wall Street merger-makers say "a perfect fit." In 1972, the consolidated company was named Sotheby Parke Bernet worldwide.

But in spite of the happy corporate marriage and the strong balance sheet, problems were forming beneath the surface. In one way, Sotheby's resistance to change served it poorly. As more and more of the multimillion-dollar art collections were sold off piecemeal to private investors or bequeathed to museums, and as more and more of the great family fortunes were dispersed over the generations or frittered away by irresponsible heirs, Sotheby's core market shrank by attrition. Compounding the problem was a gradual disenchantment with collectibles as an investment asset and a growing preference for real estate. The new generation of millionaires—recording artists and Wall Street dealmakers—favored California ranches and Caribbean islands over Ming vases or Louis XIV desks.

By failing to monitor and respond to market changes (constancy remained the firm's guiding principle), Sotheby's missed out on the first signs of this capital reapportionment. Not until 1976, with the fiscal evolution well underway, did Sotheby's consent to a major departure from its traditional markets and its traditional way of doing business. It joined the land rush.

With the launching of its International Realty subsidiary, Sotheby's committed itself to selling a new product, real estate, as a marketer rather than auctioneer. For the first time, Sotheby's would act as brokers, earning commissions for the sale and purchase of real properties.

Not surprisingly, considering Sotheby's insular management, the initiative for diversification came from outside the company. Charles Seilheimer, Jr., the former Previews' vice president and a Virginia-based broker, had the brilliant stroke of applying the Sotheby's brand name—perhaps the most illustrious in the world—to the marketing of real property. A natural born marketer, Seilheimer recognized that in a nation increasingly drawn to symbols of status and privilege, Sotheby's imprimatur was an enormously valuable asset, one that could give the auction house instant access to real estate's grandest sales and its swelling treasury of seven-figure commissions.

By stressing Sotheby's long ties to British peerage and by thus creating an aristocratic image attractive to tradition-starved Americans, Seilheimer recognized he could gain immediate acceptance in the real estate market, by-passing the substantial investment generally required to build a reputation from the ground up.

"Sotheby's sells a lifestyle," he says, reiterating the theme he used to sell Sotheby's management on the real estate concept. "People have always looked to Sotheby's for the finest art, porcelains, and furniture to fill their home. Why not turn to Sotheby's for their homes as well? Who better understands their lifestyle—who better knows how to preserve and enrich it?

"I made the Sotheby people see the natural link between their traditional markets and the proposed expansion into real estate. I said to them, 'Look, you are really a marketing firm. You use catalogs, mailing lists, and public relations to sell to people who want and demand the finest. Until now, you've limited this effort to art works but there's no reason to preserve this limitation. We can use similar procedures to sell luxury properties.' "

Seilheimer's point—widely accepted by management consultants—is that marketing know-how is transferable to a wide range of products and services. The skills developed in selling one brand or category of goods can be applied to dozens of different brands, even those in widely different industries. In many cases, the brand names change, but the fundamental sales tactics remain the same. Corporate recruiters know that an office products marketer can apply his skills to selling toothpaste, deodorant, or toilet paper. That's why when Apple Computer sought a marketing-oriented president to help the company open new markets in the

1980s, it lured away John Scully from the presidency of Pepsico's beverage unit. Learn to sell, the theory goes, and you can learn to sell anything.

Seilheimer first presented his real estate marketing ideas to an old friend at the auction house, Sotheby Park Bernet vice president Edward Cave. The two had crossed paths over the years and, although their relationship had always been informal, Seilheimer was sufficiently impressed with Cave's entrepreneurial flair—unusual for a Sotheby's man—to trust that he'd react favorably to the proposal.

"Every now and then we'd share business opportunities," Seilheimer recalls. "When I was at Previews, I'd push some leads on home contents auctions to his side of the desk and he'd pass me prospective real estate listings. We were in a good position to help each other and it worked out quite well."

"That's one of the reasons I approached Edward with my idea for a national marketing organization. He's a sharp, open-minded man, always eager to hear new business ideas—and I felt certain he'd greet this one enthusiastically.

"But he didn't—well, not at first. In fact, he hardly responded at all. There I was exuberantly describing my master plan and he just stared at me, expressionless. I'd never seen Edward that way and, let me tell you, it was disconcerting. When my wife asked me how our meeting went, I had to admit to myself and to her that I didn't have a clue.

"But the mystery, thank God, was short-lived. Edward called bright and early the next day, saying he hadn't slept a wink. My idea, he confirmed, was superb and he wanted me to return to New York immediately to meet with Sotheby's chairman John Marion."

Seilheimer's next challenge was to convince Marion that the luxury real estate market had sufficient potential in terms of gross revenues and net profits to warrant Sotheby's involvement. His most convincing argument was that the rich had become a highly mobile class, dividing their time between a collection of homes offering a mix of climates, leisure facilities and social connections.

Cave, a trained curator whose double vision views the

twentieth-century world from a historical perspective, recognized the truth in this and restated it in his own inimitable fashion:

"Two hundred years ago Louis XIV could not conceive of a trip 30 or 40 miles away—one of the greatest men of all times and he never saw Rome or journeyed to London-towne. Today a prince may enjoy a *pied à terre* in Manhattan, a villa in Monte Carlo, and an oceanfront mansion in Palm Beach, all because of the mobility afforded by the Concorde."

The Seilheimer/Cave presentation convinced Marion to give the go-ahead on the new division. Credit him with the foresight to break with tradition primarily on the strength of an outsider's recommendation. No doubt the temptation proved too great to resist. With property values soaring and percentage-based brokerage commissions rising in tandem, there was clearly money to be made. Cave and Marion agreed that Sotheby's was in an unusually good position to profit handsomely in this potentially lucrative business.

"We knew we had a built-in advantage in selling real estate because of our exclusive access to the Sotheby Park Bernet's mailing list, which is made up of 80,000 of the wealthiest people on earth," boasts Seilheimer, a large but gracefully mannered man who comes across as part country gentleman, part corporate wheeler-dealer. Before vacating* the president's office in July 1983 to become a Sotheby's regional vice-president, he criss-crossed two worlds, living weekdays in a Manhattan cooperative near Sotheby's office and jetting off Fridays to his Virginia farm, where he tends to a stable of horses and a cherished collection of early American furniture and paintings. "Our mailing list is especially valuable because it is made up of clients that Sotheby Parke Bernet, the gallery, has served for generations, in some

---

* Seilheimer claims he resigned in order to cash in on Sotheby's stock holdings as the firm was being purchased by a private investor—something he was forbidden to do as president. But he also hints at conflicts with Sotheby's senior management on the way the real estate division should be run. Sotheby's refuses to comment.

cases for centuries. Because of these enduring relationships, the families and individuals on the list are remarkably receptive to our solicitations."

Sotheby's intimate knowledge of its auction clientele has also been turned into a potent weapon for real estate marketing. From its earliest years, the firm wisely footnoted its mailing lists with semipersonal data on client hobbies and business interests. Today, when a major property comes on the market, Sotheby's taps this vein for leads. To find a buyer for a Kentucky horse farm, for example, the staff cross references the master list for those Sotheby's clients with a known passion for horse breeding, racing or polo. This gives the auctioneer cum realtor an advantage over arch rival Previews.

"The important point is that you always want to figure some angle, some clever way of reaching the target market through their most identifiable affiliation or pursuits," Seilheimer says. "Determine their lifestyle, then try to sell them real estate that matches it."

To market Hilton, a $2.5-million, 264-acre gentleman's horse breeding farm in Somerset, Virginia, Sotheby's structured a multidimensional direct mail campaign using widely available lists in addition to its own in-house cross-referencing system.

"It was felt that the property would appeal to various interest groups," says Virginia Haynes, "including foreign diplomats assigned to Washington, D.C., as the estate is only a 1¼-hour drive to Dulles International Airport and 100 miles to Washington, D.C. Because of this, we sent mailings to: Sotheby Parke Bernet's lists of U.S. and Foreign art offices, our Geneva office VIP list, and our Italian VIP list. We also mailed to our lists of European brokers, United Kingdom brokers, South American brokers, and embassy offices in Washington, D.C.

"Due to its close proximity to Washington, D.C., mailings were made to U.S. officials assigned to Washington, D.C. Lists included U.S. Cabinet Secretaries' and Undersecretaries' offices, housing officers for the Armed Forces (for

high-ranking personnel), Pentagon officials VIP list, lobby-
ists in Washington, D.C.

"We also selected lists that reflected Hilton's unique
structural characteristics. Because the manor house is a
newly restored eighteenth-century Colonial, mailings were
sent to Sotheby Parke Bernet's subscribers in Colonial and
Early American Art, Sotheby Parke Bernet International
Realty's VIP list of potential buyers of Colonial homes, and
our VIP list of potential buyers of Estates over 200 acres.

"As the property is a breeding farm for thoroughbreds
and Angus cattle, and is also a hunting terrain with Canadian
geese and ducks, additional mailings were sent to the Morgan Horse Clubs and Horse Farms, American Saddlebred
Horse Association members, Roster of Recognized Horse
Judges, Stewards and Technical Delegates, New York
Breeders membership list, Virginia Breeders membership
list, Hunt Country Virginia brokers list, and our own list
of potential buyers of breeding farms."

Again, we see the Previews-pioneered segmentation
strategy put to use in marketing real estate. But the list
selection for the Hilton estate reveals that the similarities
between Previews and Sotheby's tend to mask their differences. Though both are savvy practitioners of direct mail
marketing, and both use special lists to reach narrowly defined segments, Sotheby's prefers to choose its lists more
on the basis of personal contacts with prospective clients
than on detective work. Most important, every effort is made
to cultivate leads, and to win listings through Sotheby's long-
standing auction house relationships.

Edward Cave, a fellow who is said to have started his
career in Sotheby's warehouse but who appears never to
have soiled his hands, likes to put it this way: "Because
we have always sold what hangs on the walls, we should
sell the walls too."

This apparent play on words is actually an intrinsic part
of Sotheby's sales campaign to woo prospective real estate
clients. The pitch, well rehearsed by Sotheby's field personnel, holds out the lure of a cash windfall for those owners

wise enough to list with Sotheby's. The reasoning goes like this: "Because we are skilled appraisers, because we are trained to identify value in household assets, we may determine that Aunt Sara's hideously ugly flower vase relegated to the front porch as an umbrella stand is actually a rare Chinese porcelain worth $500,000 at auction. And heaven knows we'll be pleased to auction it for you."

Seilheimer loves to relate seductive anecdotes of his firm's "gold-in-the-attic" discoveries.

"Just when I arrived to handle the sale of Chestnut Lawn, an estate in Remington, Virginia, owned by an heir to the Wilkens coffee fortune, a set of Goya prints in the main residence was about to be sold off to a local dealer for the measly sum of $500. Because the figure seemed terribly low, I asked if I couldn't have a look at the prints before they were let go. I'm not an art expert myself, but I could tell from a cursory examination that the prints resembled genuine Goyas, and I knew that if I was correct they were worth a lot of money. So I asked Edward to fly down and give us a definitive answer."

Cave, an art historian schooled at the University of Geneva and at Columbia University, remembers the McNairey case well.

"I became extremely excited the moment I saw the prints hanging along the main staircase. It seemed that Charlie's hunch was right, that they were indeed genuine Goyas and quite valuable at that. But before committing myself, I wanted our Sotheby Parke Bernet resident expert on Goya to examine the works. We asked that the local sale be postponed until our New York staff could conduct a formal appraisal.

"It was worth the wait. The prints were deemed to be one of the few high-quality Goya sets around. They fetched $150,000 at auction.

"In another case, a local dealer offered one of our real estate clients $4,000 for what the owner deemed to be an interesting object of little value. On the hunch that the rather strange item—a figurine of a camel draped in a blue blan-

ket—might well be a rare antique, we asked that it be
brought to Sotheby Parke Bernet for professional appraisal.
To make a long story short, it brought $50,000 at auction.
I even remember a case when the contents of a house
brought more than the home itself: $650,000 versus $425,000.
I think it's fair to say that the owner profitted handsomely
by having as his real estate broker a firm capable of valuing
all of his assets—the physical structure as well as the contents."

Were there such a thing as the ideal Sotheby's listing—
one in which the physical structure is composed primarily
of antiques—certainly the twenty-one-room Manhattan triplex at 666 Park Avenue, sold by Sotheby's in June, 1982,
would fit the bill. Assigned to Sotheby's by the former owners, Leslie and Fan Fox Samuels—noted patrons of the arts
and major benefactors of Lincoln Center—the 6,000-square-
foot residence is self-consciously European, from the elabo-
rately carved cornice to the Corinthian pilasters and chimney
breast ornamented with cornucopias, garlands, scrolls and
center mantle mask. Reflecting Sotheby's penchant for collectibles, the entire 50-foot pine drawing room is a valuable
antique, having been imported from Spettisbury Manor in
England and installed stateside in exact proportion.

Sotheby's marketing brochure prepared for the triplex
waxes poetic about the property, finding in it all that has
been lost in an increasingly uncivilized world.

> Vigorous Old English influence continues in the pine
> library, elliptical in form and distinguished by masterful
> 18th-century appointments such as imported Georgian
> paneling and a mantle obtained from an early Georgian
> manor on London's Grosvenor Street. . . .
>
> Accessible from the main stairway, which rises in a
> graceful curve from the entrance hall, three spacious
> master suites include the Louis XIII Suite, reflecting
> all of the grandeur of the seventeenth century in France.
> Paneled with two polychromed *boiserie*, this suite once

served as a wing to the Château de Courcelles—a charming château built in the truculent days when Marie de Medici's son reigned on the throne and the astute Richelieu was the virtual leader. . . .

Says *New York Times* architecture critic Paul Goldberger:

This is a place that seeks to pull all of history within its grasp. Within the discreet limestone exterior of this Park Avenue apartment building, sections of seventeenth-century France and seventeenth- and eighteenth-century England were brought here out of that same impulse that motivated so much of our eclectic architecture—that sense that we might somehow command history, possess it, by transferring it, piece by piece, from its origins in Europe to the new culture of New York City.*

But even more than the grand maisonette, more than any of Sotheby's extraordinary listings, the marketing of Hever castle clearly indicates how art works and real estate can be fused in the valuation of a single property and how they can serve as two distinct profit centers for the broker skilled in auction services. When Sotheby's launched its search to find a qualified buyer for Hever, it found that the heirlooms collected by three generations of Astors and stored within the castle's gray stone walls were an impediment to a quick sale. Word has it that prospective buyers complained that they were being asked to purchase a museum. Bids coming into Sotheby's New York and London offices did not reflect a fair value for the castle's contents. To get around this problem, Sotheby's sold the property stripped of its contents** and marketed the collection in three separate auctions for the arms, works of art, and

* Paul Goldberger, in *The New York Times*, July 16, 1981, p. C10.
** Sotheby's refuses to cite the sales price.

manuscripts. Major pieces included an extraordinary array
of arms and armor featuring a Milanese mid-sixteenth-cen-
tury suit made for Henry II of France, together with a fif-
teenth-century helmet of forged steel overlaid with gold,
said to have belonged to the King of Granada, a fourteenth-
century French Gothic oblong casket made entirely of ivory,
historic portraits of Queen Elizabeth I and Edward VI, ten
contemporary drawings by Robert Adams of the Defeat of
the Spanish Armada, continental and English furniture, six-
teenth-century tapestries, letters signed by Henry VII,
Henry VIII, Queen Elizabeth I, and three of Henry's wives:
Catherine of Aragon, Anne Boleyn, and Catherine Parr.

Showings were held in New York, Los Angeles, Frankfurt, Munich, and London. When the final gavel fell, the
auction produced an additional $8.8 million, with Henry II's
armor fetching $3,041,000 of that total.

The assurance that one's real estate broker is skilled
at valuing and marketing a treasure of this magnitude is
comforting to property owners whose collections represent
a substantial, but often illiquid, component of their personal
wealth. That Sotheby can serve as a quasi-investment banker
for these arcane assets is certainly a strong selling point
in the competition for property listings.

But auctions are auctions and real estate is real estate,
and its facility for selling works of art is not the key factor
in Sotheby's success as a licensed broker. The one Sotheby's
asset that neither Previews nor any other competitors can
duplicate is the very one that inspired Seilheimer's brainstorm and that accounted for the firm's entry into the real
estate market. When it comes to attracting clients and successfully marketing million-dollar properties, Sotheby's extraordinary image does most of the work.

It's the quiet dignity of the Sotheby's name, the aristocratic air, the near magical association with royalty and tradition and fairy tale kingdoms that so enchants buyers and
sellers alike. This is another of those rare businesses whose
appeal is greater than the sum of its parts.

Factor in the firm's exclusive mailing lists, its network

of old school ties, its staff of scholarly curators, and the total—impressive though it is—does not fully account for Sotheby's rapid ascension to the heights of real estate brokerage. Something extraordinary is at work here.

"Quite often, when Sotheby's name is associated with a property; when Sotheby's name is on the brochure, the property commands a higher price than it could otherwise obtain," says Jack Mitchell, whose brokerage firm, A. T. Houlihan, served as Sotheby's first affiliate in Westchester County until it was replaced* in 1983 by Bixler, a local competitor. An entrepreneurial wheeler-dealer always on the lookout for ways to expand and diversify his brokerage business, Mitchell competes head-to-head with Sally Siano in Bedford's pricy horse country. "I've seen the Sotheby's name tack on a half million dollars or more to a property's sale price. Let me put this in the proper perspective.

"Example one: Just before Sotheby Parke Bernet International Realty became a force in the Bedford market I sold an extraordinary estate here, then owned by Gardner Cowles, to cosmetics heir John Revson. This absolute palace of a place, built in the late 1920s, had everything even the most pampered trillionaire could want and then some. I'm talking about sterling silver door handles, walnut floors, an air-conditioned movie theatre, tennis courts, pool, greenhouse, 80 acres, and a perfectly marvelous view of the countryside. It would seem that Mr. Cowles was in a position to demand many millions for the estate. But far from it. The most we could get for the property—after a full year of negotiations with various parties—was $535,000. Not quite a princely sum.

"Example two: about the same time, in the fall of 1975, we listed another perfectly marvelous home, this one built entirely of seventeenth-century bricks taken from the coun-

---

* Mitchell claims this was a mutual decision made by Sotheby's and himself. "When this market turned really strong, I found that property owners balked at paying Sotheby's marketing commission. Because Sotheby's started blaming me for this, I decided that it was best to part company." Sotheby's refuses to comment.

try house of the Earl of Essex. The lavish appointments
matched and exceeded the Cowles estate. Antique brass fixtures throughout, swimming pool, two gate cottages, six-
car garage, barn, and the best fishing stream in Bedford.
What was the best we could get for this? $565,000.

"In spite of the fact that I personally thought that both
of these sales were virtual giveaways, they represented,
at the time, the high water marks for Bedford real estate
prices. Slightly over $500,000 each for what were easily the
best houses in town.

"But a dramatic change was in the wind. Six months
after the Cowles' estate was sold, Sotheby's handled its first
listing in our market. A pleasant frame Colonial built close
to the road on 14 acres, it was a charming place but several
notches below the properties I'd just worked so hard to fetch
half a million dollars for.

"But Sotheby's was not fazed by the recent sales. They
believed that the Sotheby name could set new price levels
and to prove it they asked over $1 million for the Colonial.
Local brokers were snickering and to be honest I was among
the skeptical, thinking Sotheby's was going too far too fast.
But we succeeded in selling the property—I acted as the
local agent—not for a million but for $1,535,000. This for
a property that did not have one-third the intrinsic value
of the previous sales."

Why did Sotheby's fare so well? Because it brought
an extra dimension to the market. Specifically, the widely
held notion that any asset sold through Sotheby's offices—
be it an oil painting by Dutch masters or a colonial home
by American craftsmen—is worthy of special artistic consideration. People think it's special because the Sotheby name
is stamped on the offering circular.

"There's no doubt that Sotheby's presence here has
changed the complexion of Bedford's property market. From
the day they closed on that first listing, all subsequent sales
in town stepped up to a higher level. The Sotheby's deal
became the standard against which other prices were set."

Sotheby's PR staff credits the firm's buyer network—

clearly a clone of Previews stock exchange for real estate—for its pricing performance.

"We're successful at fetching an average sales price of $1.4 million because we reach outside the community to tap an international network of wealthy buyers. It works like this: Let's say we have a listing in Bedford that, because it is perched on a hilltop and has a magnificent view, can bring an extra $500,000 over comparable homes on less spectacular settings. Typically, a local resident will not pay an additional half million dollars for a hilltop view. To that person, it's just another home he's passed for years on the way to work or church or what have you. He thinks the view's worth a bit extra, perhaps, but not $500,000. But by introducing an Englishman, a Frenchman, or a Manhattanite to the property—one who enjoys spectacular views and is willing to pay handsomely for the feature—we can increase the sales price quite substantially. To these outsiders, the home's new and original and well worth the premium. That's why we can routinely assure the sellers more than they would have received were the sale limited to the local community."

Predictably, Previews debunks this, claiming that Sotheby's sales network is more or less a fabrication designed to impress sellers and to win listings.

"Let's put it this way, there's less there than meets the eye," snaps Bruce Wennerstrom. "What they call a sales network is mostly a publicity gimmick. Anyone who knows anything about real estate knows that you can't build a meaningful marketing system in a few years. It has taken us decades—and we're still perfecting it. The truth is that Sotheby's marketing strategy is to tell people they can get more money for their properties and hope they'll believe them. To make the pitch more appealing, Sotheby's throws in little teasers about its prestigious reputation and all but that's just snobby nonsense. We witness their gambit all the time. Enlightened sellers who recognize that they need marketing assistance will often call on Previews and Sotheby's to compete for the listing. Inevitably, Sotheby's goes to great extremes to schedule its meeting with the owner after we've departed. Once inside the home the Sotheby's executive whispers in the owner's ear, 'How much did Previews tell you the house is worth?' Regardless of what the party says, Sotheby's comes up with a figure that's above our appraisal. Understandably the novice is taken in by this. If one broker claims he can sell your most important asset for $1 million but another promises to clear an additional $250,000, who's going to get the listing? Any fool can answer that one.

"But this is counterproductive. Overpriced properties languish on the market. They take longer to sell and they go for less than if they were realistically priced from the start."

Sally Siano, a feisty competitor whose initial anxiety over Sotheby's entry into the Bedford market has all but dissipated, agrees.

"Just look at the house Peter Duchin built here in the late '70s. It's a pseudo-Tudor, constructed of modern building materials often with less than the best workmanship. The home is replete with new timbers stained to simulate centuries of wear; textured plaster designed to duplicate Old World building techniques. But it doesn't fool anyone. Pull up in the driveway and you see the nouveau-riche signs written all over the place. In Bedford, that's anathema. Wealthy people choose to live here because the town has an abundance of genuine eighteenth-century properties built by colonial craftsmen. They don't want the same mock Tudors you can find in any town in Ohio.

"It's a sad story with the Duchins' house. Peter and his wife put a lot of money into building it, but I believe they were led down the primrose path in pricing it for sale.

"At Sotheby's initial $3 million figure, the place was terribly overpriced and it remained so even after being reduced to $2.5 million. With their expectations set unrealistically high, the Duchins rejected reasonable offers that might have led to a quick sale. I brought them a buyer for $1.6 million but they wouldn't even entertain the offer. Too bad—

the place has gone vacant and unsold for more than a year. I blame this, in part, on the ridiculously high asking price."

The truth is that virtually all realtors build a modest cushion, call it a "vanity premium," into property appraisals when they believe this will help to secure a choice listing. That's the motive behind local brokers' newspaper ads promising homeowners a free estimate of their properties' market value. The thinking goes like this: get your foot in the door; play up to the owner's sense of pride (and greed); tempt him with a valuation that's slightly inflated and chances are you'll get the listing. Going to market with an asking price that's only marginally above the actual projected value is good business anyway. Savvy negotiators always build in a little padding to allow room for compromise while still closing a profitable deal.

The national marketers, Sotheby and Previews, are more prone to wholesale use of the vanity premium because they must justify the substantial override they tack on to standard brokerage commissions. The rationale is that if they charge more, they should deliver more, and what better way to assure superior performance than to net the owner a bigger return on his property.

Financial services professionals have used this tactic for years.

"Granted, our fees are higher than those charged by many small CPA firms," says William Raby, a tax attorney and partner with the Big Eight accounting firm Touche Ross. "But we tell clients to judge us not by the size of our fees but instead by the amount of taxes we save them. I say a good tax attorney trades dollars for discount. That's actually what happens when a client pays me $25,000 and I save him $100,000."

Full service stock brokerage firms also use this argument to halt the defection of major accounts to discount brokers, many of whom offer savings of 50 to 75 percent on securities trades.

"So the investor saves $200 on a round trip trade," says a vice president of retail brokerage for Merrill Lynch. "We turn the tables on him, asking that he consider what he lost to gain that $200. Because discount brokers do not offer research services, the investor may lose out on news of emerging companies, potential splits or sudden market reversals that warrant a quick sale. Yes, it costs more to do business with us, but in all likelihood you'll earn more in the process."

The caveat in quoting vanity premiums—at least when it comes to real estate brokerage—is that realtors must avoid the severe overpricing that can damage the property's marketability and its ultimate sales price. When that happens, it's usually for competitive reasons. Blinded by ambition, greed, competitive zeal, and personal antagonisms, they accept any number of deals that come back to haunt them once the property is on the market.

Conversations with dozens of brokers familiar with both national marketers indicate that both may inflate appraisals from time to time. But these same sources indicate that when Sotheby's keeps its vanity premiums within modest bounds, it is likely to secure the high prices in the marketplace.

"I'm willing to point out Sotheby's strengths as well as its weaknesses," Siano mentioned. "While I don't agree that they can single-handedly bring an entire market's prices to substantially higher levels, their name can be a potent aid in the sale of luxury properties and they may be able to get a few more dollars for realistically priced homes.

"The Sotheby name connotes social grace, old money, a classic Bentley. You can't buy that kind of cachet with advertising or brochures alone. No local broker—no other national marketing system—can match it.

"Maybe I shouldn't admit this, but I'd absolutely adore being the Sotheby's broker in Bedford. Virtually all of the homes here are in the luxury class and many of the owners have dealt with the art gallery for years. The Sotheby name would add stature to Sally Siano Associates. It would enhance the prestigious image I've worked so hard to cultivate for my firm."

Sotheby's differs markedly from Previews in that it des-
ignates a single affiliate broker as its representative in each
community. The affiliate gains local control of Sotheby's-gen-
erated listings, has sole authority to display the Sotheby
name in its brokerage offices and newspaper ads and has
its name printed alongside Sotheby's in the company's marketing brochures. Most important, should another local broker sell a Sotheby's property, the affiliate is assured one-
third share of the commission. Sotheby's and the cobroker
split the balance.

The affiliate approach goes hand-in-hand with Sotheby's
goal of creating a pristine marketing system unspoiled by
the second-rate properties or brokers.

"You build a strong marketing network by identifying
the best local brokers in every major market and then convincing them to work with you," says Hall Wilkie, former
Sotheby's West Coast vice-president. The firm's Los Angeles
office maintains an annual inventory of thirty homes with
an estimated market value of $120 million. The $4 million
average is maximal even for the real estate wilds of lotus
land.

> You look for brokers with experience selling luxury
> properties, with a fine reputation in the community and
> with a bit of panache. They have to complement the
> Sotheby's name.

By handpicking its local affiliates, Sotheby's raises the
quality of its local brokerage network and, in the process,
safeguards its corporate image. This strategy, based on the
marketing principle known as "limited distribution," count-
ers the prevailing notion that the marketer's success can
be measured by the number of sales outlets carrying or
representing his products. Adherents of limited distribution
(Sotheby's is one, Previews is not) hold that it is the quality
of distribution, not the quantity, that has the greatest impact
on the bottom line. Again, the concept of "less is more"
comes into play. By intentionally limiting the size of its affili-

ate network to a single broker in each community, Sotheby's believes it can control not only its product (it can and does refuse to list pedestrian properties) but also the channels of distribution (the brokers responsible for showing properties to active prospects).

Top drawer fragrance marketers—similar in many ways to luxury real estate marketers in that both sell snob appeal products at the high end of their industry's price spectrum— use limited distribution to shape the profile of their retailer networks. Estee Lauder, for example, disciplines itself to reject distribution requests from chain or discount stores, believing that an association with Alexander's or K Mart would do irrevocable damage to its image. Much like Lauder, Sotheby's prefers to align itself with the most sophisticated and most prominent representatives in the local community.

But Sotheby's experience in Greenwich, Connecticut, proves that even the best-planned marketing systems can unravel in the marketplace. That Sotheby's should run into a roadblock in this pocket of affluence is surprising because Greenwich seems tailor-made for Sotheby's WASPy appeal. Certainly, this was on Seilheimer's mind when he entered the market in the mid 1970s—but he was headed for disappointment. The firm has sold less than five homes since hanging out its broker's shingle.*

Officially Sotheby's executives blame this poor showing on the selection of "second-rate" affiliates. The public relations mumbo-jumbo goes like this: "When we first started out there, we did not have a good fix on the brokerage power structure. Our affiliates, although strong in Stamford and other Connecticut towns, were not at the top of the Greenwich hierarchy. As a result, they were not entirely suited to be our representatives. They were, how shall I put it, below our station. A disadvantage from which we are now hoping to recover."

But in private, Sotheby's managers admit, albeit reluctantly, that the relative strength of the Greenwich brokerage

* As of mid-1983 figures.

community is the real deterrent to the national marketer's success in the community. Says a top-level Sotheby's executive, "In Greenwich, even a bungalow by the railroad tracks sells for a half million dollars and anything halfway decent is nigh into several million. So Greenwich brokers have a good deal of experience with luxury properties. They don't have to work hard to attract buyers—wealthy people come to Greenwich under their own steam—and they don't have to be taught the finer points of catering to the rich. Local brokers there are convinced they don't need us—and in some cases they're probably right."

Add to this obstacle the same "pride factor" that turns many brokers against Previews. Greenwich realtors—especially the successful and prestigious offices that Sotheby's woos—don't sit still for the idea that an art gallery subsidiary just getting its feet wet in real estate can show up experienced brokers with deep roots in the community. Even when it is in their own self-interests to work with Sotheby's, these realtors instinctively seek to beat back the nationals as dangerous interlopers.

Sotheby's shrugs off this resistance in a number of blue-chip markets—Manhattan and Palm Beach (managed by a former Previews executive) among them—by operating its own office in these communities. But this apparent solution creates a problem of another kind. While staffing its own outlets frees Sotheby from dependence on independent affiliates, the trade-off is that it creates resentment among local realtors and confirms the image—held by skeptics all along—of Sotheby's as a brokerage competitor rather than a third-party marketing organization.

"Sotheby's moves in and corrals the best markets for themselves," gripes Palm Beach's Steve Cutter. "How can brokers even consider working with an organization like that? They're not our allies, they're our competitors."

Although Sotheby's shudders at this kind of talk, the firm may be forced to open a company-owned office if it is ever to be a factor in the Greenwich market. Its current affiliate, Jane Newhall of the firm of Ogilvy & Newhall, is not the kind of enthusiastic liaison Sotheby's can count on to further its interests.

"Not true," Seilheimer roars. "You must understand that Jane Newhall recently merged her brokerage with another firm run by a much younger man. So you have the grande dame of Greenwich real estate now sharing responsibility with another principal.

"If she seems somewhat irritated or aloof, it's because the two principals don't always agree on how the business should be run. But one thing they both agree on is that the Sotheby's affiliation is a good thing for the firm."

Wishful thinking? Seated in her soberly furnished office, appointed with banker's mahogany and stiffly starched drapes, Newhall shows little patience for making small talk with Sotheby's regional vice president Clair Martin or for meeting anyone's standards save her own.

Asked how the Sotheby's image will aid her brokerage firm, she appears perturbed by the question.

> I don't know about things like that. We just sell properties here. That's all we've ever done.

Thoroughly embarrassed by her remark, Martin seems eager to plunge out the nearest window. Typical of Sotheby's field vice presidents, he cultivates an impeccable, never-a-hair-out-of-place appearance. Together, he and the feisty gray-haired realtor make for an odd couple infinitely more disparate than Felix and Oscar.

When asked, in Newhall's presence, to describe Sotheby's most successful sale in the Greenwich market, Martin fusses and fumbles, asking for time to assemble all the facts.

"I'll have to look into that one. Check the facts. You know how it is. I want to be perfectly accurate. Let me get back to you."

Weeks pass. Phone calls go unanswered. Months pass. Still no response. No description of the sale. Finally, there is a call from the PR department.

"Er, Clair asked me to call. Er, we haven't had a Greenwich sale that we think really merits close scrutiny."

"Well, why don't you just tell me about a few of your best sales and let me be the judge."

"Er—we haven't had a sale in Greenwich for years."

"None?"

"None."

Sotheby's performance is infinitely better in those markets where the local affiliate enthusiastically embraces its venerable name and marketing system and delivers to Sotheby's a bankable collection of local listings likely to benefit from international exposure. The willingness to share listings with the national marketer is vitally important for gaining affiliate status and for maintaining a successful relationship. In spite of its exacting corporate standards on broker selection, Sotheby's is willing to stretch the limits of acceptability for those prospective affiliates who can keep the firm well plenished with million-dollar listings.

Realtors operating in Sotheby-free markets may use this marketing tactic to build a position in luxury sales. By trading a major listing in return for designation as the Sotheby's affiliate, the broker gains instant access to Sotheby's prestigious logo and its international sales network.

Jack Mitchell used this approach to hook up with Sotheby's soon after it launched its real estate division. Blessed with the kind of 20/20 double vision that distinguishes the most successful real estate entrepreneurs, Mitchell can keep one eye on the details of current business and the other on long-term objectives.

"When Sotheby first opened their doors, they tried to keep the Bedford market for themselves, servicing it through their New York office," Mitchell recalls, flashing the shy smile of a country fox who outmaneuvered the big wolf from the city. "If I looked at the real estate business strictly on a sale-by-sale basis, I'd have viewed Sotheby's as a competitor to be challenged at every turn. But intuition told me that it was the better part of valor to join rather than battle them. Sotheby's had something I wanted—incomparable prestige—and I decided to put some of that to work for my firm, A. T. Houlihan.

"So I launched a two-stage stick-and-carrot offensive:

Posing as a prospective buyer, I started calling Sotheby's about their advertised properties, asking to see this or that house only to cancel at the last minute. Each time a Sotheby's V.P. would take the Great-Four-Hour-Empty-Handed-Circular-Route, motoring out from New York, arriving in Bedford only to learn of the false alarm and then angrily pointing his automobile back toward the Triborough Bridge. Each time he killed the better part of a day and each time he relearned the same lesson: That to sell real estate you need a presence in the local market—that real estate is a local business."

Mitchell knew it wouldn't take too many frustrating excursions for Sotheby's to admit that it couldn't service Bedford from the east side of Manhattan.

"Just when I thought they were getting the message," Mitchell adds, twisting an imaginary pinky ring, "I closed in for the kill, suggesting that I become their affiliate broker. I knew it would be a hard sell so I brought along a secret weapon. Tucked in my pocket was an irresistible listing for a major Bedford property. They took the bait, sold the place for $2.5 million, and we've been working well together ever since."

Seilheimer's recollection of the episode reveals that there was another dimension.

"Our regional vice presidents were keeping some sales territories for themselves," Seilheimer admits. "They were hoping, by keeping affiliates out of the picture, to claim a greater share of the brokerage commissions. But I set up this company with the aim of operating it as an affiliate network and I wasn't going to let my staff tamper with that concept. That's what being a chief executive is all about. You want to give your subordinates some decision-making authority but not so much that they can rewrite the rules. Once I learned of the problem, I demanded that they be more aggressive in signing up affiliates. That's when Jack Mitchell came on board."

Mitchell's coup illustrates how creative thinking coupled with aggressive action can propel a broker from the ranks of the ordinary to the highly successful: One man's tactics prompted Sotheby's to rewrite its policies and to cut him in on a piece of the action.

Much like Previews, Sotheby's is set up more as a marketing firm than a realtor. Although Sotheby's does not publish a real estate magazine of its own, it lists properties in the Sotheby's gallery newsletter and spends $1 million a year advertising in a collection of upscale magazines including *The Blood Horse, Preservation News, The Economist, Historic Preservation, Country Life* (U.K.), *Town & Country* and *Architectural Digest*. Sotheby's brochures, similar in form and content to those of Previews and the Confederation of International Real Estate, have one distinguishing feature that typifies Sotheby's Old World style. Each property is christened with a haughty name meant to impart aristocratic bearing.

Just how Sotheby's marketing system makes a Cinderella out of a stepchild—how it uses creative packaging and a pretentious name to give a property an extra dimension—can be seen in its handling of a rather modest home on a half acre in Beverly Hills. Because the home's custom designed interior is its most striking feature, Sotheby's advised the owner to sell it completely furnished. Christened "Le Bijou" and promoted as an "instant home," it was designed to appeal to the handful of wealthy bicoastal New York-based executives willing and able to invest $3 million in a *pied-à-terre* convenient to Studio City. Sotheby's stroke of genius was to include, along with the art work, linens, china, plants, sofas, and chandeliers, a 1976 Rolls-Royce Silver Shadow. The burgundy Rolls—worth no more than $50,000 on the open market—served as a rich man's prize in a Cracker Jack box and effectively enhanced the property's appeal.

Ironically, domestic automobile manufacturers have traditionally used a similar tactic to sell expensive cars. When Cadillac introduced its top-of-the-line Seville, the $20,000 automobile was promoted on the basis of a $500 computerized trip odometer. The flashy gadget gave the shlocky gas guzzler a high tech image and provided it with a catalyst for impulse sales. Seville advertising focused not on the drive train or the engine, but instead on the dashboard's mini terminal. Likewise, Sotheby's "Bijou" brochure gave top billing to the Silver Shadow.

There is a lesson to be learned here. In all real estate sales—from single-family homes to commercial office towers—creative packaging and clever marketing gimmicks can make ordinary properties more attractive and can add to their selling price. Although the concept is not new to local realtors, few take it to the limit. The problem is, they think too small, limiting their actions to established and all too often ineffective procedures. When a local Bedford broker reels in a listing for a $500,000, six-bedroom center-hall colonial, he'll look only to the standard ways of readying the property for sale: a fresh coat of paint, a new roof, a dozen rhododendrons on the front lawn. But he may profit by setting his sights higher, convincing the owner to leave his Jaguar XJS in the circular driveway, and his gourmet cookware hanging in the country kitchen—all inclusive in the sales price. Taking a page from Sotheby's, the seemingly ordinary Bedford clapboard is repackaged as an "instant home" for transferred IBM executives.* Because transferees—a major market for suburban brokers—are uprooted families in search, above all else, of a sense of home, the tactic can be extremely effective, adding substantially to the owner's and the broker's bank accounts. If properly packaged, $25,000 worth of used Jaguar and Cuisinarts builds $50,000 into the sales price. Much the way a $500 computer gadget, heavy-duty shocks and the name Seville help General Motors sell $20,000 cars.

"We promoted Le Bijou on the basis that the buyer needed only a check and a toothbrush to move into his own West Coast home," Hall notes. "It would be as convenient as checking into a hotel."

---

* The company has its world headquarters only miles away in the neighboring town of Armonk.

The biggest pushovers for Sotheby's marketing machinations are not the blue bloods whose lifestyle they are designed to imitate—they see right through it—but instead the nouveau-riche who are busily jockeying for social position. Somehow it seems that buying gifts from Steuben Glass and homes from Sotheby Parke Bernet is all it takes to pole-vault through the socioeconomic strata.

"There's a predictable cycle to it all," says a Palm Springs broker who's earned millions plotting the behavior patterns of the newly rich. "Those who make the big bucks in one fell swoop want to spend it yesterday—or sooner if possible. I guess they have a lot of catching up to do. You know, all those years of being just a character actor off-Broadway or a down-on-the-luck wildcatter in the Texas panhandle. Now that they've achieved stardom, or struck oil, there's a lot of high living to do. They buy everything that isn't nailed down. And they love the glitzy stuff—DeLorean cars, coyote coats, lizard slacks, and to top it off a Beverly Hills showplace, put the accent on 'show,' ten feet from the curb and bathed in so many spotlights you could play night baseball on the front lawn.

"Well, once they gain these possessions they think they must have died and gone to heaven. To be living so beautifully—they have to pinch themselves to believe it. But then two, maybe three years go by and they start to see themselves in the mirror. A half dozen freshly made millionaires follow them onto the same Beverly Hills block, each with the identical stainless-steel DeLoreans, the coyotes, lizard slacks, and the spotlights. Always the spotlights. And they see how tacky it really is.

"Just about this time they begin to discover how the old money lives. Perhaps they've been invited to one of their intimate little dinner parties or have been guests at their clubs. Suddenly the understatement, the reserve, the preference for buying fine things and keeping them in the family for generations—these trappings of quiet wealth seem infinitely more attractive than their own ostentatious lifestyle. In one of the greatest about-faces you've ever seen, they can't wait to discard all of their schmaltzy possessions, to turn off the spotlights and to trade in the curbside-bus-tour showplace for a distinguished estate concealed behind 10-foot hedges.

"They're also off to Palm Springs in search of a proper winter residence. At this point, they're determined to buy their way into American royalty. You have to see it to believe it. I've watched them stroll by my window dressed in white suits and straw hats. These people think they can transform themselves into the likes of the Whitneys or the Vanderbilts. When they're in that state of mind, Sotheby's has them for the picking. They view Parke Bernet as much as a social connection as a broker. It's nonsense, but they believe it.

"Not that we play dead to Sotheby's. By studying this strange but wholly predictable consumer psychology, we've learned to improve our business. Most important, we've created a prestigious reputation of our own. Following Sotheby's lead, we advertise in the society pages, we harvest social connections, and we run our office more like a private club than a typical brokerage storefront. For example, when we first started out as brokers, we kept lollipops in the office. Now, perish the thought. We've replaced the candy with a humidor of fine cigars and a mini bar stocked with imported brandies. The nouveau-riche are extremely image-conscious and they adore being pampered. Sotheby's has known that from the start. I had to learn it the hard way."

Although Sotheby's publicity mill loves to crank out breathless stories about the firm's dealings with dukes and princes, if the realty division had to depend on royalty to pay its bills it would soon be in Chapter 11.

For the most part, (in spite of Cave and Seilheimer's remarks to the contrary) the true aristocrats live in the homes they inherit and pass them on to the next generation. Properties are considered heirlooms to be sold—God forbid—only if the family fortune is squandered and assets have to be turned into cash. It's the fast-track crowd—the rock stars/song writers/film producers/video game makers—who make it fast and spend it fast and who buy and sell

their way from glitter to gentility and who keep the properties moving and the commissions brewing and the money
pouring in. Bless 'em all. While Sotheby Realty boasts of
its ties to the manor-born, the firm's client list reads like
the cover of *Variety*. A list of Sotheby's most notable transactions includes a sprinkling of American aristocrats—Nel-
son Rockefeller, Henry J. Heinz II, Mrs. Edsel Ford—but
is heavily weighted with millionaires of more recent vintage:

- SOLD: Designer Kenny Taz Lane's Manhattan townhouse
  to Liza Minelli.
- SOLD: A Long Island tudor mansion to the Bee Gee's
  Robin Gibb.
- SOLD: San Diego Chargers owner Eugene Klein's $8.5
  million estate in Beverly Hills to a client from the Near
  East.
- SOLD: A Virginia estate, "Harenwood," to Jack Kent
  Cooke, owner of the Washington Redskins.
- SOLD: Lowell Thomas's 350-acre Dutchess County, NY,
  estate to Italian film producer Dino De Laurentiis.

The De Laurentiis deal came on the heels of the largest
single family residential sale in U.S. history: Sotheby's marketing of the Italian film producer's Beverly Hills mansion—
The Knoll—to singer Kenny Rogers. A look behind the
scenes of this record-setting transaction offers a revealing
glimpse of real estate brokerage Sotheby's style, in the nation's most extraordinary market, Beverly Hills.
  The appeal of The Knoll is attributed to the old real
estate saw that the three most important components of
property value are location, location, and location. And there
are few locations in the world that can match Beverly Hills.
A wedge of real estate that rose to prominence in the golden
days of film making, Beverly Hills retained its luster as
an enclave of conspicuous wealth long after the studio system and most of the early stars that were its first residents

vanished from the scene. Although the four-square-mile twi-light zone of sun-bleached art deco mansions and piano-shaped swimming pools still boasts a sprinkling of celluloid legends—and the familiar tourist buses that cruise by Doris Day's house—the '80s crop of Beverly Hills residents are a diverse group of entrepreneurs having earned their money in movie production, drugs, video games, and oil. To them, Beverly Hills remains a Mecca partly because of its still glamorous facade, but equally important because it qualifies for the stock exchange for real estate, for the land rush.

It is, above all, a superb investment. The fundamentals, as they say on Wall Street, are impeccable: a sunny climate, close proximity to a major metropolitan city plus the security of the world's most stable democracy. For these reasons, money from the world overflows into Beverly Hills real es-tate, inflating property values by more than 1,000 percent in the past decade. Here one sees in microcosm the universal rule of land: that quality is far more important than quantity. Because it is so highly prized by people of wealth—mostly new wealth—the insatiable demand for wedges of Beverly Hills soil (shares of its stock) has propelled the price of one-acre building lots to $1.5 million. Again, we see the phenome-non of too many dollars chasing a limited supply of proper-ties.

"Don't let anyone tell you anything else: the rich want to live only with the rich," says Ed Cave, the gleam in his eye signaling his endorsement of this economic apartheid. "It's no fun to put on a diamond necklace unless everyone else at the party knows it's real."

Adds Hall Wilkie. "Sotheby's clients don't want to live in Podunk, California. Tell them of the most spectacular homes in a second- or third-rate town and they won't even bother to drive out. The only time they'll even consider re-mote properties is if they are vineyards or retreats. Other-wise, most everyone wants to live in Palm Springs, Santa Barbara, Pebble Beach, La Jolla, or Beverly Hills."

Which leads us back to the value of The Knoll. Far from being Beverly Hills' most attractive residence, the surprisingly plain Georgian estate is nevertheless its most valuable because it sits on one of the community's largest preserves of residential property. Its ten acres, bordered on all sides by a heavy-gauge wrought iron fence and a sophisticated security system, creates a DMZ between the superstar owner (now Kenny Rogers) and the legion of groupies, money-seekers, up-and-coming songwriters, gawkers, and extortionists pressing to get at him. Safely ensconced in his California fortress, the country-and-western crooner can play out his cowboy fantasy as if he were living alone on the great plains rather than smack in the middle of frozen yogurt land.

"And he can be assured of a superb investment," Seilheimer notes.

"Safety is the primary factor. America's political stability and its commitment to private land ownership is unmatched by any other country. That's why American real estate is so attractive to foreigners and why Sotheby's, in turn, limits our listings—Hever Castle is the only exception—to properties in the United States, the Caribbean, and Mexico. Rich people feel confident about investing their money here.

"We know that there are new millionaires being minted every day in dozens of countries all over the world. They're creating fortunes in gems, oil, precious metals, high technology, and entertainment. They're of different colors, cultures, and currencies. The only thing they have in common is that they want to invest their money in U.S. real estate."

On this, Sotheby's and Previews agree. "For many years, we sold a number of overseas properties to Americans," Bruce Wennerstrom notes. "Then, beginning in about 1973, the pendulum swung the other way and gradually overseas buyers became more important. This was caused by the weakness of the dollar and the strong economies in countries like Germany.

"Purchasing a property in the United States doesn't have a lot of the complications that overseas purchases do. When somebody has money that they want to invest in real

estate—I'm talking about outside the United States now—
and they begin to think about what countries they want to
invest in, the United States has to be right near the top of
the list."

> In many countries there are restrictions about nonciti-
> zens buying property. Many countries will not permit
> you to take out the capital gains. If, for example, you
> buy a property for $500,000 and you're fortunate
> enough a few years later to sell it for $700,000, you
> can take out the money you brought in. But the profit,
> the capital gains, has to stay within the country, so
> that detracts from the desirability of making a purchase
> and that is true of many countries.*

De Laurentiis discovered how substantial the capital
gains can be. The producer of such films as *Serpico* and
Death Wish purchased The Knoll in 1975 for $2.5 million,
and offered it for sale four years later for nearly six times
that amount.

"Mr. De Laurentiis was in New York on a business
trip when he called Ed Cave to request that Sotheby's handle
the listing," Hall says. "I understand he had dealings with
the auction gallery over the years and was impressed by
both Sotheby Parke Bernet's style and its business acumen.
That's why he entrusted us with his home.

"Needless to say, Ed Cave was delighted to get the
listing. Although he assumed it would be a major property—
the client was, after all, a world-renowned film producer—
he wasn't familiar with The Knoll. He called me the instant
he hung up with De Laurentiis.

" 'What's it like?' he asked, clearly hoping that I would
confirm his expectations. Although I'd never inspected the
property, I knew from the real estate grapevine that it was
the finest house in Beverly Hills."

After giving Cave the good news, Hall alerted Sotheby's

---

* *Palm Springs Life.*

local affiliate, Mimi Styné, and the two rushed to The Knoll paced by visions of six-figure commissions.

Quickly, they confirmed The Knoll's reputation as a magnificent, but somewhat poorly maintained, estate. The thirty-five-room main house boasted an impressive list of amenities, including seven servants' bedrooms, electric curtain and drape openers, heated swimming pool, four-person elevator, forty-foot library, two butler pantries, five-bedroom children's wing, temperature-controlled wine cellar, marble-floored gun room, two gazebos, poolside cabana with his and hers dressing room, potting shed, mechanic's shop, screening room with two Meganon Megalite 35mm projectors, thirteen-car garage, and guard house with half bath.

With so much going for it, there was no doubt the property would shatter Beverly Hills standing record of $6 million for a single-family residence. The only question Hall and Styné asked themselves was how high to set the asking price. Its abundant acreage in the midst of Beverly Hills made it a unique property, completely free of the restraints of comparable value.

"I called Mr. De Laurentiis, to inform him of our fees and to tell him that we require an exclusive contract," Hall remembers. "Clearly he was familiar with the terms—I imagine he'd discussed them first with Edward—and he indicated his eagerness to proceed with the sale. No more than a week after our telephone conversation, he returned to me a signed contract and we were ready to launch the marketing effort."

A month later, Sotheby's unveiled and circulated to its international network a rather hard-sell brochure highlighting The Knoll's most appealing features: privacy and security. The full-bleed cover, shot with a wide angle lense directly before the front gate, presents an imposing wall of iron—as wide as two Mercedes limousines—braced by ten-foot-high brick pillars topped with stone statues of menacing eagles. The subliminal message: this is as much a fortress as a home.

Past the gates the camera has trouble finding much

to celebrate. The place is rather ordinary save for the copious size of the spread and the protective buffer it provides. The main residence, ordinarily the lead act in a Sotheby's brochure, is banished to a one-by-three-inch sliver shot on the back cover. The white boxy structure, overpowered as it is by a broad, door-front canopy, bears an uncomfortable resemblance to a roadside motel. Even a Sotheby's executive admitted that The Knoll's physical condition left much to be desired.

"Oh, those interior rooms," he moans. "Although comfortably large and nicely laid out, they were in general disrepair. Because De Laurentiis spent more time in Italy than in Beverly Hills, the place was neglected and it looked it. It was a very difficult home to photograph. There was no place for the camera to turn."

Undaunted, Sotheby's set the asking price at a heady $15 million, the rationale being that so grand and private a property only minutes from state-of-the-art sound studios, NBC president Grant Tinker's office, and Los Angeles airport could command an enormous sum regardless of its condition. But that was only theory—the market had yet to speak. In the first six months, Sotheby's received twenty-four serious inquiries, a dozen of which jelled into solid offers. But all were below the property's $13 million "liquidation value," the sum it would bring if it could be subdivided and sold off piecemeal as separate building lots. Sotheby's price, somewhat above the property's raw asset value, reflected a built-in premium for having so sumptuous a setting intact in a community where art deco mansions are typically bunched as close together as the Lilliputian Cape Cods on Archie Bunker's Northern Boulevard.

"The initial offers, although I can't reveal the precise amounts, were flatly rejected as inadequate," Hall snipes, seemingly perturbed by such pettiness. "We were confident that we had something special to offer and that our patience would be amply rewarded. We counseled Mr. De Laurentiis to hold out for an offer close to his asking price and he deferred to our experience in these matters."

Soon after the marketing team made the decision to await a more generous bid, a secretary called Wilkie's office to say that her boss wished to arrange a tour of The Knoll.

"We ran a bank check on the fellow—we do this for all new clients—and the results indicated that he was a person of means," Hall notes, "so I set up a meeting at the property. Sure enough he appeared to be enormously successful. From the cut of his clothing to his luxury car, everything about the man gave evidence of wealth. Best of all, he called back in less than a week and made a very attractive bid." Ordinarily a cause for jubilance at the broker's office, this time there was hesitancy to uncork the champagne. In spite of all the positive signs, Hall sensed that something was wrong. He couldn't believe that so wealthy a client in the Los Angeles area would be unknown to him. In any case, Hall decided to double-check the bidder's credentials.

"I ordered a second bank check—this time from another source—and the findings couldn't have been worse.

"It turned out the guy was an impostor—a low-income work-a-day fellow whose idea of a good time was playing the role of a rich man. It turned out that he had weaseled his way through the first credit check by paying a bank officer to verify his financial statement. The car was doubtlessly rented; the secretary was in all likelihood a friend who played a part in the charade. When I informed him that we were onto his ploy, he became terribly agitated, screamed a half dozen obscenities, and then hung up on me. I never heard from him again."

Make-believe millionaires, counterfeit countesses, and phony princesses infiltrate the Beverly Hills real estate scene like so many character actors in a sitcom. The harmless variety, call them socioeconomic transvestites, simply get their jollies impersonating the rich. This, after all, is the land of make-believe. But other impostors, a far more dangerous breed, are motivated by criminal intent; gaining entry to a Beverly Hills estate in the guise of a would-be buyer provides the cat burglar with a rare opportunity to steal jewels, credit cards, and negotiable bonds without having to get past the burglar alarm or the guard dogs. Brokers, to retain their entry privileges, must act as the first line of defense. Thus the checking and the double checking.

Sometimes, references are unnecessary. Slightly more than eight months after The Knoll was listed, Kenny Rogers signaled his interest in the property. This time Sotheby's knew they had a qualified buyer.

Hands down the hottest act in show business, Rogers had earned an estimated $100 million on a string of hit records, concerts and television appearances. A middle-of-the-road artist with a country-and-western flair, his sweetly romantic ballads—appealing to a wide range of age groups and musical tastes—were equally popular in New York and Nashville. With his shaggy beard and soulful voice, he appeared to women as a gentle sex symbol—a father/lover figure with a seductive balance of strength and sensitivity. Fans sold out his live appearances hours after the tickets went on sale. The money poured in.

But Rogers, who struggled for years before hitting paydirt, knew from the unpredictability of his own career that show business doesn't offer guarantees nor does it pay annuities once the voice goes bad and the records stop selling. Rightfully proud of his business acumen, he decided to invest his wealth prudently—to buy his own insurance policy against the riches-to-rags route so common to show business personalities. He invested heavily in real estate, buying a fine collection of homes and ranches. When he got his first glimpse of The Knoll—through prominent interior designer Ron Wilson, who received Sotheby's brochure in the mail and passed it on to his client—Rogers recognized it as a perfect addition to his investment portfolio and an ideal residence for his family.

"He knew what he wanted and he pursued it single-mindedly," says Mimi Styné. "That's what made the deal so much fun. Kenny is a self-confident, straightforward guy who puts his cards on the table, makes his position clear, and comes prepared to deal. Marketing a major property like The Knoll ordinarily entails all sorts of machinations, marathon negotiations, nitpicking on both sides. But not with Kenny."

Adds Hall, "Quite often the problem is with the buyer's business managers. I can't tell you how many times I've stood before a property with an oil sheik, listening to the guy rave about the place and giving every indication that he'll make an offer the very next day—at the full asking price—whatever it takes. He's a wealthy and impulsive multimillionaire and he simply wants what he wants, whatever the cost.

"But that's only stage one. Soon after, I hear from those who are paid to see to it that the sheik stays a multimillionaire. The next time I show the property to an entourage of his business advisers. These are the sheik's accountants, attorneys and financial planners. They're sharp, skeptical, and paid to fret about the kinds of things the sheik doesn't want to bother with. While the sheik falls in love with the heart-shaped pool, the advisers ask for statistics on comparable houses and the size of the lot. Then they punch a few figures into the pocket calculator and make an offer that's 25 percent below the asking price. Well, in many cases that's not acceptable to the owner and the deal falls through. It's frustrating because you know so well that if the sheik made his own decision, the sale would have been a *fait accompli.*"

Some say the brokers have no one to blame for this but the brokers themselves. Arab sensitivity to real estate rip-offs can be traced to the late 1970s when Iranian money started pouring into California. As word went out that Iranians were easy marks for sales of wildly overpriced properties, a number of brokers put $4 million price tags on $2 million homes, hoping to profit from the foreigner's ignorance of the local market. Although some of the earliest émigrés were taken to the cleaners, those who followed learned to have professionals look after their interests. Brokers saw the change come quickly. Even when naive buyers agreed to outrageous rip-offs, their advisers usually quashed the deals before a dollar changed hands.

"Sometimes, even when the buyer and his advisers

agree on the purchase and on the amount they will offer,"
Hall adds, "they still ruin the deal by insisting on exotic
payment terms. Brokers in routine, middle-class communities talk about creative financing, but they don't have an
inkling of just how 'creative' wealthy people can be. Many
want to pay for properties by trading some of the assets
they already own. One client, for example, wanted to buy
a $12 million Los Angeles property for a small amount of
cash and the rest in gypsum deposits still in the ground.

"Another promised to saw off a section of a gold bar
for the broker's commission. Fortunately, Kenny Rogers and
company didn't have any such exotic payment terms in mind.
They were the kind of clients brokers dream of."

Mimi Styné agrees. "Here I was facing a record sale
and it couldn't have been easier. As soon as Kenny and I
walked into the main residence, I could tell he was going
to buy the place. Within minutes, my hunch was confirmed.
He sat down at the dining room table, took a slow, sweeping
look around, and said 'I'll take it.' We closed in less than
two weeks. The final price: $14.5 million."

Because of the magnitude of the sale, Sotheby's had
agreed in advance to shave its standard commission two
points to 8 percent. Negotiated commissions, now common
practice nationally, have long been the norm in highly competitive Beverly Hills.

"In this case, the commission had to be split three ways,"
Seilheimer recalls. "We were informed, at the last minute,
that Rogers' decorator, who holds a real estate license, was
demanding a co-broker fee. This kind of involvement on the
part of decorators is not unusual and to be perfectly honest,
we welcome it. That's because they have wide contacts with
well-to-do clients and because of their influential position
they can make things happen. We set our standard commission at 10 percent specifically to allow co-brokers to earn
the same 3 percent commission on our three-way splits that
they ordinarily earn when splitting two ways with a local
broker."

The Rogers sale was grand enough to keep all the participants smiling. For escorting the Los Angeles cowboy through The Knoll's front door, Ms. Styné earned a shade under $400,000. More than the average Main-Street-U.S.A. broker collects in ten years.

"But don't judge Mimi by a sale like that," says a competing Rodeo Drive broker who admits, providing the compliment remains anonymous, to a grudging respect of the Sotheby affiliate. "She's a twenty-four-hour-a-day businesswoman who concocts real estate deals in her sleep. Mimi's become a major force in this town by bringing off tough deals, by ferreting out buyers for properties no one else quite knows how to sell, by developing her own referral network that runs through every vestpocket of wealth from here to Hong Kong and by keeping her name in the spotlight so that buyers and sellers think of calling her first.

"Around here, that takes a lot of doing. The Beverly Hills market is half twilight zone, half Disneyland. The deals get so big, you can't keep all the zeros in your head. In our office alone, the average sale exceeds $2.3 million, many are between $4 and $5 million. In this environment, commissions climb into the high six figures and even lunch with a client can go for $500—more than enough for brokers in most parts of the country to live on for a week. It's surreal. Mix into this crazy concoction the fact that a substantial part of our dealings are with show people. Many are rich, arrogant stars, addicted to having things their own way. Spoiled children, the bunch. Fuck up just once and they cut you out of a deal in midstream. Give them the opportunity and they'll eat you for breakfast. Thousands of brokers from all over the country are drawn here by the lure of mega-commissions, but few ever make a single sale. Some die trying."

It's easy to see how. Playing the Hollywood social scene—a route many new brokers take in search of clients— is like getting swept up in a Kansas twister and being carried, head over heels, to a land stranger than Dorothy's Oz. To a plush pinball machine known as the Polo Lounge, a popular broker hangout tucked away in the lobby of the

Beverly Hills Hotel. Here, a half million BTUs of air conditioning keeps the 200-odd revelers packed around the tiny
bar and the dainty cocktail tables preserved in the deep
freeze of their five-line highs.

From 7 P.M. to the requisite parting at 9:30, brokers,
starlets, and assorted seekers of the American dream down
white wine, cocaine, and guacamole dip, all munching and
snorting and trying ever so desperately to sell something
to someone. It's a Tommy Tune musical, book by Woody
Allen.

At center stage, a former storm trooper—call her
Shultzy for her uncanny resemblance to Bob Cummings's
TV secretary—marches through the mass of shiny hair-
pieces and heaving breasts, paging names for waiting telephone calls. As the evening unfolds virtually every name
in the house is paged.

"Ms. Lovely Lovelace, telephone call.

"Telephone for Mr. Lance Crunchfists.

"Call for Rock Handsome.

"Urgent . . . urgent . . . telephone call for Ms. Afternoon Delight. . . ."

No doubt, 99 percent of the calls are planted. Polo
Lounge regulars insist on two prerequisites before showing
up at the front door: reserving a prized table (when a newcomer called to make a reservation, he was told that "jeans
are forbidden unless, of course, they're designer jeans"),
and arranging for Shultzy's page. Experienced hands prefer
to be called ahead of the others, but not so early as to play
to an empty house.

Those who swear by the Lounge—who wouldn't miss
a night of it—insist that in spite of the apparent chaos and
the determined role-playing, business gets done. In the midst
of the partying—the flaunting of creamy cleavages goose-
pimpled by the frigid air conditioning, the dashing back and
forth to answer fantasy phone calls—contacts are said to
be made, properties bought and sold.

"But I don't believe it," says Mimi Styné, debunking
the notion that a Beverly Hills realtor has to know more

about cocaine than deed covenants. "Property buyers and sellers want one thing from brokers and that's professionalism. They know they'll get that from Mimi Styné and Sotheby Parke Bernet. They don't expect me to entertain them and they don't want to be my friend. I know that my clients would rather see me hunched over a calculator figuring a better way to structure a deal than watch me down cocktails at a bar. I don't go to the Polo Lounge. I'm too busy working."

Styné is also too busy making money to put on a show. She frowns on the notion that to sell to the rich you have to match them dollar for dollar on cars, clothes, and jewels.

"It's absurd to try and impress your clients. This isn't a competition. Some Beverly Hills brokers drive around in Rolls-Royces. How vulgar! I drive a seven-year-old Seville that gets me from place to place just fine and that hasn't lost me a sale yet. Brokers who forget what they're really in business to do are in trouble, deep trouble. I'd say those driving around in Corniche convertibles are more into acting than selling real estate.

"That shows up on the bottom line."

3

Local Luminaries:
The Art and Science of
Independent Brokerage

Real estate cannot be lost or stolen, nor can it be carried away. Managed with reasonable care, it is about the safest investment in the world.

Franklin D. Roosevelt

It all began with an innocent Sunday stroll through Beverly Hills.* So says Hollywood gossip columnist Sheilah Graham, recalling the first, rather modest, investment that drew her, inexorably, to the land rush.

Crossing North Maple Drive, where she rented a home, she noticed an "Open House" sign before a Spanish-style house and decided to have a look around. The real estate agent, a pleasant, middle-aged man, greeted her effusively and escorted her on a tour. She fell in love with the place—its soaring cathedral ceiling, big French windows, and backyard trees.

"But the price, $57,000, was much more than I could afford.

* The year was 1947.

" 'I'll think about it,' I said . . ."

Every Sunday, for the next four weeks, she visited the empty house.

"Well," remarked the salesman jovially on the fourth visit, "are you going to make an offer?"

"I made an impossible offer.

" 'I'll pay $40,000,' I gulped, 'if you'll accept a down payment of $15,000.' This was the exact amount I had in my savings account . . ."

"I'm sorry, but it's not possible. The owner might come down to $55,000, but no less."

Graham decided to stop going to the house. Instead, the real estate agent visited her. Every Sunday he'd make a new proposal. "Fifty-three thousand . . . Fifty-one thousand . . . Forty-nine . . . Forty-five . . ." and finally, "All right, forty thousand."

"I had a house!"

Here we have the three-act play that is the classic real estate sale. Note the cast of characters. As the curtain goes up, there are a dream house, a breathless buyer, a jovial agent, and a hard-nosed seller. As the drama unfolds, the characters change roles. A bit of negotiation brings together an overpriced house, a reluctant buyer, an edgy agent, and an increasingly anxious seller. Then, in the final act—once the offer is accepted—the dream house regains its luster, the buyer is once again breathless, the agent his jovial self, and the seller smiling all the way to the bank.

Aspirations, negotiations, compromise. These fundamental elements, these building blocks of real estate sales, are vital for the successful closing of property transactions. Sheilah Graham's first purchase—forget that it was consummated in the never-never land of Beverly Hills—makes for a classic case study of the residential real estate transaction as it occurs every day in countless communities across the United States. Without the presence of a national marketer, the participants are limited to a buyer and a seller—each with clearly defined and often conflicting self-interests—and a mediating force, the licensed local broker, whose overriding responsibility is to keep the personal drives and ambitions moving toward the same objective: a reasonable sale.

Interestingly, although he does not control the assets nor the capital, the broker, more than anyone else, influences the course of the transaction. He does so (witness the broker in Graham's story) by recognizing that of all the participants in a real estate negotiation, he is the only player capable of stepping back from the action and of directing the flow of events. This is possible because he does not have an "emotional" stake in the outcome (granted a substantial commission may be at risk—a commission the broker wants very much to earn—but this is not the same as having one's life savings on the line), and because he brings experience and professionalism to the discussions. His familiarity with the principal players, with the issues and with the psychology of real estate, enables him to anticipate reactions, to manipulate egos and to time the presentation of bids and offers for maximum impact and appeal. The successful broker uses this advantage to nudge both sides to the other's position and to encourage flexibility in the negotiations.

Charles Seilheimer, who wears two hats—both as Sotheby's vice president and as a broker in his beloved Virginia—puts it this way: "When negotiating a real estate deal, you must place yourself, as the broker, in the position of both parties. Feel them out. Look beyond what they are demanding—for this can often be misleading—to what they'll be willing to settle for. This expands the parameters of the discussions; it gives the broker the all-important element of operating room.

"It's important to remember that in order to act for one party, you must have the knowledge of what the other is trying to obtain, or, equally important, what they can afford. Let's say your client wants $2 million for a property and along comes a buyer with a bid of $1.7 million with $500,000 in cash. Should you take it? Well, assuming you don't think any better bids will be forthcoming, you may want to go ahead. But not without making certain that the

$1.7 million/$500,000 cash offer is the best the prospective buyer can deliver. Can he be squeezed for $800,000 cash? Will the owner accept $500,000 or $800,000 cash (plus the balance to $1.7 million in notes) in lieu of the $2 million asking price? It's the broker's job to determine, among the hundreds of variables, the best mix of terms that will satisfy the parties and make them agree to shake hands—or at least let their lawyers shake hands."

Flexibility, within the confines of established parameters, accounted for the successful conclusion of the Graham deal. The broker skillfully discounted the seller's aspirations while simultaneously determining the buyer's capacity to pay. In all likelihood, he had convinced his client to accept Graham's $40,000 offer weeks before they showed their cards, and had simply used the intervening period to try to beat the floor figure by a few thousand dollars. His offensive strategy was to manipulate the party most likely to heed his counsel (the seller) and then to bring the buyer to the best possible compromise.

Seilheimer, who has grown wealthy negotiating hundreds of major deals, applauds this multidirectional approach, but claims that most brokers do just the opposite. "Look, the seller is the broker's client so he naturally wants to please him. How? By engaging in personal flattery, by fawning over the client's property. This excessive ego boosting is counterproductive to successful real estate negotiations because it overheats the seller's expectations. By the time the broker concludes his 'you're a prince and your home is the Taj Mahal' song and dance, his client believes his property is flawless and deserving of 50 percent or more above market value. He's also made that person intransigent. Pump up a seller with all sorts of grand expectations and he is going to reject every reasonable offer that comes along. The broker's knee-jerk, please-the-client approach has produced a formidable obstacle to consummating a successful sale. That is the seller himself. The broker's created a Frankenstein.

"My advice is to remember that the buyer in every sale—

be it for $100,000 or $10 million—believes that he is the essential participant—the force to be reckoned with. If you think about it, that's only human nature. I don't care what business you're talking about—be it real estate or something as radically different as film-making—the party with the money expects to be treated deferentially. Once you recognize this, you also recognize that as a broker you best serve your client not by stroking his ego, but instead by playing up to the buyer in such a way that he accedes to the seller's terms while still believing that the settlement turned out in his favor. That's what closes deals."

Seilheimer's modus operandi is, in one sense, similar to that of Cutter, Mitchell, Siano, and Styné. The elite fraternity of successful brokers—those who consistently close million-dollar deals—bring personally devised marketing principles (i.e., Seilheimer's "multidirectional negotiations") to the real estate marketplace, both to close deals and to find an operating niche that will assure their firms of sustained profitability over the years. This systematic approach to real estate—this determination to substitute strategy for luck—is the hallmark of the big moneymakers.

Although they profit by occasionally working with international marketers, they know they cannot rely on Previews, Sotheby's or the Confederation of International Real Estate for the bulk of their fees. Instead, they find a success secret—be it a way to bring buyers and sellers together, to cultivate special markets or to establish their presence in the community—and they use this to profit from the land rush.

Steve Cutter's rise to prominence as one of Palm Beach's stellar producers can be traced to a clever marketing strategy formulated in the first days of his career. Born to a mom-and-pop brokerage firm established in the opulent seaside community, Cutter grew up around the real estate business, but found it unappealing and declined his parents' invitation to join the family firm. When he turned college-age, he left Palm Beach to take up residence in Boston, believing that his decision to forgo a career in real estate was irreversible. But in a pattern familiar to many ultimately successful brokers, he found himself propelled to the business through an unexpected turn of events.

"Mom and Dad always worked hard enough to support a comfortable lifestyle, but not too hard to interfere with their leisure pursuits. They'd come to Palm Beach partly to retire and partly to dabble in real estate, and they wanted to enjoy life. Whenever they made enough to cover expenses, they'd close up shop and play tennis. In those days—before real estate became the fiercely competitive business that it is today—you could get away with that kind of casual, work-a-day, play-a-day style of brokerage. There were more than enough sales and few enough brokers to allow for this self-indulgent approach. The problem is, my parents never built a foundation to fall back on. It was a hand-to-mouth business, one without a cash reserve or a sales organization to keep it going in tough times. So, when Dad took ill in the mid-1960s, the company suffered. But rather than close up—it's terribly hard for brokers to write off a business they founded—Mom and Dad asked if I wouldn't take over. My initial reaction was the same as it had always been—a polite but firm "no, thank you"—but this time, after considerable soul-searching, I believed that I should consider more than my own career goals. I felt I owed it to Mom and Dad to try to resuscitate the business, so I left Boston and headed back to Palm Beach."

As a fledgling broker in an increasingly competitive market, Cutter had one advantage and one handicap. On the plus side, he was a local boy with a wide circle of relatives, family friends, and school buddies turned local homeowners. His was a brand name in a business that puts a premium on personal contacts and that pays big dividends to those with a high profile in the community. Previews' slogan of "the broader the exposure the easier the sale" is, on a smaller scale, as true for local realtors as it is for international marketers.

On Cutter's debit column, the Palm Beach brokerage community was not about to roll out the red carpet for a

young and inexperienced upstart out to play catch-up ball
at their expense. Through the years of mom-and-pop Cutter's
tenure, aggressive competitors were gobbling up the better
listings, increasing their market share and establishing
themselves as Palm Beach's premier realtors. By the time
Steve put his name on the Cutter letterhead, the family firm
was clearly behind the market leaders.

Much to his credit, the budding entrepreneur created
a marketing plan to compensate for his competitors' dominance in residential sales.

Imitating the high tech start-up companies that rise rapidly in the computer field not by challenging IBM, but by
pinpointing a market the giant considers too small to bother
with (the way Apple established a beachhead in microcompu-
ters while IBM was still focusing on main frames), Cutter
zeroed in on that segment of the Palm Beach real estate
market that was all but ignored by the established brokers.

"Shortly after taking over the company's reins, I did
some research to determine the local market's fastest-grow-
ing segments. My investigation revealed that there was intense competition for residential sales at all points on the
price spectrum but little competition for property rentals.
I decided, immediately, that this would be my specialty—
that I would work to dominate the rental market.

"The big, highly profitable brokers frowned on rentals
because they paid lower commissions than sales. But I looked
at it differently. To me, rentals spelled opportunity. The very
fact that there was a vacuum in this part of the market
meant I could claim a major share of it with little resistance
from my cash-rich competitors. I could use rentals to improve
my cash flow, generate referrals from other brokers and
generally revive the family business. But this was only to
be phase one of a major rebuilding program. I viewed the
rental market not as an end-all but as a medium for bolster-
ing my resources and capabilities before challenging the
established brokers for residential sales."

Cutter's strategy worked remarkably well. By staking
out a narrow segment of the market, he secured a corridor

of growing room safe from competitive encroachment. By taking his specialty seriously and by bringing a new professionalism to the rental business—once a stepchild function handled by part-timers—he won a growing reputation in the community and, perhaps more important, gained the grudging respect of his fellow brokers.

"Once we proved our capabilities as rental specialists, other brokers started referring listings to us. What started out as a trickle accelerated to a heavier and heavier flow of business. This dovetailed perfectly with my marketing plan. The commission revenues provided the resources to hire sales associates, to advertise, to extend my firm's reputation and its presence deeper and deeper into the community. With our organizational strengths gaining parity with competitors, we started moving more and more into property sales. Partly as a result of the firm's natural evolution and partly because of the steps I took to encourage it, sales gradually became the predominant part of our business."

Today, though his firm is a leader in Palm Beach sales, Cutter still accepts rentals and still credits this ancillary business with helping to resurrect the family firm and for leading to its ultimate success. "Savvy brokers must recognize that what at first may seem like a minor deal can lead to more substantial transactions somewhere down the road," Cutter advises. "Take the case of this interesting transaction. It all began with a routine telephone call to my associate Ben Johnson."

"Hello, this is Mrs. Green calling from New York. I'm responding to your advertisement in *The Times* for a beachfront Spanish mansion. The one you are renting." Johnson gazed through his office window at the standard lunch-hour motorcade of white Corniche convertibles. Puffy cumulus clouds floated above, gingerly sidestepping the dazzling midday sun.

"Would you like to see the property, Mrs. Green?" Johnson asked. "Are you coming to Palm Beach?"

"Perhaps. Tell me more about the house. Your ad was rather sketchy."

Johnson knew he had a wonderful listing. The only question in his mind was if the caller could afford it. He'd learned
over the years that those of real means made the initial
broker contact through attorneys, aides-de-camp, and assorted intermediaries. Still, he wouldn't dare jump to conclu-
sions. He'd also learned well enough that the wealthy were
given to eccentricities.

"It's one of our finest properties, Mrs. Green. Two acres
on the water in what is considered Palm Beach's premier
location, between the Everglades Club and the Bath & Tennis
Club. The residence, built in the 1920s by one of the Vanderbilts, has two swimming pools, a ballroom, every conceivable
amenity to assure your total comfort. Need I say more?"

A moment of silence was broken by the caller's distinc-
tive purr. "I plan to be in Palm Beach in two weeks. I'll
call you when I arrive."

Two weeks turned into three without word from Mrs.
Green. Johnson, preoccupied with dozens of local clients,
never gave it a thought. Until the phone rang again.

"Hello, Mrs. Green calling. Do you remember me?"

"The rental property, right?"

"Right. As you may have guessed when you didn't hear
from me, I rented another house. But it's completely unsatis-
factory and I must find a replacement immediately. Won't
you drive by this afternoon? Show me what's available?"

Green's drop-everything-and-service-me-now telephone
manner rubbed Johnson the wrong way. He eyed a swollen
Rolodex bulging with names that had to be called. "You're
in Palm Beach, Mrs. Green?"

"Yes, yes, it's been a disaster. I detest this house. Come
by today."

"Look, Mrs. Green. I can't reschedule my appointments
simply because you want to go out on a moment's notice.
I'll be pleased to show you properties but I'll need time to
prepare. Let's make an appointment for—"

She cut Johnson off in midsentence. "My name really
isn't Green. I'm Yoko Ono."

Johnson rescheduled his appointments. Within hours he

was sitting in the rear of a limousine talking houses and dollars to the avant-garde songwriter/artist/wife of a Beatle. Johnson found her icy-cool, all business.

"Fortunately, the Spanish estate was still available," Johnson recalls, "and I thought it would be ideal for her. So I directed the driver to take us there. As I expected, Yoko adored the home and agreed to rent it on the spot. She had one warning: were we to tell anyone that the Lennons were in Palm Beach, they'd never do business with us again. Of course, we respected their wishes.

"Theirs was only a one-month rental—and they didn't even stay the full month. So I thought I'd heard the last of Yoko Ono. But about a year later she called again, saying this time that she wanted to buy the estate. We wound up selling it to her for $800,000.* Here's a perfect example of how the attention to seemingly minor deals has rewarded us with one of the biggest and most prestigious sales in this town. It has helped us to earn millions over the years."

Cutter's success is clearly atypical. Only one in ten of the nation's brokerage firms earn a substantial profit (measured as 20 to 30 percent of "company dollar."** This is very much a pyramidal industry: at the base, the vast majority of brokers struggle to survive, to close a major sale before the local newspaper cancels their advertising contracts, to hold on through the economic down cycles just long enough for credit to ease and housing starts to pick up again. But at the apex, seemingly insulated from this precarious existence, top brokers earn exceptional sums regardless of prevailing economic conditions. The reasons for this striking contrast can be traced to the brokers themselves, to the mind set they bring to the market, to their professionalism.

Ask a hundred brokers what it takes to succeed and all mouth a weary cliché about hard work, dedication, and

* Current value is $3 million.
** Company dollar is the funds remaining from gross income after all sales and listing commissions, including those to cobrokerage firms, are distributed.

ethics. Those blessed with 500 sales associates and a stable
of Mercedes will utter the same corn as their bush league
colleagues scratching to make ends meet. But they are
wrong. Observations of a wide cross section of brokers reveals a clear pattern of success that distinguishes the super
achievers. Although truth, honesty, and the rest of the Boy
Scout code are admirable characteristics, they may not always serve a broker well and—more to the point—they are
not enough to assure success. No, those at the pinnacle didn't
get there because they rub their nostrils closer to the grind-
stone, but instead because they are crafty, aggressive, and
creative, and because they bring to the land rush the all-
important business discipline that helps them identify and
cultivate growth markets.

Forty-one-year-old Peter Kennedy is typical of the
breed. A lifelong resident of suburban Chappaqua, New
York—an affluent community of predominantly $200,000 to
$500,000 homes nestled in northern Westchester County
about thirty-five miles from Manhattan—Kennedy is a familiar figure around town. His successful brokerage firm,
Holmes & Kennedy, is housed in a postcard-lovely clapboard
colonial at the foot of quaint King Street, just steps away
from the town's red brick post office and within a short
walk of Chappaqua's only landmark, a statue of favorite
son and former resident Horace Greeley.

Seated behind his warped and slightly tilted oak desk—
topped with blueprints, Polaroids of homes in various stages
of construction, and sales contracts—Kennedy exudes the
boyish charm of a Norman Rockwell Sunday school teacher
waiting patiently for his students to assemble before the
Bible class begins. But the image is deceptive. Behind the
parochial exterior lies an aggressive broker, an entrepreneur
with a Midas touch for major residential real estate transactions, and a shrewd business strategist. Since launching their
fledgling business fifteen years ago, Kennedy and partner
Bill Holmes have built it into Chappaqua's leading brokerage
office, handling property sales of over $30 million yearly.*

* This figure is somewhat inflated. As is traditional with local brokers,
properties are counted both when they are listed and sold.

Certainly hard work and old-school ties have played a role in the partners' success, but both agree that much of the credit belongs to a marketing strategy developed in the company's infancy. Much like Cutter, Holmes & Kennedy decided to corner a single segment of the Chappaqua real estate market—in their case, new home construction—by building bridges to local developers.

"Bill and I started our business quite by accident," Kennedy recalls, counting himself among the successful brokers who credit fate rather than lifelong ambition for bringing them to their present calling. "It all began when we bought this modest frame office building in the center of Chappaqua, intending to manage it as income property. But we soon learned, to our great displeasure, that we couldn't rent enough space to make the investment pay. At the time, I'd been selling real estate for about a year in nearby Armonk and Bill was doing the same a few miles away in Pleasantville. We decided, as much to fill the building as anything else, to join forces and start our own brokerage firm. It was a case of the tail wagging the dog."

The year was 1968 and the young partners faced a formidable obstacle. The brokerage firm of A. T. Houlihan, then run by its hard-driving and highly competitive founder Art Houlihan (who would sell to Jack Mitchell fifteen years later), was Chappaqua's predominant realtor, controlling 40 percent of the market. In Houlihan's shadow, seven minor competitors fought among themselves for the balance of local sales.

"When we told Houlihan we were opening up as the ninth realtor in town, he greeted us with a combined warning and prediction. 'Hell, you'll never make it here.'

"I saw that as a partially veiled threat—and it frightened me. Considering that Art had all the best contacts in town and that his firm totally dominated the market, a determined power play on his part would have squeezed us badly. But he made a fatal error. Convinced that Bedford was northern Westchester's up-and-coming market, Art opened an office there and lavished it with most of his attention, to the extent that he virtually ignored his Chappaqua interests.

While he was off frying other fish, we had the chance to gain a foothold in the market he controlled. We capitalized on that opportunity by working twenty-four hours a day to claim the business he was losing by default. And this opportunism paid off. We gained listings and, most important, we earned a reputation for closing sales. By the time Houlihan realized what had happened, we were on our way to supplanting him as Chappaqua's leading broker. Art learned the hard way a lesson that we'll never forget. If you want to expand, you must first protect your home flank with strong and capable management."

Just how Holmes & Kennedy broke through Houlihan's Maginot Line is interesting. Blessed with some quick sales—which they credit as much to their chief competitor's laxity as to their own brokerage skills—the partners moved rapidly past the break-even point and found themselves out of the fiscal hot seat just long enough to engage in short-term business planning. Wisely, they set out to answer the one question crucial to all new ventures: Where's the business going and where *should* it be going?

"We conducted some informal market research," Kennedy recalls, "and the findings indicated that there was real opportunity for brokers who could cultivate strong relationships with the local home builders. We had reason to believe that this sector would experience explosive growth."

Chappaqua's superb school system—recently rated by *Money Magazine* one of the nation's top ten—was fast becoming a drawing card for young professionals and corporate executives seeking refuge from urban crime and the escalating cost of Manhattan's private schools. With a shortage of homes to meet this urban migration, but with choice parcels of undeveloped land still available, Chappaqua was ripe for a wave of new construction. When this occurred, a dozen or so contractors would control an increasing percentage of residential listings. By reaching out to this loose-knit collection of seat-of-the-pants entrepreneurs—by making it clear that Holmes & Kennedy was interested in serving their needs—Kennedy recognized that he would be in an excellent position to benefit from the housing boom. Wise beyond his years in the business, Kennedy also realized that contractor accounts were likely to produce multiple opportunities—listings for raw land, condominiums, custom and speculative homes—and that this diversified customer base would lead to fast track growth and a stable long-term income stream.

It has worked out precisely this way. Kennedy's first major builder/client, Homes by McKenna, found an enthusiastic pool of buyers willing to pay two and three times the national average for its natural cedar, architectually creative, contemporary homes—most with soaring angular roofs, cathedral ceilings and wrap-around decks.

"We've been Tom's exclusive broker from the outset," Kennedy says. "To date, we've sold about fifty of his new homes, regained the listings for many when they went back on the market for resale, and picked up business from other builders as a result of our work for Tom. The relationship has been an extremely lucrative one for the broker and the developer. We grew in tandem. Tom became Chappaqua's number one builder and we became the leading realtors."

Even Kennedy's competitors agree. "Although I wish I could say differently, Holmes & Kennedy are the top sales producers in Chappaqua," admits Jack Mitchell with a hungry look in his eyes that signals his intention to change that—someday. "Certainly, their links to the builders are valuable. Contractors have been major factors in the Chappaqua market in recent years, and they've provided Holmes & Kennedy with a substantial base for growth. Also, contractor business tends to multiply itself—to generate new business spontaneously. Builders have a wide radius of contacts and are involved in many new deals all the time, many of which benefit their brokers. My hat's off to Holmes & Kennedy for perceiving that from the outset. They went after the contractors and they've made that business succeed. They've learned what it takes to serve local builders."

What does it take? Brokers active in this market point

to two prerequisites: flexibility and opportunism. Most important, the broker must be willing to accommodate the builder's often erratic and volatile business operations. Most contractors experience sharply cyclical business patterns: a burst of sales activity marked by positive cash flow is often followed by a precipitous decline in new construction and corresponding drought of working capital.

"If you know the builder, if you can vouch for his integrity, you bend your payment terms to accommodate his business cycles," Kennedy explains. "The last thing you want to do is to dog him for commissions that may be a few months overdue. Construction is a capital intensive business. If the guy needs his capital to build, taking that away from him when his back's against the wall damages the client and the broker as well. That's what it means to think like a builder; you have to understand their finances and you have to have the patience to wait for their cash flow to turn positive.

"In 1982, for example, we closed fifteen sales for one of our major builders. Can you guess how much he paid us that year? Not a penny. All the cash he could muster went directly into another, even bigger development that was experiencing significant cost overruns. He asked if he could postpone our commissions until he satisfied his heaviest capital commitments and arranged for additional financing. Because we'd worked with him for years, we agreed without a moment's hesitation. Some would say that's not prudent business practice, but I disagree. We know who we're dealing with and we intentionally establish our policies to be responsive to their needs. As it turned out, the builder sent us a check for the full amount in early '83.

"You can't treat local builders the way you would a giant corporation. We don't even ask our builders to sign brokerage contracts. If a builder we've worked with in the past assigns us as exclusive brokers for an entire development, we'll spend considerable sums of money on logistics— perhaps opening a trailer office at the site—and promotions without any guarantee that we won't be replaced. If you're a worrier, this kind of relationship may not be for you. But I must say that a major builder has never double-crossed or defaulted on us. Just the opposite. They like the fact that we operate on trust, that we're flexible, and they reward us for it."

The second prerequisite—the broker's opportunism—comes into play in his role as a behind-the-scenes deal maker. Rather than simply waiting for the contractor to announce new projects and then moving in to sell the properties, the successful broker acts as a catalyst, creating development opportunities for his and the builder/client's benefit. For example, should the local rumor mill leak word that an octogenarian dowager—the owner of a twenty-room Victorian surrounded by thirty acres of woods—has outlived the family fortune, aggressive brokers will be pounding on her hand-carved oak door with offers of $1 million for her backyard forest. If she agrees to sell (most in her situation do) the broker calls in his most active builder, draws up plans for a forty-unit housing subdivision, and negotiates a deal with the old lady.

Should the development be built, the broker profits in three ways: on the sale of the land to the builder, the sale of the homes to the first-time buyers, and many of the resales to subsequent buyers.

But the broker/catalyst benefits in another way. By structuring the deal, by gaining the right to sell the land and the houses, he locks up part of the town's geography. All sales within the development's borders fall into the broker's exclusive domain. The more developments he initiates and the more sites he represents, the more he dominates the community and assures himself of a steady flow of commissions. By controlling geography—even if that control is based solely on his relationship with a builder—the broker commands a percentage of all the real estate transactions within that sphere.

Holmes & Kennedy used this approach to engineer its first major sale—one which still ranks as one of the biggest real estate coups in Chappaqua history. In doing so, the brokerage firm profited on a single tract of land four times and catapulted itself to the top of the area's real estate hierarchy.

"It all started in 1968," Kennedy recalls, "about six months after we went into business. A broker friend of mine called to moan and groan about the headaches he was having trying to sell a 220-acre tract of land. The property, nicely situated on the Chappaqua/Mt. Pleasant border, seemed ideally suited for new homes but the broker couldn't interest a single builder in acquiring it. Why? Who knows. There are mysteries in this business, as in any other, and my friend was clearly dumbfounded as to why he couldn't make a sale on what seemed to be an attractive parcel.

"I guess it set me wondering too because our conversation replayed in my mind over and over again. Busy as I was with a thousand and one other things, the lure of such a large, challenging sale was irresistible. I believed I could find a buyer. But, as I've found throughout my brokerage career, a little research was in order.

"I found that the land owner had died and that the property, now part of the deceased's estate, was being administered by an attorney who, I recall, wasn't much of a talker. When I asked if he'd assure me a commission should I find a buyer, he made some wishy-washy comments without committing himself to anything. He was the kind of guy who answers a question without saying yes or no.

"Still, I decided to proceed on the confidence that I could sell the property and that I'd get paid for doing so. I've always accepted risk as a necessary part of the brokerage business."

Kennedy's inspired marketing campaign extended beyond the most obvious market, housing developers, to financial advisers who might recommend the property for client investments. "It was one of those hunches that panned out," Kennedy says. "As it happened a local attorney heard of the property and thought it ideal for one of his clients, a wealthy Manhattan-based stockbroker and real estate investor. The lawyer contacted me, suggested that his client see the property, and I naturally agreed to meet him at the site.

"It was a day I'll never forget. There I was leaning against my car on a dirt road that ran along the property line when a badly bruised Lincoln smoking like a chimney and sounding every bit as loud as a locomotive came to a grinding stop a few feet away. Out stepped a rather disheveled-looking guy dressed in sneakers and blue jeans. I hadn't the foggiest idea of what he wanted. My best guess was that he was lost and needed directions. But surprise, surprise he turned out to be the Manhattan millionaire. Talk about misjudging a book by its cover: He agreed to purchase the property on the spot for $750,000."

The sale brought in Holmes & Kennedy's first big commission, $40,000, and it sparked a chain of events that would enrich the young agency for years to come.

At first, the property remained dormant in the new owner's hands. But Peter Kennedy—always the real estate catalyst—recommended that the investor consider various development schemes. "A development would give us something to sell," Kennedy explains. "Sure, we could have simply congratulated ourselves on selling the raw land, but to succeed in the brokerage business on a long-term basis, you have to replenish your property inventory. We commissioned plans for developing the land into detached houses, cluster units, and several other configurations. But in the end, the landowner felt that real estate development wasn't his game and he declined our recommendations. Instead, he asked that we find a buyer for the land five years after he'd purchased it.

"This time I had an excellent lead in selling it to a local builder. During the first go-around, I'd written a letter to Henry Paparazzo—a major housing developer who'd put up the extremely successful 3,000-unit Heritage Village condominiums in Southbury, Connecticut—saying that I thought our property was ideal for a similar project. But he never responded.

"Fortunately, now that the land was back on the market,

I received a call from another broker, Billingsley in nearby Katonah, New York, saying that Paparazzo was interested in acquiring some Westchester land and did I know of any attractive sites.

"From that point, things moved very quickly. I briefly described the Chappaqua/Mt. Pleasant property, noting that I'd had it in mind for Paparazzo from the start. Because Paparazzo was in the broker's office, I suggested that they come down to see the site immediately. It turned out to be a match made in heaven. Paparazzo was eager to buy, agreeing to a price of $1.1 million. Naturally I couldn't have been more pleased. Our share of the commission came to $50,000—the second check we'd received for the same undeveloped tract."

Paparazzo's plans called for building a cluster housing complex of detached residential units around a recreation area and with its own private road. To preserve much of the property's wooded area in its natural state, the homes would be tightly spaced on small building lots, leaving the balance of the tract for public use. This environmentally sensitive approach had proven to be increasingly popular with zoning boards. Accordingly, the plan seemed likely to glide through the local approval mill. "But for some mysterious reason the town turned thumbs down," Kennedy recalls. "The idea of a private road and cluster development simply made people uncomfortable. When the town vetoed the private road, Paparazzo decided to proceed with a standard subdivision, calling for 176 separate homesites. Just a mass of homes in a community to be called Heritage Court. He thought it the path of least resistance and he was right. This time the town gave its stamp of approval."

Immediately, Holmes & Kennedy's builder connections paid handsome dividends. Determined to act before the powers that be rescinded their approval, Paparazzo commissioned the brokers to sell all of the Heritage Court lots.

"We sold virtually all of them to other builders—mostly in multiple parcel deals—including fifteen to Tom McKenna," Kennedy says. "Within two years, the lion's share of the lots had soared in value from $30,000 to $90,000 and were developed as single-family contemporary homes selling for $150,000 to $400,000. We were the exclusive agents for almost every one.

"So you see, we profited on that beautiful hunk of land on the sale to the Manhattan investor, then to Paparazzo, then to other builders and finally to homeowners."

Heritage Court proved to be a turning point for Holmes & Kennedy, giving the partners periodic infusions of capital to expand their advertising and sales staff and to gain ever-wider presence in the market. But it is interesting to note that as Holmes & Kennedy moved out from Houlihan's shadow, planting their flag on consistently larger tracts of Chappaqua's geography, other more experienced brokers who had languished in the background for years remained firmly in place. Profiles of dozens of brokers across the nation reveal that this pattern is widespread. Realtors who view the brokerage business solely on a house-by-house basis (what's up for sale today and how do we sell it) are destined to live hand-to-mouth. Without the monopoly mentality—without a strategy for cornering limited sectors of the market (e.g., Holmes & Kennedy's builder connection)—they fail to score the major coup that helps more aggressive brokers pole-vault above the competition and into higher levels of exposure and financial resources. Their careers make up a patchwork of small-minded ideas and misguided marketing strategies. What success they achieve is limited by their own narrow view of real estate brokerage. The poor results show up on the bottom line.

The broker's personal earnings, known as the "owner's cash flow" is derived from three major sources: the firm's net income, the broker's personal commissions, and his salary for nonselling services. Although it is widely believed that the broker should work to boost each component of cash flow, this is myopic. Astute brokers recognize that they can actually increase their total return by foregoing one of the cash flow contributors. The idea is to reduce sharply or eliminate the owner/broker's selling activities. Growing firms need an executive manager, a planner and a strategist. This is the broker/owner's primary role. He must see himself not as a salesman, but as a businessman.

"I'm too busy running a company to do much selling anymore," says Peter Kennedy. "Oh, I'll handle this or that property if the circumstances demand, but for the most part our staff does the selling and Bill and I do the managing. We have a vision for the firm—one that will be achieved only if we don't get bogged down with the day-to-day puzzle of trying to bring together buyers and sellers."

Vera Aguzzi—a smartly tailored, likable broker with a winning personality and a firm commitment to salesmanship —appears to be content with far less ambitious goals than her neighboring colleagues Peter Kennedy, Jack Mitchell, and Sally Siano. Starting her career as a saleswoman for a northern Westchester broker, Aguzzi entered the business just about the same time Holmes & Kennedy were getting their feet wet working for others. Unlike many other married women who venture into suburban real estate to "keep busy and earn some extra money," Aguzzi always viewed her job as a stepping-stone to self-employment.

"I knew I'd have to establish a network of contacts before I could open an office of my own, so I set out to meet as many people as possible and to sell, sell, sell. Although I don't mean to brag, things went beautifully from day one. I guess it's because I had the sixth sense it takes to produce sales. My greatest strength was, and still is, the ability to size up buyers' lifestyles. I can tell after a few minutes of small talk what kinds of homes they'll like and what will leave them cold. And that's crucial to establishing a good rapport. Show an artist a raised ranch, he'll write you off as a tasteless clod. Conversely, show a corporate executive a converted barn or a windmill, and he'll race to the broker across the street. You can misjudge buyers' economic capabilities—they'll forgive you for that—but guess way off on their tastes and they'll take offense. You don't have a prayer of working with them."

Aguzzi's solid track record led to her appointment as office manager of Blueprint Realty, a multibranch Westchester brokerage. Her duties—to motivate the sales staff and to guide pending sales through the legal, financial, and psychological hurdles that can often cause them to come apart after the buyer and seller shake hands—proved ideal for the would-be entrepreneur.

"A lot of sales people want to be brokers without having a thorough understanding of what the latter entails," Aguzzi says. "It's one thing to be a good salesperson and another to be a manager/administrator. While the former is highly individualistic, the latter must take a team approach. Many top sales producers aren't cut out for the paperwork and the politics that go with the management positions. But I found that I loved it and, more important, that I was damn good at it. So with the Blueprint experience under my belt, and with the knowledge that I was cut out to be a broker, I opened my own office in Armonk in 1972."

Aguzzi immediately set her sights on the same market segment—new home construction—that Bill Holmes and Peter Kennedy were pursuing five miles away in Chappaqua. Here, she had a built-in advantage. Married to a local contractor, Aguzzi had first-hand knowledge of the builder's trade.

"Before turning to brokerage, I was an administrator for my husband's construction firm. My assignment was to sew together the loose threads on land transactions, architectural plans and whatever else threatened to slow a project beyond its scheduled completion date. In the process, I learned all the little secrets of the home building business— most importantly, as it turned out, what a broker has to do to successfully serve it.

"First, I found that you must have a keen eye for selecting commercially viable land. This means evaluating properties from the standpoint of the developer rather than the user. From the builder's perspective, a given property has to be priced so that he can put up a home suitable for the market and sell it for a reasonable profit. That's his major concern. A novice broker may see a beautiful lot, level, wooded, with a marvelous view—and recommend it to the builder on the basis that it's well worth the $100,000 asking price. And it may well be. But the builder has to consider more than the land's intrinsic value. If it happens to be situated in a community of $80–$110,000 homes, it may be too much of a good thing. Any house the builder puts up on it will have to sell for more than two times the community average.

"Second, you have to be able to educate prospective buyers on the dollars and cents implications of their dream house fantasies. First-time buyers of custom homes traditionally start the planning process with visions of Windsor Castle, only to find, after learning how much it all costs, that they have to settle for something less. Brokers familiar with the builder's economics can instruct them on how to keep some semblance of the dream—enough to want to buy the home—while staying within their $250,000 budget. He can show them that they may have to drop from 4,000 to 3,000 square feet, make do with two cathedral ceilings instead of four and finish the basement a few years down the road. By getting all of this straightened out before the actual negotiations begin, the broker helps the builder save valuable time and even more important, reduces the likelihood of friction between the parties. When an intermediary is involved, the buyer doesn't think the builder is trying to rip him off.

"Third, you have to think and act quickly, often committing to projects without the benefit of market analyses. Successful builders are decisive and they expect their brokers to be the same. Yes, this means accepting uncomfortable levels of risk from time to time, but it's the price you pay to be a major factor in this market."

No doubt about it, Vera Aguzzi is a skilled and successful broker whose business is the envy of the thousands of realtors who huff and puff themselves to near exhaustion just trying to keep the lights on and the phones connected long enough to make that one monster sale they know, they dream, will put them over the top and on to bigger and better. Aguzzi Properties has grown from a one-woman shop to a modest-size brokerage firm employing eight full-time sales associates and six part-timers. In a major reversal of family roles, Vera's husband has closed his contracting firm for a position in his wife's company, where he now specializes in serving other builders, principally in the land selection process and in guiding zoning matters through the local board.

But unlike Holmes & Kennedy, Aguzzi has never made the colossal deal that springs local brokers from the grind of day-to-day sales and that builds a rock-hard base for accelerated growth.

Perhaps this can be traced to Aguzzi's apparently narrow view of the brokerage business—one that limited her firm from its earliest days. "I wanted to run a very small business, just big enough for myself. My over-riding goal was to be able to provide the highest caliber of service— and that, I thought, meant servicing all customers personally."

Small thinking threatens the broker's long-term prospects. By setting limited objectives, he checks his firm's growth potential and prevents it from achieving the stability and the competitive strength that size affords. Although the broker may find personal satisfaction with his quaint, easily manageable operation, he is all the while vulnerable to forces beyond his control. Sooner or later, an unexpected event makes him fear for his survival—and makes him grope for a quick fix to assure his firm's status as a going concern.

"I attended a real estate seminar a few years ago hoping to pick up a few pointers about management, marketing, and so forth," Aguzzi recalls, the lines under her eyes apparent for the first time. "But I left the session disheartened and worried about my business. The speaker's theme was that mom-and-pop brokers were on the way out—that the future belonged to national franchises.

"After that seminar, it seemed that every article I read, every talk I heard, echoed this theme. And the arguments for it appeared to be well-founded. Increasing competition, the need for creative financing and the explosive growth of the franchises themselves seemed to threaten the independent brokers. I felt isolated, vulnerable, and ultimately convinced that I couldn't survive alone—that I needed to tap the resources of a national organization. It was at this point that I decided to buy into a franchise. Because exposure was important to me, I picked the franchise that I knew best and that I believed was most familiar to the general public. That was Century 21. I bought into the franchise with great optimism, thinking that this would be the cure-all for my business problems and the vehicle for my firm's future growth."

Aguzzi was not alone. The Chicken Little syndrome that spread through the brokerage community has delivered more than 7,000 brokers into the Century 21 camp since its founding by Art Bartlett and Marsh Fisher in 1971. From an initial base of seventeen affiliates in Orange County, California, this loose-knit network of independent brokers mushroomed into a real estate phenomenon linking 65,000 salespeople, generating more than $20 billion in annual sales and accounting for roughly 10 percent of all real estate transactions in the United States and Canada.

At the outset, Century 21 worked on three levels: a tiny corporate staff headed by the founders, an elite corps of master franchisers, and the swelling ranks of local franchisees. Power flowed from the corporate office to the master franchisers to the locals; money moved in the opposite direction. The founders profited by selling territorial (master) franchises to investors, who gained the rights to sell individual franchises in specific states or regions, and by claiming 25 percent of the master franchises' annual revenues. Master franchisers, in turn, profited by selling the individual franchises and taking an average of 6 percent of their yearly gross. The mom-and-pop realtors who shelled out the up-front franchise fees and the 6 percent royalties were led to believe that they too would profit from their franchise affiliation. They would sell more homes.

The Century 21 system has worked well for the entrepreneurs who brought it to life and who viewed its greatest potential, not as a real estate venture, but as a marketing system.

The early investors in territorial rights paid as little as $500, only to sell them back a few years later for staggering profits. This appreciation—which ranged to 1,000 percent or more—was fueled by headquarters' decision to buy back the masters in an effort to boost corporate profits. This produced an even greater bonanza for the master franchisers. "A group of real estate people in St. Louis, Missouri, bought one of the franchises in 1975 for about $100,000, and last February sold it back to the company for at least $1.7 million."* Century 21's founders in turn hit paydirt in 1977 when the company went public and scored again in 1979 when the corporation was acquired by the Trans World Corporation for $89 million.

Dick Loughlin, Century 21's current president, has also profited handsomely. Moving to Century 21 after serving as executive vice president of the San Francisco Board of Realtors, Loughlin was one of the first master franchisers, claiming rights to the northern California region for $60,000 in 1972. Eight years later, Loughlin sold the franchise back to the company for "several million dollars"** and took his position at the company's headquarters.

Peering beneath Century 21's carefully constructed image, one finds that the master franchisers and the founders achieved extraordinary success, in part, because they developed a formula for selling franchises. Their master stroke was in positioning real estate franchises as an idea "whose time had come." Like all crafty marketers they had an instinctive feel for how people respond to a given stimulus, in this case the prospect that the sun was setting on the era of successful independent and unaffiliated realtors. That to survive in the eighties and beyond, mom-and-pop would have to join an organization—the national franchise—whose

* David Pauly and Martin Kasindorf, in *Newsweek*, July 3, 1978, p. 59.
** Loughlin refuses to specify the exact sum.

big budget advertising and brand-name awareness would provide a buffer against the nasty realities of the marketplace.

Brokers in Vera Aguzzi's position responded predictably. Alarmed that the businesses they had built from scratch could not compete with "the idea whose time had come," they rushed to add ERA and Century 21 and *Better Homes and Gardens* to their family names. What many failed to recognize, however, was that the franchisers had created the image of a threat they were warning brokers to defend against. Upon close examination, we can see precisely how the brains behind the franchise systems accomplished this. Their clever marketing strategy featured the following components:

- Plant the idea that centrally owned multioffice brokerage chains were poised to seize control of the nation's real estate market. Take the story to the press. Confirm the dire predictions with quotes like this from the *New York Times.* "By 1984, ten concerns will control sales of single-family houses." Reprint the *Times'* warning, slap it on the cover of direct mail brochures and send to every realtor in the country.

- Convince the most easily swayed brokers to join the fledgling franchise organizations and announce that a bandwagon is underway. Go back to the press (great lovers of trends), placing more quotes like this from the *Times*, ". . . many small brokers are being squeezed out of the business . . . brokers are just beginning to appreciate the long-term implications of the trend."

- Enlist more franchisees. Spend heavily on advertising, public relations, and sales promotion. Continue the media blitz, landing passages like this in *Marketing and Media Decisions* magazine: "Even the wealthiest and most powerful independent will have trouble working against the heavily funded advertising campaign of the nationals."

- Dominate news coverage of the land rush by encouraging editors and reporters to contact the franchiser, whenever a real estate article or feature is underway.

When they do, the message is constant: independent brokers are an endangered species. They must band together (in a franchise) to survive. The question is, do the franchisers offer more than protection against themselves? Do their national advertising campaigns produce results at the local level? Does a brand-name logo affixed to the realtor's shingle sell homes? And, most important, can an independent thumb his nose at the "ten concerns" and beat them at their own game?

The answer varies from broker to broker. Michael Nash, Chappaqua's Century 21 broker (his office is diagonally across King Street from Holmes & Kennedy), credits the franchise with helping him carve out a "respectable" share of the town's brokerage business. But again there is the question of expectations. Is Nash's definition of "respectable" the same as Peter Kennedy's? As Jack Mitchell's? Unlikely.

Nash, a modest, even-tempered man, admits to a lifelong dream he has never fulfilled.

"I always wanted to be a merchant—to own a small shop. But somehow I wound up in sales for the International Paper Corporation. One day, in the early 1970s, my supervisors abruptly informed me that my position was being eliminated and that I had two equally unpalatable choices: to take a transfer or to accept severance pay. I took the latter, hoping to use the money to fund my dream of entrepreneurship. When it turned out that I didn't have enough cash to open a store, I decided to try my hand at real estate. It seemed like a related field and, all things considered, the next best thing to becoming a merchant."

Nash launched his midlife career at Holmes & Kennedy, joining the staff the very day the bottom fell out of the local real estate market. In six months, he began to hate the telephone. Hundreds of calls went out; few were returned. Although he scoured the community for leads and pursued even the faintest prospects, his efforts produced little more than an occasional flurry of interest that would inevitably dissipate before a sale was made. His bank account drained, his confidence jolted by the interminable dry spell, Nash questioned his ability to make it in the business. "But then one of those leads—one of those countless leads I had floating out in the market caught fire. Suddenly—and somewhat inexplicably because it seemed too good to be true—all the elements of a deal were in place."

In an eleventh-hour triumph reminiscent of a Frank Capra film, the hard-working man on Main Street made his first sale (a $42,000 Cape in Chappaqua Ridge, one of the town's more pedestrian sections), pocketed his first commission ($800) and found himself on a roll that produced a string of successes and a cushion of financial security.

"At the time, it seemed as if my luck had just turned but when I look back at it now, I recognize that there was more to it," Nash says, as he fiddles with a stack of papers in his neat but cheaply appointed office that appears to have been furnished with Salvation Army chairs and desks. "All the meeting and greeting and cold calling I'd done over the previous months made me a known quantity in town and led to people seeing me as a real estate professional. Once the housing market turned around, all of that exposure and good will paid dividends. I started making sales and earning money and forgetting that I ever had a beginner's slump.

"But success did have its price. Once again I was haunted by the desire to have a business of my own. Try as I did to curb that urge and to focus on my work at Holmes & Kennedy, the aspiring entrepreneur within me just couldn't be contained. So I faced what I came to recognize as the inevitable and opened my own firm, Michael Nash, Real Estate."

"You could tell at first glance that I was not a man with a grand design. My first office was not much bigger than a refrigerator, which is just right for a broker who wants to stay small. You can't hire a staff when there's no room for another desk."

But Nash's humble aspirations grew somewhat more ambitious with the first tastes of entrepreneurship and with the knowledge that high-caliber service is more a function of standards than of size.

Just as he was stretching his suspenders, taking the lay of the town and thinking of ways to claim more of its real estate sales, Century 21 came to town to enlist franchisees. Although most of his competitors considered the franchise concept inappropriate for Chappaqua's affluent demographics, Nash saw an opportunity to grow and he seized it.

"I'll admit, I was the laughingstock of the other brokers when I first bought the Century 21 franchise. They thought I was falling for a hard sell—getting into something that wouldn't work in this community. But I proved them wrong.

"I believed from the outset that a nationally known name would be a super drawing card to attract corporate transferees. With IBM and other major corporations headquartered within striking distance of Chappaqua, there's always a parade of executives riding the career shuttle in and out of the area. That makes for a steady, reliable market. I knew that even if Century 21 didn't mean much to our more sophisticated local residents, it would have a hell of a lot of credibility with midwesterners and others who come here for career relocations. Those newcomers from Illinois, Michigan, or Nebraska are looking for one thing—a familiar name—and it's on my door only. I've carved out a niche in the relocation market and I credit much of that success to my affiliation with Century 21."

Saturation advertising—and the brand awareness it buys—is an integral component of Century 21's marketing strategy.

"We are spending more than $20 million a year in national advertising," boasts Dick Loughlin. "You know what that does? It makes us better known than some presidents. A Gallup poll has found that 99 percent of all home buyers know our name. Meaning: when they're ready to buy or sell they will turn to the company they know best. Century 21 of course. This gives our brokers a tremendous advantage."

Proud of his association with Century 21, Nash uses "farming letters" like this one to establish his identity as the franchise's local affiliate.

December 1982

Dear Neighbor:

The social season is here and again one of the topics of conversation will be real estate. (It always is!) Please do me a favor. If the subject comes up tell them for me, Century 21 Michael T. Nash R.E., Inc. is completing its best year ever in sales. I know, all the reports in the newspapers, TV, and word of mouth will tell you it has been a disastrous year. NOT SO!! As a matter of fact, we are currently in need of listings. If you have any thoughts, or know of someone who has a "move in their future," we would love to talk with you. Many will want to wait until after the holidays, but may I suggest that this is a good time to get your appraisals done and paper work completed so that when January arrives, you will get an early start on the market.

There was a good real estate article in the *Reporter Dispatch* the other day. It commented on the fact that there is currently a "window" in the real estate market. That is, the interest rates are still coming down and the prices have not started up yet. The market is good right now and mortgage money is readily available. It may be hard to believe now, but they are predicting a drying up of funds next summer if the trend continues.

When I say we have had our best year ever—I mean it. Maybe it is because we are Century 21 and affiliated with over 7000 offices across the country. Maybe it is because we have *TOP* sales people who are personally concerned in all their transactions. Maybe it is because we have grown to be one of the major factors in real estate in Chappaqua. What ever it is, we would love to talk to you about anything that concerns you with real estate here or anyplace else in the country. After all . . . Century 21 is America's TOP seller!!

Sincerely,

Michael T. Nash

Michael T. Nash

Note the seductive lure of "readily available" mortgage money. This is a cornerstone of the great franchise promise: that the collective might of the national organization can deliver dollars where independent, unaffilliated brokers cannot.

"No question, I was led to believe that the franchise had substantially more clout in securing real estate financing," Aguzzi says, "and that's one of the major reasons I joined. It seemed to me that the mom-and-pop independents came up weakest in this aspect of brokerage. When interest rates soared and mortgage lending all but dried up, financing became the chief barrier to sales. I'd hoped that the franchiser could muscle its way into the money markets in good times and in bad and could keep the funds flowing to us. But they can do nothing of the kind. A strong relationship with a local bank is still the local broker's best financing source."

Adds Don Blair, president of Putnam Trust, a commercial bank active in nearby Greenwich, Connecticut's, real estate lending market, "Our responsibility is to the local market. We would never give special consideration to an organization based outside the Greenwich area just because it was big. In a recent year, we made $79 million in real estate loans—out of a total loan portfolio of $107 million—most of it went to sales involving established local brokers. You can accent the word 'local.'

"A relationship develops with those brokers you've done business with over the years. It's a two-way street: if they hear that American Can is bringing in a new executive, they'll send him to us for banking and trust service. If we learn of the new executive first, we'll send him to the brokers we know to help with the housing search. These are the people that get first call on our money."

The truth is that Century 21 does not have privileged access to the Federal Reserve or, for that matter, to the Main Street banker's loan portfolio. It cannot unilaterally reduce interest rates or increase the money supply.

But where the franchiser does excel is in the development of alternative financing strategies. Put simply, this refers to real estate transactions structured without standard bank mortgages. Savvy brokers learned long ago that they were in a numbers business—that mathematicians were as important to their success as architects. Take any two realtors marketing the same property at the same price to the same prospective buyers. The one with the most attractive payment terms makes the sale. He knows how to fuse applied mathematics, tax know-how, and business sense into hybrid financial structures that effectively match the seller's demands with the buyer's ability to pay.

Century 21's real estate investment staff provides the local affiliates with a smorgasboard of practical and creative financing schemes. In booklets, brochures, seminars, and the company's newsletters "The Neighborhood Professional," and "Investment Journal," the franchiser's resident financial gurus reel off dozens of ways its brokers can close deals when the banks say "no" or when the parties involved prefer to circumvent high interest rates. The franchiser also sensitizes its affiliates to the importance of financing, not just as an obstacle (which they already know from market experience) but also as a marketing tool. Note the following from a Century 21 presentation:

• "An old axiom in the real estate industry is that 'if you can't finance it, forget it!' The statement has never been truer than it is today.

• "Indeed, for most investors, the availability and cost of financing can be either the feature attraction or primary deterrent to any investment opportunity. . . ."

Valuable though this information is, it raises a major question: are timely articles worth the cost of franchise affiliations? Is this ammunition enough to catapult affiliates to the top of their markets? The evidence, in Chappaqua and Armonk, is to the contrary. Although Century 21 has helped Nash—through advertising and alternative financing plans—to develop a modest presence in a rather limited market segment (relocation), he has never challenged the local heavyweights. Visionary brokers in the Mitchell/Siano/Kennedy mold are barely aware of his presence. They have not been "squeezed out of the business" and have not begun to appreciate "the long-term implications" of a fearsome trend. Nor has Vera Aguzzi. Her experience with Century 21 has proven radically different from Nash's.

"I found myself on a one-way street going in the wrong direction. How else would you describe a situation in which I was sending Century 21 franchise fees but they weren't sending me new business in return. The referrals I received from them were pretty much limited people looking for $100,000 homes. What are you going to do with that in a town like Armonk where there aren't many homes available for less than $150,000? To compound the problem, I had to pay Century 21 a percentage on the $250,000 sales I was making selling local properties to local clients who'd been with me before the franchise affiliation."

Aguzzi measures her comments carefully, taking great pains not to knock the franchise concept for fear of the impact it will have on fellow brokers still affiliated with national systems. Smoothing out imaginary creases on her cream-colored silk blouson, she emphasizes that her Century 21 experience was an isolated business mistake. She makes no indictment of the franchise, its executives or their optimistic pitch to prospective affiliates. But Aguzzi has come away from the experience with something far more valuable than anger.

"For this broker, in this community, the system just didn't work. It didn't damage my business—and I didn't lose anything except a small initial investment. I simply recognized that I was better off taking the money I was sending

to the franchiser and investing it in my own advertising
and brochures. This way, I can tailor promotions to the Armonk market and make more productive use of my capital."

Not the kind of talk the franchisers like to hear. Not
only because it counsels against joining a national system,
but also because it undermines the argument on which they
build their membership drives. Think about it. Aguzzi's Century 21 experience brought her full circle to a renewed faith
in the virtues of independent brokerage. Driven by the fear
that she could no longer go it alone, she joined Century
21, only to recognize in less than two years that independence
held the best prospects for long-term success.

Others have decided similarly. Between 1977 and 1980,
more than 10,000 brokerage firms dropped their franchise
affiliation. Most complained that the high fees—an average
initiation of $10,000, 6 percent of gross residential commis-
sions, and $200 per month for national advertising—did not
produce a compensating increase in profits. Studies of the
profitability of residential brokerage firms conducted by the
National Association of Realtors show that nonfranchised
firms often do as well as franchised firms and sometimes
do a bit better.

> While franchising has grown phenomenally over the
> past several years, firms which join are not permanently
> wedded to their organization. Indeed, nearly 9 percent
> of the firms in our survey had at one time belonged
> to a franchise but for one reason or another grew dissat-
> isfied and dropped out of the franchise arena altogether.
> In addition, a small number of franchised firms have
> switched allegiance.*

Most of the brokers terminating their franchise affiliations cite the high costs, disappointing sales, poor referrals,
and dissatisfaction with advertising and sales training.

Many brokers react negatively to the highly regimented

* "Profile on Real Estate Firms," National Association of Realtors, 1982.

approach of franchising. "We're the last bastion of independent contractors," says Norman Kailo, former president of the New Jersey Association of Realtors. "We don't like regimentation. Many of our people don't feel comfortable wearing the same jacket or being associated with just anyone. You can clone a hamburger but you can't clone professional people so easily."*

Thoughts like this are likely to unravel the myth of

**REASONS FOR TERMINATING FRANCHISE AFFILIATION
FOR FIRMS THAT DID NOT JOIN ANOTHER FRANCHISE
(Percentage Distribution)**

Reasons	Very Important	Somewhat Important	Not a Factor	Total
High costs	70.4	16.9	12.7	100.0
Didn't increase sales as expected	70.0	21.4	8.6	100.0
Poor referrals	55.7	25.7	18.6	100.0
Advertising did not meet expectations	48.5	19.7	31.8	100.0
Sales training program did not meet expectations	41.8	19.4	38.8	100.0

In contrast, firms that switched allegiance to another franchise terminated their previous arrangement for different reasons. Generally, these firms considered the failure of the sales training program to meet expectations and poor referrals as very important factors in the firm's decision to terminate its previous franchise affiliation.

**REASONS FOR TERMINATING FRANCHISE AFFILIATION
FOR FIRMS THAT JOINED ANOTHER FRANCHISE
(Percentage Distribution)**

Reasons	Very Important	Somewhat Important	Not a Factor	Total
High costs	44.4	5.6	50.0	100.0
Didn't increase sales as expected	47.1	23.5	29.4	100.0
Poor referrals	50.0	11.1	38.9	100.0
Advertising did not meet expectations	41.2	29.4	29.4	100.0
Sales training program did not meet expectations	50.0	16.7	33.3	100.0

Source: National Association of Realtors. Reprinted by permission.

* *New York Times*, December 27, 1981, Section IX, p. 1.

franchise invincibility and to lead many more affiliates to return to the ranks of the independents. They may recognize that franchising—save for the benefits its accrues to the franchisers—is not the best way to profit from the land rush. In the author's opinion, the corporate blazers, pitches, and sales slogans are nothing more than placebos for small-minded brokers seeking the quick fix of collectivism in a business that heaps the greatest rewards on individualists.

Independent brokers can learn more from their success-ful colleagues than from franchise executives, some of whom have never sold real estate. The best role models are those land rush leaders who've managed to achieve double-digit commission growth in spite of competition from the franchis-ers. How do they do it? What are their success secrets? What can other brokers learn from them? Interviews with twenty leading brokers in major real estate markets reveal the following:

Success Secret Number One: Recruiting Sales Manag-ers

"The most important sales people are your sales manag-ers so I spread the word around town that I'm willing to overpay to get the best," says a Beverly Hills broker.

"Yes, I bribe them with salaries that are 20 percent above the going rate, with their choice of company car— up to and including a Mercedes—and with an office and secre-tary of their own.

"This costs $40,000 a year in extra expenses. Appar-ently, my competition considers that to be extravagant be-cause no one's ever tried to match me. I couldn't be more pleased. For $40,000 I'm able to lure away the best manag-ers, those who can contribute to my firm more than $1 million a year in incremental commissions. I don't know of a better return on an investment.

"I have four offices now—all of which are managed su-perbly by sales managers I've recruited from competing bro-kers. If I were asked to list the factors that have contributed to my success, this would be high on the list."

Success Secret Number Two: Market Timing

"Brokers in every town can identify a handful of exceptional properties that can sell virtually the moment they're listed," says the president of a brokerage firm in the fashionable summer community of Southampton, New York. "Well, I believe in manipulating the market by keeping these sought-after homes on ice for a short time after they're available for sale. When such a premier residence is available—providing I'm fortunate enough to get the listing—I leak word that the owner is just about ready to take offers. But I try to convince the seller to hold off for a month or so. We don't allow anyone to tour the house and we don't take bids. What does that do? It teases the other brokers and their clients, creating tremendous pent-up demand. The salespeople know the house will go fast and they want to be sure that their clients have first crack at it.

"This works wonderfully in our favor. When I finally do throw open the doors there's a rush to see the place. The offers are usually substantially above the asking price, netting the owner significantly more than if we'd rushed the property to market.

"A strange psychology develops when a hot property is withheld from the market. Buyer and brokers together fashion strategies to claim it as soon as the wraps are off. The most common tactic is to make a preemptive bid. One so substantial that it immediately has first option on the property. Wonderful. That plays right into my hands."

Success Secret Number Three: Less Is More

"Most brokers seize every listing they can get, but I contend that in some cases, less is more," says Sally Siano. "This prompts me to reject some listings that are priced substantially below a half million dollars.

"I do this for two reasons: First, I've established a reputation that could be damaged by taking on what in this town are perceived as ordinary homes. Second, the hard sells in Bedford are not the $3 million mansions but the $250,000 to $300,000 colonials. Why should I devote time and resources to relatively small commission deals when the more profitable transactions are easier to make? Were I not selective in this way, I could be diverting my staff's attention from the $100,000 commissions to chase after those for $10,000."

This "less is more" selectivity demands that the broker exercise extraordinary discipline. For a natural-born salesperson, saying no to a deal, any deal, is the ultimate in abstenance. But the virtue is rewarded. By controlling the urge to rush after every modest listing, the broker automatically trains his efforts on the major deals, earns a reputation as a successful marketer of luxury properties and nets the megacommissions that provide the capital for *Town & Country* ads, sophisticated brochures, video tapes and the full complement of sophisticated marketing tools.

"You've heard of the vicious cycle," Siano says. "Well, this is the beneficial cycle. Once you sell the better properties and earn the bigger commissions you have the name and the financial muscle to get to the top. All you need is the discipline to stay there."

To this breed of broker, success is a function, not of joining franchises, but of beating them.

4

Merrill Lynch Realty Associates: Wall Street Takes On Main Street —And Loses?

Like the bull in the china shop Merrill Lynch pictures in its TV ads, the Wall Street giant may be out of place in real estate. This is one market you can't overpower.

Charles Seilheimer
Vice President, Sotheby International Realty

Local brokerage superstars may have a more difficult time rejecting the amorous advances of another would-be land-rush power—a pillar of the financial community—that is now actively assembling successful brokers into a network of its own. But one with a fundamental difference.

While Century 21 is selling its way into the real estate market—profiting from franchise sales as it builds an ever-wider chain of affiliates—Merrill Lynch is trying to buy its way in. In a move that has sparked wide imitation on Wall Street, the firm that calls itself "a breed apart" is reaching beyond its traditional preserves of stocks, bonds and tax shelters to become a financial services warehouse. The underlying objective is to provide the typical American family with a cradle-to-grave shopping list of money management products including life insurance, annuities, Keoghs, IRAs, convertible debentures, municipal bonds, zero coupons, limited partnerships, tax anticipation notes, common stocks, mutual funds, money market accounts, options, commercial paper, government securities, and. . . .

"Real estate!" says Weston E. Edwards, chairman of Merrill Lynch Realty Associates. "We see real estate as a way to build relationships with the American consumer at an early stage in his life cycle. The traditional Merrill Lynch client—a securities investor about fifty years old—tends to reduce his investment activity with us as he ages. With this in mind, we recognized that we had to hook into the consumer well before middle age—to get the person into a growing list of financial services when he or she is in the initial stages of the career- and family-building periods. Money market funds are viewed as an effective hook but they don't compare to real estate. Because buying a home is a person's first major investment, those who use our real estate brokerage services will likely start with Merrill Lynch in their thirties and stay with us. That's our plan."

Dakin B. Ferris, Merrill's executive vice president in charge of its real estate and insurance group, explains the corporate strategy this way:

"Merrill Lynch entered the real estate business for two reasons: The first—very bluntly—is to make money. Each year Americans put more money into real estate than into securities and commodities commissions. That caught our eye. The second reason is that an active real estate operation helps us develop life-cycle relationships with clients. We want them to come to Merrill Lynch for a wide array of financial services, rather than seeking those services with a wide variety of individual providers. If we serve their housing needs well, we will attract home buyers to return to Merrill Lynch for additional investment and insurance needs. If we serve a commercial real estate need well, that opens the door to other deals with that client, including individual services for its owners.

"We believe that being part of the Merrill Lynch operation, with total access to all of that organization's great strengths in the marketplace, gives us an unparalleled potential."*

Ferris also notes that, "Between 1945 and 1965, 80 million babies were born. Those babies are now adults, or will be presently. The older half is exactly the market we seek—the twenty-seven-to-thirty-seven-year-old. The younger half will be entering the market during this decade. In the 1970s, 32 million Americans reached the prime home-buying age of thirty. In the 1980s, 42 million will turn thirty. And in the decade, there will be from 13 to 15 million new household formations. It's a vast market . . . We know there's an opportunity to approach that market with the quality image and reliable reputation of a nationally known brand name—the Merrill Lynch brand."

Merrill Lynch is not the only business superpower hoping to capture a commanding share of the real estate market. At the other end of the corporate spectrum, Sears, Roebuck, the Chicago-based retailing behemoth, is also establishing itself as a financial services supermarket, acquiring in recent years Previews, Dean Witter, Allstate Insurance, and Coldwell Banker. Sears customers in the chain's stores shopping for Craftsmen power drills or Die Hard batteries can also pick up 100 shares of General Electric, a whole-life policy or a yellow-framed colonial on Main and Elm. Because Sears condenses all of the components of a money-management supermarket into a retail setting, it provides the most graphic example of the financial synergy that is the prime mover behind a growing number of corporate marriages. But Merrill Lynch's program is most interesting because of its heavy reliance on real estate as a cornerstone of its diversification plan and because of its campaign, ambitious even by Wall Street standards, to become the dominant force in residential brokerage.

But how did Merrill Lynch get started in real estate

* Speech to the New York Real Estate Board, Grand Hyatt Hotel, March 10, 1983.

and why did it choose to acquire existing brokerage firms? "When the corporation began exploring the real estate field as an avenue of growth, it considered three points of entry into the market: direct brokerage, that is establishing its own offices; franchising, something akin to the Century 21 format; and relocation companies," Edwards explains, talking in the deliberate, highly controlled manner that reflects his conservative bearing. "At first blush, management was attracted to direct brokerage, but they soon recognized that this was radically different from securities brokerage—that they couldn't just march in with a lot of fanfare, open their own local offices and make an instant success of them. They needed education—hands-on experience to go that route.

"Franchising was also considered because it was simpler to structure and far less capital intensive than building a direct brokerage organization—but it too was rejected for several reasons. Most important, management realized that franchising was not a good way to go about improving existing brokerage practices—which was one of our goals. Instead, it would simply be a case of putting a new image on an old and often inefficient business. Merrill's executives also feared that franchising might damage the firm's vaunted reputation. Because the investment house would be lending its name and logo to thousands of independent brokers essentially free of the corporation's control, it risked having its good name tarnished by unethical or unprofessional realtors.

"Relocation—the business of transferring (including buying and selling their homes) corporate executives around the country, had none of these problems. So Merrill made its first major approach to the real estate market by acquiring, in 1977, Ticor Relocation Management—a firm I had founded. My company was a perfect match for Merrill at this early stage of its real estate activities. Why? For three basic reasons. First, Ticor's clients were blue chip corporations—more blue chips than Merrill had in its investment banking arm—so there was no reason to fret about Merrill's reputation. These were the kinds of companies Merrill had always sought. Second, the acquisition was a perfect fit for both Ticor's and Merrill's long-term needs. Merrill Lynch needed a platform for growth which we could provide, and Ticor needed capital which Merrill could provide. Ticor had been relying on bank financing to fuel its growth; Merrill's cash could lower its financing costs and thus its over-all operating expenses. Third, Ticor gave Merrill a window into the real estate business. With our inventory of 3,000 homes, and a volume of 15,000 corporate transfers annually, we put Merrill smack-dab into all the major real estate markets. Merrill's management valued this not only for the revenues it would produce but also because it gave them the opportunity to work with and evaluate the best brokers in the country. They could learn firsthand what it takes to succeed in residential brokerage.

"The experience proved to be invaluable. Quickly, Merrill learned that it could transfer its marketing skills to real estate, that it could bring new sophistication to the field, and that its management prowess and financial resources could bring improved profitability to existing ventures."

With its confidence clearly soaring, Merrill was ready for its next major move, the acquisition and subsequent control of big, market-leading brokerage firms throughout the United States. The master plan was to assemble, through purchases, a far-flung, but centrally owned and managed, brokerage organization. Two years after acquiring Ticor (and renaming it Merrill Lynch Relocation Management, Inc.), the company that is "bullish on America" launched its primary real estate arm, Merrill Lynch Realty Associates, and, through it, unleashed a stampede that brought its executives thundering into every major city in search of profitable, multioffice brokers willing to trade their independence for prime shelf space in Merrill's financial supermarket.

The corporation's entry into real estate has had all the finesse of a bulldozer. Although the PR hype called for infusing its acquisitions with superior management tools, training and corporate facilities, the emphasis was and still is on building market share by gobbling up an awesome collection

of local brokers. To date, Merrill has acquired thirty brokerage firms with a total sales force of 8,000 associates.* In
just four years, Merrill Lynch Realty Associates has become
the largest residential brokerage firm, selling 60,000 houses
a year. A heady demonstration of big business's ability—
by way of its enormous financial resources—to compress
generations of growth into a remarkably brief time span.
But according to Merrill executives, it has only just begun.

Dakin Ferris says this of his plans for a continued blitz-
krieg of the residential market: "Let me say right off that
I realize our entry probably is not universally hailed. The
real estate industry is one of the last refuges of individual
entrepreneurs and small organizations.

"Some may feel as if they are in that national park in
Africa where a warning sign is posted beside a ladder of
steps running up a large tree. The sign says: 'In case of
rhinoceros charge, climb at least eight feet.'

"I don't know about rhinoceroses, but you can expect
a charge of bulls because we are determined to become a
dominant force, nationwide and worldwide, in real estate—
a premier company . . ."

Adds Weston Edwards, "By 1985, we intend to be the
recognized leader in U.S. real estate. That translates into
major representation in fifty markets and a sales agent force
of more than 20,000 strong. That's what we are aiming for
and with the enormous resources and talent of Merrill Lynch,
I'm quite certain we will achieve our objectives."

Edwards' confidence may be misguided. Seated cross-
legged on a nubby sofa in his spacious corner office—decorated in the middle-American chic of an airport VIP lounge—
he is Central Casting's version of the straight-as-an-arrow,
born-in-a-white-shirt corporate executive. Surrounded by secretaries, staff assistants and assorted climbers of the corporate ladder, he appears to suffer from an illusion common
to many chief executives: the conviction that his organizational power extends to a world beyond the steel and glass
walls of Merrill Lynch Realty Associates offices in a Stam-

* Figures are as of fall, 1983.

ford, Connecticut, corporate park. One gets that impression because Edwards believes he can impose his will on the real estate market and have it obey his commands like a snake in a genie's basket. But he may be wrong. Some objective observers believe that in real estate, Merrill Lynch may be investing a fortune in a losing proposition.

From day one of its brokerage activities, Merrill has applied the George Steinbrenner pennant race formula to residential real estate. The controversial sports mogul scouts the big leagues for the best players from Boston to Los Angeles, spends millions to get them under contract and then fits them with Yankee pinstripes. In much the same way, Edwards identifies the best independent brokers, buys them out for cash and stock options and incorporates their operations under the Merrill Lynch banner. It makes for a gutsy, high-risk, and potentially high-reward strategy. By acquiring large, well-established, multioffice brokerage firms, Merrill becomes a major force in the largest cities virtually overnight. The customers, sales associates and listings are all in place: the Wall Street giant simply nails its name to the door.

The question is: has Merrill made a sound investment? Has it purchased a foundation for long-term growth or is it building on a base of quicksand? Can Merrill achieve its stated objective to "become the recognized leader in real estate?" Or will its foray into the land rush produce the kind of devastating losses that turn stock market speculators into determined bond clippers.

Those who doubt Merrill's ability to weld its purchased patchwork of brokerage offices into a highly profitable and market-dominating force form two skeptical camps: those who reject the notion that the Wall Street bull can improve current brokerage practices, and those who insist that the business will always be led by aggressive, locally connected independents.

Merrill Lynch is staking its growing prestige and earnings on a bid to revolutionize the real estate industry by servicing every aspect of home sales and financing.

It is an attempt at horizontal integration never tried before in an industry of specialists. Merrill Lynch subsidiaries already relocate customers to new communities, find their houses and provide them with financing while insuring both the mortgage borrower and lender. But last year—the first full year in which all the pieces were in place—real estate losses trimmed $34 million from Merrill Lynch's pretax profits. . . .

Some independent-minded agents say they find Merrill Lynch's strict corporate policies and command structure too stifling and they feel that the parent company has done little to bring new services to the table. This is still a one-on-one meet-me-on-Saturday-afternoon business with a big personal factor," says Kenneth A. Kerin, an analyst with the National Association of Realtors. "Those that have gone to Merrill Lynch have hoped to get superior access to the capital markets and greater ease in getting financing for their clients. But I don't see Merrill Lynch doing that kind of thing right now.*

Adds Sotheby's Charles Seilheimer, "Merrill Lynch has come to recognize that real estate is the ultimate investment vehicle, with far more potential than marketing stocks and other paper assets. So they've gone beserk spending a king's ransom in acquiring and homogenizing brokerage offices according to the Merrill Lynch formula. But their massive undertaking is bound to fail. What the boys from Wall Street do not recognize is that residential real estate—for all its cumulative wealth and potential—will always be a local business.

"Successful brokers get to the top not by applying McDonald's-type formulas but instead by having roots in the community, by knowing the town and its people and by earning their trust and respect over the years. Our current Greenwich affiliate, Jane Newhall, is a superb example. When anyone who is anyone has a property for sale, Ms. Newhall is at the top of the list of brokers they call to handle

* *Business Week*, April 13, 1981, p. 128.

the listing. She can gain entry to houses even before their owners have decided to sell. They'll seek her advice in making a decision on when to sell and at what price. McDonald's formulas are O.K. for marketing cheeseburgers but not for handling what most people consider their most important asset.

"Consider this: for a mere pittance of the cost of Merrill Lynch's program, Sotheby's has plugged into 400 of the best brokers in the country while Merrill has only 30 brokers. What's more, by bringing central management to these acquired offices, Merrill strips them of the operating style and the local flair that made them successful in the first place. Does this make sense? I think not. You have a Wall Street company with virtually no experience in real estate instructing real estate professionals on how to conduct their businesses. Crazy. Imagine Merrill taking instruction from realtors in selling convertible debentures."

Such heresy makes Edwards raise his hands to the sky, as if to ask God to enlighten the congregation.

"No! No! No! We have no intention whatsoever of tampering with our brokers' local identification. Whoever says to the contrary is sorely misinformed or just plain malicious. We know full well the importance of preserving local identity and of harnessing the individual brokers' skills and experience. Our approach leaves all of that intact. We simply fill in the cracks where the local operations are weakest."

Merrill's objective—one common to acquiring companies in many industries—is to strike a delicate balance between central control and local autonomy. The mechanism for achieving this—a minority stock ownership plan—gives the acquired brokers continuing equity in the firms they owned, and in many cases founded, but now manage for Merrill Lynch.

It works like this: When Merrill Lynch purchases Smith Realty,* Bill Smith is paid in cash and notes or a combination

* Merrill Lynch refuses to divulge its purchase prices and forbids the acquired company to reveal this information. Edwards apparently fears that word of high prices will set a precedent, forcing higher terms for future acquisitions.

of both for his interests and Merrill Lynch Realty Associates gains control of the firm. But to keep Smith's incentive high—to dissuade him from taking the proceeds of the Merrill Lynch acquisition and spending the rest of his days on the golf course—Merrill makes Smith a minority stockholder in the newly acquired firm, letting him keep a maximum 20 percent of his stock.

Although the acquired broker is no longer the principal owner, he retains a piece of the action and thus a vested interest in seeing to it that the parent company succeeds in the local market.

"This is the only part of Merrill Lynch where local entrepreneurs own a share of the business," Edwards says. "When you think of it, that's really quite extraordinary. It is done so that we can attract and motivate the best brokers in the country."

Even with the sweetener of stock participation, the transition from business owner to corporate employee can frustrate long-time entrepreneurs accustomed to making all of the management decisions and collecting all of its rewards. Some need time to adjust; others never will. Aware of this, Merrill generally sets aside the first five years as a "honeymoon," during which it monitors the individual's performance to determine if both parties can work together on a long-term basis. Through the trial period minority stockholders do not have the contractual right to sell their shares back to Merrill Lynch (unless they leave the company during this period) nor can Merrill force a sale of the stock. At the conclusion of the five years, the stockholders can require that Merrill buy back their shares based on a set formula, and Merrill reserves the right to make such a purchase even if the stockholder prefers to keep his equity position.

"During the honeymoon period, we use what I call 'shadow management,' " Edwards says. "This means letting the local firm have considerable freedom in running its affairs. We simply shadow them to make certain things are being done according to Merrill Lynch's standards. If business declines or other problems develop we switch to a hands-on approach. Should local management prove itself unable to produce, we assume control and search for a replacement. We're tough and demanding, but we are also fair. Our motto to brokers sums it up nicely: 'Profits give you freedom.' "

What Merrill considers poor performance brings freedom of another kind. Or so Paula Stringer has discovered. A Dallas broker whose firm became Merrill's first acquisition (Spring, 1979), Stringer ultimately found herself as little more than a community goodwill ambassador for Merrill Lynch Realty Associates. A competitor in the Dallas real estate grapevine holds that she did not score well on Merrill's honeymoon report card. Questioned about this, Stringer seems to both confirm and deny it.

"I was never much of a business person and a business of this size needs someone who is. My son served in that capacity but when he chose to leave Paula Stringer Real Estate to go off on his own, Merrill Lynch brought in someone else to run the business. Their first appointee didn't work out and I told them so. Some of my best managers were threatening to leave. That's when Edwards brought in one of his long-time associates to take the top spot.

"I chose not to serve as chief executive any longer. But Merrill still pays me a compensation and bonus package worth six figures just to serve as a consultant."

When asked for his side of the story, Edwards appears to confirm the rumors that Merrill forced Stringer out while couching them in a bouquet of compliments. "Paula's a lovely lady . . . a lovely lady. Yes, it has seemed best to relieve her of the terrible responsibility of day-to-day management."

"Whose decision was that?" he is asked.

"Paula's a lovely lady. I'm sure she agrees that everything is fine just the way it is."

It must be said that Stringer does not appear to be terribly upset with the circumstances. Like many small business owners faced with a fat-cat offer from an acquisitive giant, she viewed the opportunity to sell her eighteen-office, 750-sales-associate firm to Merrill as a once-in-a-lifetime chance to turn the trappings of commercial success into cash.

"I sold to Merrill because I wanted time to smell the roses. They made an offer I couldn't refuse and it came at a time in my life when I wanted more than just business success."

Not that the free-spending bull always has its way. Merrill's first acquisition candidate, Stringer's Dallas competitor Ebby Halliday, rejected the wealthy suitor as an unwelcome interloper.

"Merrill Lynch thinks everyone has a price—I guess that's the way they work in New York—but we can't be bought and we told them so," snaps Halliday. "I didn't want to sell to Merrill under any terms because I enjoy running my own business my way. When that was clear, they turned to my competition, Paula Stringer, and acquired her firm."

Edwards, obviously shaken by Halliday's remarks, responds cautiously. "We interviewed four Dallas brokers and . . . well . . . and . . . well . . . we led each to believe they were our first choice. Paula is a lovely lady. Ebby is a lovely lady. But Ebby is wrong. We never asked her to go with Merrill Lynch and so she never had the opportunity to reject us. I guess she likes to flaunt her ego by saying she turned us down, but I . . . I . . . she's a lovely lady . . . I must say her statement is not true."

Brokers inclined to sell to Merrill to achieve liquidity— only to coast through the next five years like a pampered film star resting at poolside between pictures—are short-sighted. The stock repurchase formula is keyed to the broker's performance during the honeymoon period. Because this equity is a major component of the broker's buyout, most will take it very, very seriously.

"It's our view and theirs," Edwards adds, tilting his shimmering eyeglasses to the light to fuss over a lintspot, "that the 20-percent stock can, in five years, be worth more than the entire firm at the time Merrill acquired it."

But Richard Cope, who sold his Clearwater, Florida, real estate brokerage—Roger & Cummings—to Merrill in September, 1981, says, "The jury's still out on that one. It's too early to tell if the shares will be equal in value to the acquisition price by 1986. I'm not optimistic and I'm not pessimistic: I just don't know. I will say that for the Merrill affiliation to be a success, the shares must grow to at least 50 percent of the company's value at the time of the sale. That's because our growth curve indicates that we would have reached that level even without Merrill.

"Of course, our pre–Merrill Lynch growth rate may not have been sustainable had Merrill acquired one of our competitors, thus forcing us to compete against a very formidable opponent. Although Merrill never made any such threats—and we didn't need our arms twisted to agree to the buyout—the specter of facing them as competitors certainly played a part in my decision to go with Merrill. If a local firm was going to be a Merrill Lynch realtor, I wanted it to be mine."

Cope is more sanguine about Merrill's value as a financing source than about the ultimate value of his minority shares.

"Clearwater is a bedroom and recreational community outside of Tampa. For years, we wanted to establish a presence in Tampa but, considering that we had marginal capital, that would have required a slow build and I'm not the kind of entrepreneur who likes to work that way. Fortunately, after we were acquired by Merrill Lynch, an old-line Tampa broker announced that he wanted to retire. Merrill is now set to buy him out and to add that market to our territory. With this one transaction, we'll leap-frog the entire business-building process, quickly becoming a significant factor in Tampa brokerage. That's what capital resources can do.

"Let me add that before Merrill Lynch came along, we were approached by a half dozen or so franchise outfits. Realty World even offered to waive the initial franchise fee. But we turned them all down because they were offering us nothing but a brand name and we already had that in our market. Merrill's appeal was in its financing capability and that, more than anything else, convinced us to go with them."

John Olita, senior vice president of Carl Burr Real Estate, Merrill Lynch's Long Island, New York, acquisition, also credits the parent company for helping Burr expand beyond its traditional power base as Suffolk County's dominant broker to take up strategic positions in the more populous and affluent towns of adjacent Nassau.

"We now have offices in Plainview, Massapequa, East Meadow, Valley Stream and other key Nassau County towns. One of the primary reasons for forging our association with Merrill was to achieve rapid expansion and this has certainly worked according to plan."

The same sources who praise the power of Wall Street financing suddenly become tongue-tied when queried about Merrill's performance as a dispenser of management training and marketing know-how. Questions are met with barely audible mumblings about "the difficulty of comparing management styles" or of the need "to give long-term programs ample time to take hold." One gets the impression that the former independent brokers—now Merrill Lynch employees—have learned a thing or two about creative financing from their new bosses, but precious little that they didn't already know about the trench warfare tactics of gaining listings and turning house hunters into buyers. Cope, more candid than the rest, says it best:

"They helped considerably with the application of financial controls—and God knows we needed it. Like the vast majority of brokers, we paid little attention to cash flow, credit and the like. When times were good, we just spent money helter skelter and when they were bad, we pulled in the reins. That was the extent of our financial controls. We reacted to problems rather than anticipating them. Once a brokerage firm passes a certain growth threshold—say more than 200 sales associates—this kind of seat-of-the-pants management is unacceptable.

"Merrill has taught us to be much more bottom-line-oriented. For example, we've learned to project our cash requirements for the fiscal year, to plan for a possible downturn and to make the necessary provisions for additional credit should it be required. We can also identify our least and most profitable types of transactions and can use this data to determine which parts of our business deserve the most attention and resources. In short, we know a good deal more about this company's inner workings than we did before the acquisition.

"But as to selling real estate, per se, let me put it this way. Many, if not all, of the brokers Merrill Lynch has acquired could teach corporate management more about real estate than they ever thought there was to learn."

While agreeing that the brokers are best informed about their local markets, Edwards intimates that this is more a matter of exposure than ability. "Once we've had an opportunity to sink our roots, we make up for any shortcoming we may have. The thing to remember is that real estate brokers were never known for their management capabilities. Fine people, but not sophisticated managers. That's the missing link we are bringing to local brokerage and it has a direct impact on sales."

Edwards cites three examples of Merrill's contribution to improved salesmanship:

• The publication and distribution of *Fine Homes.*

Another four-color aren't-these-drop-dead-homes magazine, *Fine Homes* is similar in appearance to Previews' *Homes International.* No doubt the properties are attractive and the book draws attention to the firm's upscale listings, but it is hardly a Merrill Lynch exclusive.

What's more, the advertisements—paid for by Merrill sales associates—are for properties clearly above the company's average middle-class listings. One issue featured:

A 6,500-square-foot contemporary—*Architectural Record*'s house of the year (1978)—in stately Westbury, New York. Price: $2 million. Broker: Merrill Lynch/Carl Burr.

A pastel-pink Spanish villa in exclusive Paradise Valley, Arizona. Price: $389,000. Broker: Merrill Lynch Realty/ Tom Gannin.

A Montecito, California, plantation home, complete with breakfast lanai with fireplace, a sparkling fountain in the patio, and an automatic greenhouse (whatever that is). Price: $895,000. Broker: Merrill Lynch Realty (company-owned office).

What value this will have to the great bulk of sales associates is questionable.

- The addition of mortgage officers to many of Merrill's major offices.

"These people are experts in real estate financing," Edwards explains. "They are trained to help our sales associates utilize every possible financing option. Before we brought them in, our offices looked primarily to their local savings and loans as sources of financing information. But Merrill Lynch's market research revealed that the thrift people limited their recommendations to the handful of financing services they could provide. Quite often, the latest, most creative options were not utilized."

- More effective deployment of sales associates.

Edwards notes, quite accurately, that few local brokers rate their sales associates according to sound business or motivational systems. Instead, the man or woman selling the most houses in any given month is viewed as the top producer until a colleague goes one better and inherits the crown.

To improve on this what-have-you-done-for-us-today method of evaluation, Merrill teaches its offices to use a "quartiling system" that grades associates according to their cumulative sales performance. The staff is divided into four quartiles, with the star producers in the top 25 percent, the dullards in the bottom quarter and the rest in between. By ranking associates along this spectrum, management can see at a glance which of its people are most productive,

which need additional training and which should be dismissed. Generally, those who remain at the bottom quartile
for a year are asked to leave, thus making room for fresh
and hopefully more productive replacements.

The problem is, many brokers claim that they don't need
a textbook system to gauge staff performance.

"If a broker doesn't know instinctively who is making
his money and who isn't, he hasn't been in business for
very long," says a highly successful Westchester independent who does very well, thank you, without the benefit of
quartiling. "That's a big business affectation that's unnecessary in a local real estate agency."

Merrill's Cope makes a similar point when he alludes
to the friction that develops when the parent corporation—
with its highly developed infrastructure of rules, regula-
tions, and procedures—absorbs what were once free-wheel-
ing entrepreneurs into its system.

"Headquarters has to learn that it cannot treat local
sales associates the same way it governs salaried employees
in the executive office. Real estate people thrive on a diet
that's heavy on incentives, light on controls. I find myself
having to remind Merrill of this from time to time, and I
must admit that it's a problem not easily solved. You have
two different mentalities here—the entrepreneurial and the
bureaucratic—and they rarely see eye to eye."

But will corporate bureaucracies—the likes of Sears and
Merrill Lynch—coddle their real estate brokerage subsidiaries like precocious children in need of a loosely structured
environment or will they be forced to comply with the same
fifty-pound policy book that governs the other lines of business?

If history is any guide, the corporate parent will stamp
out creativity rather than encourage it. A central tenet of
modern management holds that to control bigness—to oversee far-flung operating units active in diverse fields and industries—top executives must reduce a multiplicity of production, marketing and financial practices into uniform
procedures that can be easily monitored by headquarters

staff. The greatest fear of the men in the executive suite is, not that the business will be unimaginative, but instead that "It will hold surprises," as International Telephone & Telegraph's legendary chairman, Harold Geneen, used to say. This has become the rallying cry for an entire generation of corporate chief executives. The CEO responsible for managing a multinational conglomerate with 100,000 employees in fifty divisions making or selling 2,500 products knows that his 800 divisional managers routinely camouflage business problems hoping to correct them before headquarters catches on. In most cases, however, this sweep-it-under-the-rug syndrome only compounds the problem. When it surfaces—as it inevitably will—the effects are devastating. Typically, the organization is drained of millions of dollars, its reputation is tarnished and in some cases, its very existence is threatened. The fear of waking up in the middle of the night to this kind of nasty surprise is what makes the CEOs press hard for uniform controls.

But in its headlong rush to join the land rush, Merrill Lynch has been unable or unwilling to admit that its emphasis on conformity (treating, as one broker says, "real estate associates like employees in the stock trading department") may well prevent surprises and it may assure the chief executive of a restful eight hours, but it will not ignite the entrepreneurial spark that is essential to building a dynamic real estate business.

The major flaw of diversification through acquisition—often the pattern for conglomeration—is that it assigns those with the least amount of experience and expertise in a business subspecialty to manage those who founded and built the companies from scratch. In case after case, the crafty founders of entrepreneurial ventures acquired by conglomerates find that the policies that made their companies worth acquiring are supplanted by the arcane formulas of corporate MBAs, who've never run a business and who've been schooled to eliminate risk, rather than to accept it as an integral component of the business-building process. To these numbers crunchers, companies can be guided almost entirely by computer projections: entrepreneurial visions that do not assure a minimum return in a specified period of time are written off. Fortunately, their domination of the American corporate scene postdates the likes of Edison, Disney, and Paley, whose dreams would have been gleefully quashed by today's calculator-carrying divisional managers.

If Merrill Lynch is to claim its stake in residential real estate successfully, becoming the industry's preeminent force in spite of its entrepreneurial shortcomings, one factor will be responsible: the Merrill Lynch name. Much as Sotheby's trademark lends an aura of Old World elegance to carriage trade brokers, Merrill's logo connotes security, credibility and financial clout in middle-class markets where these qualities are of paramount importance. For all of its faults, Merrill has a chance of achieving its objectives because the name on the broker's shingle is instantly recognized and widely respected. It is a modern American trademark that ranks in stature with the titans of the breed: Coca-Cola, Chevrolet, and IBM.

Says Joseph DeSimone, a Merrill Lynch Realty/Carl Burr competitor in Suffolk County: "Merrill is beating the pulp out of the little John Doe realtors out here. And up till now they've been doing it on name and image alone. When the average family goes out to buy a house they're strapped for cash and hoping like mad that someone will be able to assemble a financing package that will stretch their buying capacity. And who do they think can perform this miracle? John Doe Realty or Merrill Lynch Pierce Fenner & Smith? Right you are. That's why they've been turning to Merrill and Merrill's been writing the business."

Not that DeSimone is folding his tent. A well-established broker with five offices and a solid client base, he's been able to hold his own against the Wall Street interloper, but only by besting Merrill at its own game.

Much as Steve Cutter and Sally Siano match the glamour marketers (Previews and Sotheby's) brochure for brochure, press release for press release, DeSimone—a Brooklyn-reared business street fighter with a solid grounding in real estate finance—is matching Merrill Lynch with a wide range of financial services.

"A lot of brokers see the boys from the big city coming their way and they panic. They close up, sell out, or join the enemy. They don't know what else to do because they're not business people, they're salespeople.

"But I'm here to tell them that there is a way to wage war against financial service giants and to offer the public much the same products and services they do—perhaps more. The answer to our problems is right there on Main Street at the bank and the savings and loan. These institutions are also being hurt by Merrill Lynch. As Merrill and its subsidiaries move increasingly into financial services—by arranging mortgages and offering money market funds, for example—the local thrift institutions are suffering a corresponding decline in business. The way the real estate market is evolving today, two local entities—banks and independent realtors—are being damaged by outside forces.

"But there's no reason to abandon the market. The little guys can unite, pool their services and retaliate against the national outfits. An aggressive realtor, for example, can give his bank a commitment for a minimum number of mortgages and the bank, in turn, can commit to a guaranteed volume of funds. This way, when a customer needs financing the realtor can handle the deal through his established mortgage pipeline rather than sending the buyer off, hat in hand, to shop the banks."

Although DeSimone is respectful of Merrill Lynch's name and resources, he is convinced that creative, well-managed independents can continue to prosper in the real estate market. The National Association of Realtors' Kenneth Kerin agrees. "Aggressive independents will find their own ways to tie into the capital markets and they'll be strong competitors for Merrill Lynch or any other national organization. Merrill, after all, has no monopoly on money.

"Sure Merrill Lynch will be one of the key players in

residential real estate. But I don't think it will dominate. Not in any way. The good independent brokers won't let it happen."

To assure that his seven-year-old firm ($10 million in annual commissions) continues to flourish in spite of Merrill's presence, DeSimone has repositioned his brokerage as a local financial services supermarket, much the way 7-Eleven stands against (and in many ways outmaneuvers) A&P.

"I've changed the company name to First Federal Realty–DeSimone. This is for image purposes—it tells people they can bank on us for financial services in buying and selling properties—and it also reflects the fact that we have more to offer than just properties. Through affiliations with local financial sources, we now serve as a conduit for mortgage funds, we sell mortgage insurance and we have a full line of general insurance products.

"This is not only a competitive posture. Expansion into financial services makes good business sense regardless of the competitive situation. Consider the effect it has on advertising costs, a growing expense category for local realtors. By offering a wider range of products and services, we can spread the advertising costs over more profit centers, hopefully reducing the ad cost per transaction. Sales productivity is another factor. Because we sell insurance, we can turn virtually every property sale into an insurance sale as well. Realtors are fast beginning to recognize the wisdom of integrated marketing: that by becoming financial services centers, they can profit several times in service to a single customer. The problem is that independents who haven't started moving in this direction are going to have a hard time catching up. The Wall Streeter is making significant inroads in geographic coverage and total sales."

Merrill Lynch Realty Associates' profit performance is improving, with red ink of $17.9 million in 1980, narrowed to a $7.6 million loss in 1981, and a slim $4.9 million profit in 1982. Some say this is a harbinger of the future.

"Merrill's entry into the Long Island market is one of those good news, bad news situations," DeSimone adds.

"Yes, I've been holding my own against Merrill—actually expanding my business since they acquired Carl Burr. I attribute this to one thing: Merrill Lynch doesn't yet know how to sell real estate, thank God. They can sell stocks and bonds—no one holds a candle to them there—but in real estate they have a lot to learn.

"For example, when you have several offices and a few hundred associates, accurate and timely management information systems are vital to running the business effectively. Sophisticated brokers require that their associates report the acceptance of binders just as they do for contracts and closings. By statistically analyzing binders, you can project, in advance, how many negotiations will produce actual sales in a given period. And you can spot problems in the making: like why an exceptional number of good deals are not closing. But Merrill doesn't always include binder information in their sales reporting and that makes them less effective in the field."

On a dime, DeSimone's ebullient mood turns somber.

"The bad news is that Merrill Lynch is learning fast. Everyday, in little ways, you can see across-the-board improvements in their operations, from better sales training to more comprehensive reporting systems. I'm enough of a realist to admit to the world—and more importantly to myself—that the edge I hold over Merrill will soon vanish. They're gaining knowledge and experience at an accelerated pace. That's the sign of a first-class organization and Merrill certainly qualifies for that designation.

"In a couple of years, Merrill will be as good as anyone in real estate sales and they'll have the advantage of a prominent name and a financial services capability. That's why I'm taking steps now to compete with them on an equal footing. To fight fire with fire."

A securities analyst and Merrill Lynch watcher for the Wall Street firm of Jessup & Lamont, is another true believer in Merrill's long-term prospects. "In five years, they'll be one of the most important factors in American real estate.

In twenty years they'll be as important in real estate as they are in securities.

"This is not a company that behaves impetuously. Merrill studied the real estate business for years before committing themselves to it. They went in with a blueprint for building their position in the market and they're moving along according to plan. Those who insinuate that their diversification into real estate has been a failure don't understand that they got started in a dismal housing market and needed some time for the economy to reward their efforts. The real estate division turned profitable in the last quarter of 1982, is profitable in '83 and, I think, will be a major contributor to Merrill Lynch's profits in 1985.

"Plus . . . plus Merrill is taking steps to boost the productivity of sales associates and to bring more financing clout to the marketplace. They'll be heavily involved in first and second mortgages. Consumers will find this immensely attractive and it will prove, for Merrill, to be a strong competitive advantage. The little guys are really going to feel the presence of this giant and it's not going to be pleasant. Not at all."

Observers who share this viewpoint are both right and wrong. Yes, Merrill will continue to muscle its way into the real estate market, purchasing brokers and opening offices in a growing network of cities. Money and determination will see to that. But the Merrill boosters overestimate the importance of financial services in the most affluent (and profitable) markets and underestimate the feisty competitiveness of independent brokers who'll fight like hell to protect the turf they've worked so hard to claim.

For all the awesome capabilities Merrill brings to the market, it will never stamp out the best of the independents. Real estate is too personal a business for that. In a nation awash with franchised gremlins and corporate offspring produced from a Jell-O mold, creative, highly individualized businesses will always enjoy a loyal following among those who prize these qualities over sheer size or a nationally known logo. Contrary to the fearmongering the behemoths use to scare independents into their camp, savvy local brokers don't have to buy in or sell out to stay alive in real estate. They can compete. They can win.

"Maybe I'm just a stubborn boy from Brooklyn," DeSimone says, "but I don't let anyone take what is rightfully mine. I respect Merrill Lynch—I don't deny it—but I'm going to make them respect me in return."

II

COMMERCIAL REAL ESTATE

5

Howard Ronson and the Rise
of the European Connection

Jesus Christ died on the cross and if we accept that gift, we have little choice but to accept this one, the land we sit on . . . our resources. To make a parish an end in itself is garbage and blasphemy.

The Reverend Thomas Dix Bowers
Rector of New York's St. Bartholomew's Church, and
an active proponent of leasing the church's real estate
to New York developer Howard Ronson for the
construction of a fifty-nine-story office tower.

It's an hour's drive from Joe DeSimone's Smithtown office to Merrill Lynch's corporate headquarters in New York City. A stop-and-go odyssey that winds along the Long Island Expressway, passing through a split-level postwar sprawl that stretches to the tip of Queens. Down the triple-lane highway, a bumper-to-bumper procession of cars and trucks inches past Plainview's tightly spaced, aluminum-sided Capes, past Great Neck's stately colonials, past Forest Hill's china wall of ten-story rent-controlled, middle-class ghettos, and funnels through the Midtown Tunnel into Manhattan.

In distance it is forty-five miles. But in the context of the land rush, it is an enormous gulf separating two widely different spheres of power and influence: commercial and residential real estate.

That this is a different world is plainly obvious from the first glimpse of the landscape that comes into view on the west side of the tunnel. The carefully manicured greens, the quaint clapboard cottages, the weather-worn timbers that are part and parcel of Sotheby's and Previews' marketing fantasies are replaced by sixty-story steel and glass towers rising shoulder-to-shoulder on plots of land too small for Bedford barns. But the surface dissimilarities are only cosmetic. The most striking differences between residential and commercial real estate are in the underlying economics, the risks and the power of the individual. Most important, in commercial real estate, David and Goliath change roles. Here, the independent entrepreneur—the David on the residential side—is the dominant force, structuring the biggest deals and dictating terms to the giant organizations that line up to participate in them as joint venture partners. The borough of Manhattan—epicenter of commercial real estate—is home to this extraordinary genus of land owners and developers, who, aided by tight-knit familial organizations, own and control the most valued parcels on earth. *Forbes* magazine's list of the 400 richest Americans includes sixty-three who have earned their fortunes in real estate—all in the commercial sector and many in Manhattan.

"They piss ice water," says James Austrian, president of Jones Lang Wootton, a British-based commercial real estate consulting firm that has developed an impressive clientele among Manhattan's premier landlords. A bright and engaging man with a Trumanesque flair for turning simple phrases into illuminating statements, Austrian is confidant to a covey of the world's wealthiest and most sophisticated developers. Reclining in the high-backed, leather chair that cradles his rather delicate frame, he swivels from side to side before the plate-glass walls of his corner office, pointing his finger at the adjacent buildings along upper Park Avenue.

"Within a few blocks of here there must be 50 men who, within an hour of my call, could put up $100 million of their own money should I inform them of an interesting real estate deal. They do it without boards of directors, committee meetings or the usual bureaucratic trappings of corporate America. Even with my years of experience, I can still be awed by their gutsy, decisive actions.

"Just last week—right here in this office—I presented one of my clients with the details of a fast-breaking deal that required a rapid decision and, should he accept, a multimillion commitment on his part. Well, he listened intently to the terms, stroked his chin, and then removed a rather worn-looking slide rule from his briefcase. Yes, I said a slide rule. Fiddling with the thing for a few minutes, he made the necessary calculations, stroked his chin again, and agreed to the deal. His mind figures the angles of commercial real estate transactions faster and more accurately than an IBM computer. You must understand: successful commercial developers are born to real estate the way Mozart was born to music."

Although Austrian's clients are as different as the buildings they create, to a man they are gifted, aggressive, pugnacious, egocentric, ruthless, greedy, tyrannical, cunning, obsessed, driven, immensely rich workaholics who enjoy little in life but the buying and selling of land. In a city so tangled in bureaucracy that it can take months to win a street peddler's license, these savvy deal makers manage to get the banks, the politicians, the zoning boards, the tenants, and the construction unions to agree to projects that will change the skyline, the tax base and the way of life.

Says a Manhattan banker, long active with New York's leading real estate families: "When people ask me what developers are like, I never answer them directly. Instead I suggest that they take a taxi to the Essex House hotel, ask for a penthouse suite with a view of the park, take the elevator to the top, and throw open the drapes. They'll see a narrow strip of grass and trees—Central Park—bordered on all sides by columns of buildings lined 100-deep to the Hudson and the East Rivers. Beyond the park line, a person can't extend his arms without bruising his knuckles on brick and mortar. Virtually every inch of land is bulldozed, leveled with concrete and sent roaring to the sky as a hotel, office building, or luxury co-op. Only the water and the park—one a natural barrier, the other political—stop the crushing march the developers call progress.

"But you can sense from that hotel view that they haven't given up—that they never will. The buildings appear to be alive—waiting for a signal to continue the assault. To developers, Central Park is not an oasis of green in a dark and dirty city. It is simply a waste of space. Idle capacity. Opportunity lost. Here's the most valuable chunk of soil in the world and they can't touch it. God, that smarts. Something deep inside can't accept the sight of vacant land. And, implausible as it may seem, I can envision the day when the park will be paved over. It'll start as a luxury hotel in the Sheep Meadow and end with another World Trade Center."

Should the banker's long-shot prediction prove out (James Watt would have to be elected mayor of New York for that to be possible), the creative energy and the business acumen would come from a high-powered group of New York, British, and Canadian developers—commercial real estate's Goliaths—backed by billions of dollars of investment capital from banks, insurance companies, and pension funds.

"At least ten times a day I get calls from the world's most prominent financial institutions asking me if I'll be kind enough to accept a hundred million, two hundred million, a half billion dollars of their money," says real estate wunderkind Donald Trump, a thirty-seven-year-old megalomaniac who in recent years has developed two of New York's most important projects, the Grand Hyatt Hotel (started in 1977—when he was twenty-nine years old), and the Trump Tower. "They want me to turn their money into more money—to earn them the kinds of high yields they can't earn for themselves. I have the skill, the experience and the intuition to accomplish what these huge companies with their teams of lawyers, accountants and real estate executives cannot. It's up to me to determine who I'll work with and I'm goddamn selective."

Just why the tables are turned, why huge cash-rich institutions must go hat-in-hand to "selective" entrepreneurs can only be explained in terms of the contrast in organizational form and style between commercial real estate developers and the financial services industry (the joint venturers).

Major insurers—the likes of Prudential, Metropolitan Life and Aetna—are awash with billions of premium dollars that must be put to work to produce income for insurance settlements, administrative expenses and dividends. Typically, insurance companies profit, not by beating the odds on underwriting risks—here they hope to break even or to squeak by with minor losses—but instead by making profitable investments with the cash pools that are held until they are paid out as death or casualty benefits.

Generally speaking, these prudent institutions seek balanced, diversified portfolios with major positions in money market instruments, publicly traded securities and real estate, which in recent years has commanded a growing percentage of their investment dollars. Their move to the land rush, spurred by the mid-1970s fear of rampant inflation, dissatisfaction with a sluggish stock market, and a general disillusionment with paper assets, has accelerated in spite of subsequent improvement in the money markets.

"The institutions —always disposed to take a long term view—see commercial real estate as an inflation hedge, as a relatively safe investment vehicle and as an excellent opportunity to achieve capital appreciation," Austrian says. "But they also know that these benefits accrue only if the project—the hotel, the office building, whatever—is built on budget and on time. And they are aware—thank God—that they don't have the in-house expertise to make that happen. That takes a ballsy real estate developer who'll accept enormous risks, will make decisions on a dime and will devote himself to the project—twenty-five hours a day if that's what it takes—until the ribbon is cut."

Adds John Minicus, former assistant general counsel

for Equitable Life, now a Jones Lang Wootton partner: "We tried a few developments on our own at Equitable but they didn't work out well primarily because we didn't have the right people on staff. Insurance company executives are workaday types who want to earn a good living, be assured of a comfortable pension and have time for themselves and their families. All well and good, but that's not the kind of person who can develop a $200 million office building. For that you need a Howard Ronson."

Howard Ronson? Who is Howard Ronson? Why do Minicus, Austrian and dozens of observers throughout New York's realty circles regard him—often with envy—as the epitome of the 1980s aggressive and successful developer? Why has he become the darling of prominent consulting firms and blue-chip financial institutions? How has he managed in a few short years to earn tens of millions on a string of multinational real estate deals? What can we learn from him?

Since invading New York in 1978 with a business staff not much bigger than a coffee shop's, Ronson—a British-born Concorde jockey who keeps homes and offices in New York, Paris, and Monaco—has proven that a lone ranger without ties to the established New York realty families can succeed there. He is little known outside of Manhattan's real estate community, but his rise to power is interesting precisely because it has detoured the local power structure, has been built on innovative strategies, and has moved in tandem with the huge financial institutions' race to the land rush. What's more, Ronson's tactics provide an interesting how-to case study for would-be commercial developers seeking a share of their industry's enormous rewards.

But let's start at the beginning.

Born to a wealthy British family with interests in furniture manufacturing and residential home building, Ronson was educated at Carmel College—a private boarding school—took some courses at Harvard and the Sorbonne, and joined the family business in 1962 hoping to develop his managerial skills gradually. But in 1965, a development of more than 1,000 modest suburban homes, the major project of his father, Gerald Israel Ronson, encountered serious difficulties. A soft market caused a steep drop in demand, leaving many homes unsold. As a result, the project's subcontractors suffered a cash squeeze (which they blamed, in part, on Ronson's fixed-price contracts) and were forced to liquidate. Gerald Ronson, seeking a way out of the mess, launched his own company, Dwell Constructions, to take up where the subcontractors left off. A sister company, Yorks and Lane Construction Company Ltd., had already been formed to build homes at other Ronson sites. In what turned out to be a disastrous debut as a business executive, Howard, now twenty-two, was made managing director of the family construction firms. Although home-building activities proceeded for the next two years (1966–1968), buyers claimed that quality standards were sacrificed for the sake of speed and the builder's quest for windfall profits. When the crescendo of complaints reached scandalous proportions, the National House Building Council removed the Ronson companies from its register of builders, Britain's Department of Trade launched an investigation (which would haunt Ronson later in his career), and the roof caved in on Dwell and Yorks and Lane. Liquidators were appointed in October, 1969.

Like all catastrophes, this one too had a silver lining. Ronson learned two lessons: to steer clear of residential real estate and to keep his lips sealed about the past. One of the two served him well; the other found him involved in another controversy years later.

Turning to commercial development, Ronson struck out on his own, building the small—even quaint by New York standards—office buildings Europeans favor. He saw France as an untapped territory for quality commercial space, and, operating as a sole entrepreneur, achieved enough success to interest Chesterfield Properties Ltd., an English company quoted on the London Stock Exchange, to launch a joint venture with him in 1971. With Ronson serving as managing director and 50 percent owner of Chesterfield Ronson (Europe) Ltd. (a subsidiary of the parent company), the firm put up twenty-seven buildings over a period of nine years, twelve of which were joint ventures with the Unilever Pension Fund, an institutional investor in European property.

One problem: Ronson never told his new business partners about his family's home-building disaster. Because it had been years since the Department of Trade started its investigation, Ronson thought the matter would just fizzle out in the massive bureaucracy. But in 1976, after seven years of research, the DOT stunned the now successful commercial developer and his new partners by issuing a four-volume report accusing Howard and Gerald Ronson of "arrogance, callousness, and inefficiency" and "a ruthless pursuit of profit without any adequate resources to justify it. We have been reluctantly compelled to view that neither of them is a suitable person at the present time to act as a director of a company."

Although refusing to admit wrongdoing, Howard Ronson responded to the DOT report by paying $450,000 of standing claims against the family's now-defunct development business. At first, Chesterfield Properties found itself in a sticky wicket. There were concerns about the propriety of Ronson's position in the firm ("not fit to serve as a director of a company") and a good deal of hand wringing about the public company's credibility. But when Ronson offered to resign, Chesterfield, thinking him too valuable an asset to lose, would hear none of it—saying that in light of "the fact that the directors of Chesterfield Properties have found nothing in the behavior of Mr. Ronson during his association with them which could possibly give them the right to ask for his resignation, they have decided not to accept it."

Today, Ronson still tries to conceal the goblins of the past, even though the DOT report has no bearing on his U.S. activities and does not prohibit him from serving as a corporate director in the United Kingdom. When asked about his family's background, he tells a first-time visitor that their interests were limited to the furniture business. When confronted with the facts, he looks like a schoolboy found cheating on an exam and delivers what is obviously a practiced speech.

"It was wrong of me not to tell Chesterfield about the problems with the home-building developments," Ronson says, rubbing his hands over the polished conference table at his 30 Broad Street, New York, headquarters, a building he now owns. Head bowed at the admission, he then thrusts his arm in the air, sunlight reflecting like laser beams from the face of his gold Bulgari watch. "But you must remember, I was a very young man at the time Dwell and Yorks and Lane ran into trouble. I was an officer of the companies in name only. Most of the events that tarnished my reputation were a fait accompli before I had much to say about running the businesses. It's not fair to be tainted by that for the rest of your life, so I try to forget. To bury it."

Supported by Chesterfield's board, Ronson came through the second major controversy of his career without serious damage to his business affairs. But the episode did force him to reflect. He started feeling the insecurities of wealth.

"It was about this time that I recognized that there was probably something to the theory that the last capitalist would die in America," he says, "and perhaps more importantly, I realized that many European businesses were subscribing to this idea as well.

"You see, the United States is one of the last true free-enterprise economies. Not many Americans seem to grasp this as vividly as European businessmen, but it's true. Investment money from abroad is coming into this country not only because the United States is large and rich, but also because compared to the dominance of other governments in business and private affairs, generally this country is a relatively unencumbered place to do business, even in real estate. I thought I could profit here by carving out a niche as a European-minded American developer."

Ronson's vision of European-style developments in the United States called for modest-sized buildings (roughly 500,000 square feet or less), with small floor space (5,000–

20,000 square feet) located in prestigious settings convenient to the corporate and investment communities. Exterior and lobby designs would more closely resemble premier hotels than office buildings.

But, first, there was homework to do. Uncertain of where in the United States to introduce his ideas, he asked Jones Lang Wootton's New York office to help him research the U.S. market from Wall Street to Rodeo Drive. During an eighteen-month period, from 1977–1978, he flew across the Atlantic roughly forty times, spending ten days of every month meeting with U.S. brokers, bankers, developers, investors and consultants in New York, Chicago, Atlanta, Houston, Dallas, San Francisco—forty-eight cities in all.

"Everyone was down on New York at the time—saying that bankruptcy and its gradual decline as a commercial center were inevitable—so I decided to look elsewhere for a good place in the United States to invest my money," Ronson says with the confident air of a gambler who guessed right. "But the more I looked, the more questions I asked both here and abroad, the more I realized that the pessimists were wrong. New York had great potential. It was in a state of transition, yes, but its long-term prospects were bloody good."

The year was 1978. Manhattan's office building market, always cyclical, was slowly emerging from a five-year collapse brought on by overbuilding in the early 1970s. During the ensuing period, rents fell drastically (50 percent downtown, 35 percent midtown) and developers were sitting on their hands waiting for some sign of an upturn. But they found nothing to cheer about. News from trade press, the leasing brokers, the always-active real estate grapevine was gloomy, gloomy, gloomy. Ronson, however, looked elsewhere and found a positive sign the others missed. He looked abroad. Aware that European financial institutions were planning to invest in and open offices in New York, he believed that downtown Manhattan would emerge in the 1980s as the world's premier financial center and that an influx of foreign businesses would bolster rents and property values. He was determined to be in the vanguard of the movement.

Turning again to Jones Lang Wootton, he asked for a list of properties with good turnaround potential. "I turned down the first dozen or so buildings they showed me because they didn't meet my investment criteria. I was determined to hold out for a neglected building that could be purchased for a bargain price, refurbished and rented for top market rates. The property also had to be in a prime location in the Wall Street area. At first, all the buildings I was being shown failed to live up to one or another of my investment prerequisites. But then, while in New York on a rare all-pleasure, no-business trip—my wife and I were stopping over in Manhattan on our way to a vacation—I received an excited call from the boys at Jones Lang Wootton, asking me to stop by their place to discuss an important matter. Because it sounded urgent, I decided to take the short stroll from my hotel to their offices only blocks away. As soon as I walked through the door, the Jones Lang Wootton people grabbed me by the elbow.

" 'So good of you to make it. Come take a cab ride with us, we have something to show you.' That something was a sixty-year-old office building at 30 Broad Street. As it turned out, it had all the ingredients I was looking for. Although I walked the full sixty floors that day—personally examining each and every one—I knew by the twenty-fifth that I'd buy it. It became my first U.S. investment."*

Then owned by a syndication group, the building was in shabby condition cosmetically and nearly 50 percent vacant. But Ronson believed that its location in the heart of the financial district made it a natural beneficiary of New York's emergence as a world financial center.

"He was able to buy into the building very cheaply," says Simon Milde, an articulate Briton and Jones Lang Wootton's chief deal maker. "That's because syndication groups,

---

* A joint venture with the William Kaufman organization.

as passive investors, are into real estate primarily for the
tax benefits. They are groups of doctors, dentists, and other
high-bracket earners joined together in limited partnerships
so they can take operating losses on their personal tax returns. Because the properties mean more to them as tax
losses than as investment assets, they often neglect the
buildings they own.

"Because 30 Broad was in trouble in its then sorry state,
the syndicate had to sell for a low price. But the commitment
to refurbish the property changed its fate. Based on that
guarantee, most of the vacant space was leased to Morgan
Guaranty within two months of Howard's taking title.

"Soon after, Ronson entered into a joint venture for
the purchase of 50 Broad Street, a similar property with
equally good potential. Again, on the basis of a commitment
to refurbish, a substantial amount of the vacant space was
promptly leased to Irving Trust.

"Both investments proved to be enormously profitable
for Howard. In less than a year after he closed on them,
the downtown rental market improved dramatically and the
Wall Street area started to regain its prestige as a first-
class business address for a wide range of corporate tenants.
These positive trends—which Ronson was wise enough to
spot in their infancy—have propelled the value of both buildings to about eight times their purchase price."

Adds Stanton F. Roth, senior vice president of Landauer
Associates, the city's premier real estate consultants, "1979
was the best year I've ever seen in New York real estate.
Rents shot skyward. With all the previously vacant space
suddenly gobbled up, landlords were doubling and tripling
rents as soon as leases expired. They could do it because
tenants were lined up for space. If someone didn't want to
pay the increase, the next in line would. This tight space
condition was due to the fact that very little building went
on in the mid-1970s. Those in control of existing space in
1979 did very well."

Ronson's early success was due to not only timing, but
also a shrewd eye for undervalued real estate and an instinctive feel for how to turn around a depressed property. Once

a building comes under his control, he sets in motion a series of management procedures designed to boost its income and to keep it performing well regardless of prevailing economic conditions. Most important is the introduction of his European-style leases.

Historically, New York developers have lured commercial tenants by granting long-term leases at fixed rentals or with provisions for modest increases after ten years. In periods of high inflation, this ceiling plays havoc with cash flow—expenses outpace revenues—and reduces the landlord's return on equity below the yield on virtually risk-free instruments such as bonds and commercial paper. To prevent this, Ronson negotiates leases based on the practices he grew up with in England and Paris. Basically this calls for reviewing rents every five years and for adjusting them to reflect either going rates for similar space or increases in the Consumer Price Index.

This inflation-sensitive approach—effective as it is for keeping up with galloping expenses—has another more important effect which relates directly to commercial property's value as an investment asset. While the politicians, the steel workers, and the chairman of the Federal Reserve bemoan inflation as if it were a swarm of locusts, sophisticated developers recognize that inflation can work in their favor. It forces the institutions to seek growth in real value (inflation-adjusted value) investments, and commercial real estate has proven to be the best vehicle for this.

> . . . if the rate of return doesn't outstrip the inflationary spiral, the buying power of the income is quickly eroded. This erosion is further compounded by the impact of the income tax. Therefore, investors are looking for that special combination that provides protection from inflation, capital appreciation, and tax incentives, or tax shelters. Investments in sound real estate development projects could meet all these criteria.*

* Diane Gill, *Viewpoint*, Main Hurdman CPA, p. 29, 1980, first edition.

Adds Gordon Glagett, vice president in charge of Equitable Life Assurance: "In our former role as mortgage lending institutions, we used to be proponents of long-term leases. That's because we wanted the certainty of income flow. But we've come full circle on this one. Now that we are primarily joint venture equity participants, we favor short leases— no longer than five-year reviews. We like the inflation protection this affords . . . You look at property differently when you are an owner rather than simply a mortgage broker."

Equitable's Asset Management Annual Report (1981) spells out the company's inflation-buffer strategies:

> Properties are leased under arrangements that protect against inflation and take advantage of rising property demand. Such mechanisms include net leases or gross leases that require the tenant to pay increases in operating expenses, indexing short-term leases and participation in the retail component's sales.

Ronson's perspective on the subject is direct and to the point. "Many tenants object to rent revision; however, I have a standard argument for them. Are they prepared to fix salaries for ten years? Hell, no. If not, why should a landlord have a fixed income for ten years?

"When you could get long-term money at fixed interest rates, there was some justification for having fixed income, but that is no longer the case today and will not be in the future."

With his refurbishing and European leasing practices bringing new life to 30 and 50 Broad Street, Ronson struck again; this time taking on his first from-the-ground-up building development in the United States. With it came a rude introduction to the bitchy competitiveness of New York's real estate arena. Once again, Ronson found himself involved in controversy and, once again, he emerged at the other end richer and more successful.

This time the bad blood ran between Ronson and the

Kaufman brothers, middle-aged offspring of one of New York's old-line builders, William Kaufman. Melvyn and Robert, partners in the William Kaufman organization, first met Ronson through matchmakers supreme, Jones Lang Wootton. The parties were brought together for the purchase of 30 Broad Street.

"We showed 30 Broad to the Kaufmans first and they wanted to buy with the participation of a money man," Milde recalls. "That's when we introduced them to Ronson, who upon inspecting the property, agreed to put up most of the capital. With this, a deal was struck."

Surprise of surprises, the savvy European and the hard-boiled New Yorkers hit it off and a new business alliance was christened. Everyone got along so well—dinner on the town with the wives and all—that when the Kaufmans decided to turn a parking lot at the corner of 48th and Third into an office building (767 Third Avenue), they asked Ronson to invest in the deal. The terms: Howard to put up the bulk of the capital, $8.5 million, in return for 50 percent equity in the development. That clear to all sides, it was soon obvious that everything else about the deal was as murky as bouillabaisse. Things went bad after the final handshake and then fell faster than a hard hat dropping fifty floors. Feelings turned so bitter and the points of contention so numerous that it is hard to point to a single factor that led to the feud. But several key issues are clear:

While the developers' European and American concepts could coexist on a relatively simple refurbishment à la 30 Broad Street, the gap was too wide to bridge on a full-scale start-from-scratch construction. Ronson, for example, was aghast at Mel Kaufman's plans for decorating the side of an adjacent building they'd purchased in order to assemble the building site for 767. Rather than having lower-floor office workers stare out at a blank wall, Kaufman proposed an enormous chess board with huge pieces to be moved weekly to simulate classic matches. Ronson viewed this as bizarre and distasteful. He saw Kaufman's plan as a grave mistake.

Surprising as it may seem, considering all the steel, mortar, granite, and glass that rises miraculously from the ground when an office tower goes up, developers make it their business to devote considerable attention to the decorative features as well as the structural components. They know prospective tenants judge a book by its cover—a building by its image—and that everything that comes before can come to naught if the image doesn't sell.

Mel Kaufman and Howard Ronson couldn't have more wildly different notions of what sells. Hands down the most flamboyant developer in New York, Kaufman fancies cowboy hats, ascots, and a black-painted office decorated with T-shirts and a sign informing visitors, THIS IS NOT A SCHOOL . . .

His concept of salesmanship tilts toward the exotic or outrageous touch that makes a Manhattan tower stand out from the other boxes on the block. ". . . One building in particular, that at 127 John Street in the financial district, with its neon-lighted entrance tunnel and highly visible building machinery painted in strong primary colors on the fifteenth floor has inspired most comment and debate. Completed in 1971, the thirty-two-story building," Melvin Kaufman recalled, "produced a real downtown war about whether we should take the tunnel out." They did not, and, Mr. Kaufman said, "four of the five companies who said they couldn't move in, did."*

Ronson's more subtle approach is limited to finishing off the interior space according to the tenant's instructions.

"A major difference between European and American practice has to do with the degree of interior finishing provided by the developer," he says. "In Europe, regardless of the size of the building, tenant space is finished. The ceilings, lighting, air conditioning, carpeting and decoration are prefinished to a grid system which allows a tenant total flexibility in partitioning out his space when he moves in. We believe this is important as a tenant is not in the construc-

* *New York Times*, September 21, 1980, Section 8, p. 6.

tion business and shouldn't be. He should merely provide the layout of partitioning he wants and the color scheme. The landlord should provide the rest."

Developers are convinced that they alone can do things the right way. When they clash, even on relatively minor matters, there is rarely an opportunity for reconciliation.

"Ordinary people they are not," James Austrian explains. "Most are descendants of strong-willed Jewish families imbued with a trader's mentality and with a distrust of outsiders. All have hundreds of millions of dollars in assets. Instead of viewing this wealth as reason enough to go fishing in Maine, they keep trying to make more and more."

Both Ronson and Mel Kaufman—their differences in style aside—seem to fit this mold. Any shrink will tell you that two raving egos of that magnitude can't live together without soon going for each other's throat. In no time, the parties came to blows over their differing views of the partnership. According to Kaufman, Ronson was to bow to the brothers on all major decisions concerning 767's development and ongoing management.

"How the hell could he think I'd have it any other way," Kaufman explodes. "Me with an international reputation and he just learning on the job. My God, whatever the hell that bastard knows now he owes to being in my presence.

"His company name is HRO International. Do you know what the O stands for? Organization, that's what. And where did he pick that up? From the Kaufman Organization. He imitates everything we do."

Fired by his own monologue, Kaufman shifts into overdrive, beet-faced, screaming.

"And let me tell you something. There is no Howard Ronson. You hear that. No Howard Ronson. There are lawyers and shell corporations and more lawyers but no Ronson. He comes in and causes trouble and when you want to reach him he disappears. He has no roots, nothing. He's bad for New York. Very bad."

Although Kaufman produces documents purporting to prove that Ronson agreed to play second fiddle—and his claims seem to be supported—it was naive to expect another active developer to twiddle his thumbs while Kaufman called all the shots. In addition to the chessboard, Ronson claims he contested Kaufman's plan to review rents every ten years (as against Ronson's European preference to review every five) and other operating and administrative matters. Finally, Ronson sued.

"At first it seemed as if we could patch up the relationship and I was often called in as a mediator," Milde says. "But then it got too vicious. When the suit was filed we suggested that a partner be found to buy out Howard's interests. Everyone agreed and we brought in JBM Realty, a Chicago investment group, to make the purchase. No one was right in the dispute and no one was wrong. Both were honest men who couldn't live together."

But they could profit together. The Kaufmans were left with a prime building, throwing off hefty revenues, and Ronson walked off with a payout said to earn him between $15 and $17 million.

The two have since gone separate ways. Ronson, a consummate workaholic, devotes evenings and weekends to business meetings at his East Side co-op. His wife of three years works with him doing interior designs for his developments' model offices. "Work is my only interest," Ronson says, rather pridefully. "It is my sport, my hobby, my entertainment."

His continued faith in New York's position as the world financial center keeps him piling steel to the sky. And his faith has been rewarded time and again, although never more generously than at 175 Water Street.

A wedge of earth about five blocks from the New York Stock Exchange, the Water Street site was shown to Ronson by Williamson Picket Gross, a New York real estate firm. Ronson saw the property as an ideal spot for his European brand of office building: a modest 580,000 square feet with

20,000-square-foot floors suitable for a foreign company's executive offices. Along with Williamson Picket Gross (whom he has since bought out), Ronson acquired the property, then a parking lot, for $11.5 million. He planned to put up a building on spec (without the commitment of a major buyer or tenant), risking the vagary of New York's rental market on the bet that his optimistic projections about Wall Street were on target.

But he didn't have to hold his breath. Once again Jones Lang Wootton, the British white knight, proved its skills as a matchmaker. When National Westminster Bank (a Jones Lang Wootton client in the United Kingdom and parent company of the National Bank of North America) indicated its desire to consolidate its U.S. operations in a single headquarters location, Jones Lang Wootton saw the possibilities. They believed that Ronson's Water Street building—then in the earliest planning stages—would be ideal for National Westminster's offices, and they sought to convince the developer to change his plans from a spec project to one designed for the bank. Within six weeks after JLW brought the parties together, National Westminster signed a lease for all the floor space in the yet-to-be-built Water Street property, assuring Ronson of a minimum of $1.65 billion over seventy-five years, making it one of the biggest leasing deals ever. While the building was still a shell of steel and concrete, the "man without roots" could drive by in his newly minted Rolls-Royce guaranteed another round of millions for his bank accounts and the glowing satisfaction of showing New York's real estate barons how to make money in what some consider to be their private preserve.

Ronson's big bet, on which he based Water Street and his other developments including those at 45 Broadway Atrium, One Exchange Place, and Tower 56, is that the Manhattan real estate market will be a prime beneficiary of America's transformation from a manufacturing to a service economy. Until the mid-1970s, landlords in New York, Chicago, and other metropolitan cities were dependent on Fortune 500 headquarters offices for much of their tenant base.

But these heavy industrial firms—the likes of Texaco and Union Carbide—had no meaningful business in the cities and in many cases no genuine rationale for staying there. As leases expired and CEOs decided to move headquarters closer to their operating units—or to lower-rent suburban corporate parks—downtown real estate markets were left with millions of square feet of vacant space. Space that— owing to the rules of supply and demand—put downward pressures on rentals. But with the vacant inventory increasingly filled by the fast-growing service firms, the prospects for continued high rentals—and soaring property values— are strong. Corporate lawyers Paul, Weiss, Rifkind, Wharton & Garrison; CPAs Deloitte Haskins & Sells; and investment bankers White Weld Capital Markets Group cannot flirt with the suburbs when lease reviews bring rising rents. For them, being in New York—the world financial center— is a mandatory cost of doing business.

> Lawyers and accountants may complain a lot about soaring office rents. Judging from a recent survey, however, the present office market is not creating serious problems for them. The study indicates that many firms simply raise their fees to compensate for large rent increases, and they give little consideration to cost-cutting possibilities, such as moving the firm (or part of it) into cheaper space . . .*

Long-time developer Seymour Durst, whose newest building, a forty-one-story granite tower at 1155 Avenue of the Americas, recently rented up, put it this way: "There'll soon be a shortage of space and that's due primarily to the insatiable appetite of the service industries. Advertising, law and accounting are growing steadily, must have more space and cannot abandon their clients by moving to the suburbs. White & Case, a big law firm, for example, has committed to the top third of our new building, a total of 250,000 square feet."

* Diane Henry, *New York Times*, July 28, 1983, p. D8.

Clearly, Ronson guessed right on New York's ability to attract and maintain enthusiastic tenants, especially those in the services sector. His other prediction, that a new wave of foreign capital would flow to the city for property investments, has also proven accurate.

"In a world shaken to its molten core by political and economic upheavals, the United States appears relatively safe from the dual terrors of leftist control and armed invasion," says Simon Milde. "And of all major U.S. investments, real estate has proven, over the long term, to be the most resilient and the most profitable. As a result, an increasing share of the world's great fortunes—personal and institutional—is flowing through a one-way cash pipeline from Asia, Europe and South America to America's premier property markets."

Much of this is attributable to landlords and developers liquidating real estate holdings abroad for reinvestment in the United States. Hong Kong entrepreneurs, for example, have suffered through a 50 percent drop in property prices as concern grows about the colony's fate once Britain's lease on the land expires in 1997. Although negotiations are underway between London and Beijing, the specter of a Red Chinese takeover haunts the business community and makes property holdings a risky proposition.

Foreign pension funds—especially those based in the United Kingdom—are also becoming major players in the U.S. realty market.

"The British fund managers look at their own country and they look at ours and they recognize right off that this is the place to invest in the land," says a Jones Lang Wootton executive who advises that the funds do just this. "Merry old may be a more civilized, dignified place to live but it's not really good as a place to make money. More than a half billion a year in British pension funds are now flowing into U.S. real estate and I think this will accelerate.

"The real beneficiaries are those who already own property here. In some markets, like Manhattan, enormous sums will be competing for choice properties. Owners will find that their interest will appreciate very substantially for as far into the future as I can see. This will add to their personal wealth and will give them the fiscal base to expand their development activities."

That fits nicely into Ronson's scheme of things. And does he have a scheme. The more you talk to Ronson, the more you observe him cruising from property to property in the cushy comfort of his ebony Rolls, the more you hear him firing off orders to his retinue of advisors, the more clearly you recognize that he hatched that scheme through all the years and all the deals in England and France and that every minuscule puzzle piece was in place the day he set foot on the parcel the Indians sold for $24. And when you stand back and see how well it all came together, it's clear that his top priority was to trade in his initial power base for one with more lasting influence. He was determined not to remain an outsider. Not with those who really count. Although the second and third generations of New York's landed families still view him as a foreigner likely to depart at any moment ("He keeps a Lear Jet warmed up and ready to go," says one), Ronson has established close ties with some of the world's most powerful financial institutions. All indicators are that he is here to stay. As for Ronson, citizen of England, entrepreneur of New York and Paris, resident of Monaco, perhaps the surest sign of his success is the school of rabbis seen filing out of his office.

Peering up from his conference table, seemingly dazed, Ronson folded his checkbook into his pocket. "God, those guys can negotiate. You have a certain contribution in mind and they get you to double it." He gazes across the narrow rectangular room, looking out the window to a construction crew running heavy cable through the upper floors of one of his nearby buildings. "I guess it goes with the turf."

6

The Business of Development:
Managing the Managers

There are three rules for success:
   Always Borrow as Much Money as You Possibly Can;
   Always Pay It Back on Time;
   Always Have a Tan.

Aristotle Onassis

The marble gray office towers that line New York's financial district eclipse the morning sun, turning the streets below into darkened canyons. Striding through the shadows, Howard Ronson sets out on a daily inspection tour of his urban Ponderosa, zig-zagging through sidestreets and alleys from HRO's 30 Broad Street headquarters to his subdivisions at 45 Broadway, One Exchange Place, and 175 Water Street. Weaving through the maze of double-parked Yellow cabs, street vendors and cliques of brokers passing rumors of the day's high flyers, he blends in like another paunchy, grey flannel banker on his way to Chase Manhattan's weekly credit meeting. Few who pass him on the street recognize that this is one of the handful of men with the power to shape the city's skyline.

Ronson's days begin with a 6:30 A.M. alarm, a light breakfast and a cruise in the Rolls down the FDR Drive to lower Manhattan. Office hours, which begin at 8:30 sharp with a checklist of the day's activities, are divided among the three major components of development: financial deal making, project management, and marketing. The first—the economics of his business—remains mostly under Ronson's control; the others are managed day-to-day by aides and intermediaries. This personal control of the purse strings reflects Ronson's philosophy that the way a developer raises, invests and recoups his money has the greatest impact on his profitability—or lack of it. It also impacts on his ability to stay in business by turning brick and mortar into cash infusions for new developments that continuously widen his property holdings.

Among real estate developers, Onassis's advice to "always borrow as much money as you possibly can" is religion. With the risks and the capital requirements so great, savvy developers strive to operate on a highly leveraged basis—to keep their own cash commitments to a minimum. Just how successful they are at this depends on their track record in putting up profitable projects. Banks, always concerned with protecting their capital, want borrowers to have a personal stake in the deals they finance. With his own funds at risk, the thinking goes, the developer will be more committed to making the project succeed. Just how big of a stake he must take to win bank financing depends on his track record. Generally speaking, the size of the developer's cash requirement decreases in an inverse relationship to the bank's level of confidence in his abilities. In effect, the developer's past performance is a form of quasicollateral. As a newcomer in New York, his clout with the banks virtually nil, Ronson was forced to serve as a banker in his own right, partially financing his projects with Kaufman in order to gain participation in a major Manhattan deal and to prove his capabilities to the city's financial establishment. With the completion of 767 Third Avenue—and the successful rehabilitation of 30 and 50 Broad—he could point to concrete examples of his development skills, thus parlaying his success into a basis of borrowing power for future developments. The bank took notice of the Englishman both for his growing string of profitable deals and his novel approach to commercial development.

"You must have high-powered financial connections to make it as a top-ranked developer and those connections don't come by way of a simple phone call or an introduction at a dinner party," says Frank Bryant, vice president of Manufacturers Hanover Trust. "We don't open the vault for everyone who comes in here because they have a dream of seeing their name splashed across the top of an office building. That would be a sure path to ruin.

"We fund Ronson because he has more than dreams and aspirations. He has experience. He's a proven entity and most important, he has a sound marketing plan for making his projects profitable. I call Ronson's strategy a 'retail approach.' That's because he studies his market first, identifies his tenants and then puts up a building to meet their needs. Take his sliver building* at E. 56th Street, Tower 56. It's designed specifically and exclusively for the prestige small space user, mostly foreign corporations seeking a statusy presence in New York. I think it meets their needs well and for this reason, I'm confident of its success as a commercial property.

"Banks prefer Ronson's approach because it is more intelligent and less risky than the way a good many other builders operate. Typically New York developers throw up a mass of space and then pray like hell that it will rent. Look up and down Park Avenue—that's exactly how most of those buildings were born. Although this build-and-pray approach can produce extraordinary profits if everything happens to click, it makes the developer highly vulnerable to changing market conditions. Should demand suddenly

* A type of building wedged into a narrow space between two existing structures.

slump, the general purpose mass space building will likely suffer a swift and dramatic decline. But a modest structure designed to cater to a specific market will be less susceptible to shifts in the wind.

"It's like the dress business. Women always want dresses but when the economy bottoms out, dress sales flatten. Still, some manufacturers keep selling throughout the bleakest periods. They're the ones who stake out that sector of the market most impervious to recessions and who design especially for it. When the mid-priced lines are flat on their faces, the expensive designer dresses may be selling out faster than they can be stitched together. Their market is smaller and more thoughtfully defined."

Aware as he is that real estate lenders are haunted by fears of a market collapse, Ronson, in his role as financial impresario, intentionally structures his projects to conform to an underlying development philosophy designed to minimize risk, reassure capital sources and ultimately to keep the capital and the credit flowing.

"Let's take the example of a 300,000-square-foot office building," Ronson explains. "A major tenant of that building may occupy between 20,000–40,000 square feet and that property will be made up of something between 10 and 20 tenants. If there was a downturn in the market, at the worst you lose 20 percent, maybe 28 percent, of your tenants. You can safely assume that of the 75 to 80 percent who remain, some of them will need some expansion space, or at the very worst, you have a modest vacancy.

"If you take the same pro-rated figures to a 1,500,000-square-foot building, your major tenant occupies between two and three hundred thousand square feet and if you have a 20 percent vacancy, you are talking about 300,000 square feet, which is a much heavier burden to carry."

The enormous risks and rewards of commercial real estate demand that developers live with a rare form of business schizophrenia: they must be bulls and bears, optimists and pessimists simultaneously. Only a fool would commit himself to a major project without being bullish on its prospects;

but so too will a fool commit his capital without taking steps to protect it.

Ronson's spreading-the-risk strategy reveals his bearish side. He knows that long-term success as a developer comes not from guessing right on hot properties or being in the right place at the right time when a British bank is looking for a North American headquarters. This sixth sense for the big deals is important, yes, but it is the ability to weather the tough times—the market downturns—that keeps developers solvent and their bankers content.

"I design my buildings not only to cater to specific markets—mostly advertising agencies and law firms—but also so that they'll be in the best position to come through recessions without suffering serious financial damage," says the scion of a Manhattan real estate dynasty that owns more than $2 billion in midtown property. "I do this by worst casing my projects while they're still in the planning stages. I list every possible thing that could go wrong with the development—every what if—projecting what would happen if any or all of these negatives occurred. If the building could not sustain itself for three years under any one of these worst case scenarios, I won't build. Period.

"Don't get me wrong. I'm not saying we can insulate ourselves from all risk. If we could, everyone who invests in Treasury Bills could be in commercial real estate. No, I learned about real estate risk at a tender age. I remember all too vividly the frightening episodes around the dinner table when my father would grasp his chest wailing about how he was dying and my mother would call the doctor who'd arrive just in time to give Dad a shot of something to keep him alive. Then a month or two later we'd go through the same harrowing ordeal. It seemed that every time Dad was about to top off a building, the economy would nosedive and there'd be rumors of a collapse in the rental market. Now I know what he was going through because we all live in fear of that. As a developer, you justify an investment in a building on the basis of an anticipated yield, which in turn is keyed to a projected dollar figure per square foot of rental space. But if over-building or a drop in demand cuts that actual rental rate substantially below your projection, the development may start in the red and stay that way. For every year that an 800,000-square-foot building that is budgeted to rent for $40 per square foot commands only $30, the project is off by $8 million. You can bleed to death pretty quickly that way."

"That's the dark side. It's what keeps most of the people with sufficient resources to enter the commercial real estate business a thousand miles away from it. But, my father's angina aside, when you look at it objectively rather than emotionally, you have to admit to yourself that a market collapse is highly unlikely. The worst you're likely to experience is a recessionary downturn from time to time, and you can use product planning and worst-case analyses to get you through these troughs in strong enough shape to take advantage of the booms that always follow."

Adds Donald Trump: "We don't go into a project blindly and we don't act on a hunch. There are risks, of course, but skillful analysis and preplanning help in determining if we are proceeding on a sound basis. If the initial concept must be revised, we can make the necessary changes before construction begins. The net effect is that we can design the development so that it is right for the developer and right for the market. That makes everyone involved in the project—including the bank and the joint venturers—pleased to be part of it."

Frank Bryant agrees. A burly but cordial man, he has a way of demystifying the seemingly complex relationships between developers and their capital sources.

> Lending money to builders isn't really all that risky as long as you understand the business and do things to shift the odds in your favor. We rely on three safeguards to minimize the dangers of construction lending. A thorough check of the developer's operating techniques and track record; an appraisal of the building's proposed location; and a review of current market conditions.

The nature of today's banker/developer relationships can be traced to a cataclysmic event that occurred in October, 1979—an event that dramatically changed the very nature of development finance. It was then that the Federal Reserve Board, acting to curb dangerously high inflation, started substantially increasing the rate of interest it charges to member banks, thus kicking off a rise in the prime rate that would see it soar to record levels beyond 20 percent.

Before this meteoric rise, standard development financing was based on a combination of long- and short-term lending. Typically, short-term bank loans—secured to cover construction and building costs—were retired when the structure was complete and ready for occupancy. At this point, the bank would be "taken out" by another mortgage lender, usually a pension fund or insurance company. This long-term capital source would replace the bank's short-term note with a 25–30-year fixed-rate mortgage (which was usually at a lower interest rate than the construction loan).

"But this type of arrangement all but disappeared with the onset of volatile interest rates," says Jones Lang Wootton's John Minicus. "Just as the thrift institutions got badly burned on their portfolios of fixed-rate residential mortgages, the banks suffered even heavier losses on the larger commercial financings. Fixed-rate loans in inflationary times can be disastrous for lenders because the cost of funds can easily exceed the sums they are earning on outstanding loans. Put simply, they take in less than they pay out and because the loans are fixed, there's little they can do to change this.

"With the Fed's action, long-term development loans went the way of the dinosaurs, and commercial real estate moved full swing into so-called joint venturing. In the broadest sense of the word, this refers to any arrangement where the supplier of capital shares in the risks and the rewards of the project that is being financed.

"From a legal standpoint, a joint venture is a partnership launched for a particular purpose. Two parties becoming partners in a coffee shop is not a joint venture because this qualifies not as a 'particular purpose,' but instead as an ongoing business. But two parties joining together to build a shopping center is a joint venture.

"And it is in this latter type of arrangement that the former long-term lenders now participate. To protect themselves from the ravages of inflation, they assume equity positions in the developments they finance, thus securing the opportunity to increase their returns as rents and property values rise over the years. They are partners in inflation rather than victims of it."

"We have been accelerating our movement away from mortgage lending," says Equitable Life's Gordon Clagett. "In 1981, we committed about $1.5 billion to real estate acquisitions. About 90 percent were equity related. Just five years ago that was reversed; then it was 90 percent straight financing and 10 percent equity.

"The underlying objective in all of our deals is inflation protection and we think we can get this with quality buildings put up by top developers in predominant locations."

Equitable's Corporate Asset Management strategy is revealed in its Annual Report for 1981:

> The investment objective of the Real Estate account is to achieve a stable rate of return over an extended time horizon with the potential for growth of rental income and appreciation of property value. The performance objectives of the account are to attain time-weighted rates of return which are:
>
> 1. Above the average for comparable equity real estate funds;
> 2. Greater than a portfolio of high-quality bonds; and
> 3. Greater than a portfolio of high-quality mortgages.
>
> The investment policy of the Real Estate account emphasizes the acquisition and long-term ownership of high-grade, income producing commercial real property located in strong markets. The portfolio is diversified by property usage and location. We look for property holdings that enjoy excellent rental markets and continuous resale potential.

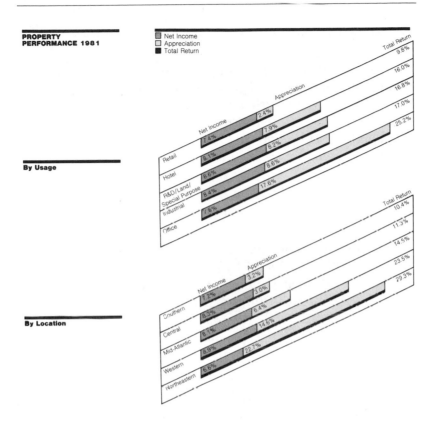

PROPERTY
PERFORMANCE 1981

☐ Net Income
☐ Appreciation
■ Total Return

By Usage

By Location

"When we invest in real estate today, we look for early year rates of return of* 10 to 12 percent and 15 to 18 percent long term," Clagett continues. "The long term factor that we try to build into a deal varies with our inflation pro jections.

"Trump Tower is a good example of what we are trying to do. It is a stunning multi-use tower located on one of the best pieces of real estate in the world and it is developed with a highly successful joint venture partner, Donald Trump."

As of year-end 1981, Equitable's real estate portfolio included approximately 38 million square feet of office space, 30.5 million square feet of retail properties, 34.5 million

* 1983 figures.

square feet of industrial and special purpose properties and 17,000 hotel rooms.

The company's major joint venture projects—developed under the auspices of regional real estate offices (assigned primarily to work with local developers) in Los Angeles, Chicago, New York, San Francisco, Dallas, Atlanta, Miami, Washington, D.C., Denver, Philadelphia, Boston, and St. Louis—include:

- The Ala Moana Shopping Center, a 1.5-million-square-foot retail complex, Hawaii's largest. (Joint venture with Daiei Inc.)
- The Four Seasons Boston Hotel and Condominium Complex, a 290-room facility with an adjacent 100-unit condominium residence. (Joint venture with Garden Plaza Association, Galbreath-Ruffin Corp. and Macombes Development Association)
- 333 Wacker Drive, an 860,000-square-foot Chicago office building. (Joint venture with Urban Investment and Development Company)
- One Post Office Square, a 40-story, 750,000-square-foot office tower in Boston. (Joint venture with Beacon Companies of Boston)

How is a typical joint venture structured? Consider this example: A developer and a financial institution are equal parties in a just-completed $50 million property. To take out the construction loan, the financial institution makes a $50 million mortgage loan to the joint venture. In consideration for this capital commitment, the institution, as a mortgage lender, gets the agreed upon mortgage coupon rate ($5 million at a 10 percent rate), plus amortization on the mortgage and is partners with the developer on the building revenues, sometimes taking the first 10 percent of earnings. Although the developer gives up the first call on income, he has still done very well. He succeeded in getting his property fully financed, his personal cash stake—which was part of the construction financing—has been repaid, and he has $25 million to depreciate because the loan was made to the partnership.

In order to realize a liquid gain and to get cash for new projects, developers will often sell out five to six years after the building is leased. In a hypothetical case, the property might sell for $75 million, netting him a joint venturer's share of $37.5 million minus his $25 million mortgage allocations, for a gain of $12.5 million. Add to this the developer's five-year tax-sheltered earning stream of $15 million plus $8 million in depreciation that can be used to reduce or eliminate taxes on other income. All of this for a typical cash investment of $10 million (on a $50 million project), which will likely be repaid when the construction loan is taken out.

The new realities of the capital market—most notably the importance of joint ventures—figure prominently in the way sophisticated developers structure their deals. They are careful not only to design projects that will allay lenders' fears of a market downturn but also to match the investment budgets of the widest possible range of equity-participating financial institutions.

Ronson explains, "I prefer to have five 300,000-square-foot buildings under construction at a given time rather than to devote all of my resources to a single 1,500,000-square-foot structure.

"There are still a number of major institutions available in the market to buy a $50 to $75 million project, or to joint venture the same. There are very few buyers, you can count them on one hand, who have the capacity or desire to buy or to joint venture on 1,500,000-square-foot projects, which today can cost anywhere between $200 million and $300 million.

"An institution does not like to put its total annual investment fund into one enormous building. If an institution has say $100 to $300 million in a given year to invest, they would prefer to diversify that investment money into a number of projects rather than into one monster. Their policy is to spread risk and that is what the developer's policy should be."

This concern with how a project will be sold before it is built is a hallmark of the professional developer. While the land rush has brought thousands of amateurs into the development business, the vast majority fail because they never consider financial strategies that can be used to reduce risk, generate fresh capital and reward themselves, as entrepreneurs, with a handsome return.

The consensus among successful developers is that it is best to opt for a balance of marketing/financial arrangements designed to provide a mix of yields: presales, preleasing, and speculation. Let's explore the differences, in terms of Ronson's projects.

HRO paid $11.5 million cash for the Water Street property (then a parking lot), originally slating the site for a speculative building. Under Ronson's standard formula for a project of this sort, the financing plan called for HRO to contribute 20 percent in cash with the balance of development costs covered by a five- to seven-year bank loan. Once the building was fully rented and therefore "stabilized" as an income producing property (generally two years after construction), HRO would arrange with an institution to purchase the property outright or take a 50 percent stake in its equity.

With the sale of a spec property, the developer's return is influenced by two crucial factors. How closely the project conformed to time and dollar budgets (additional funds spent out of pocket to complete the project will be subtracted from his gain on the sale) and how successfully it has rented. The ultimate sales price of the building—or the amount the institution must pay to gain equity participation in it—depends on the property's performance as an income producer.

This speculative approach is both the riskiest and potentially the most rewarding method of development. Should the project fail to perform as expected, the developer, devoid as he is of up-front partners or tenants, must single-handedly absorb the losses. On the other hand, if the property exceeds projections—if it rents quickly at premium rents—the developer claims 100 percent of the income or can sell the property for a substantial markup that reflects the building's long-term earnings power.

As things turned out, Water Street was transformed at the earliest stages of construction from a purely speculative development to a preleased building. At the very moment Westminster Bank signed a seventy-five-year lease for all of the building's rentable space, Ronson's risk in the project was greatly reduced, but so too was his potential reward. To gain a single tenant for the course of the building's useful life, he had to offer a preferred rent and a cap on rental increases. This trade-off is inherent in preleasing.

"My return on Water Street," Ronson says, "is respectable, to be sure, but it is not extraordinary. In fact, it may be a bloody bit less than I'd have earned had I rejected preleasing and rented instead to a number of tenants based on market conditions and a regular schedule of rent reviews. But I accepted the Westminster deal because it was fair and because it conformed to my policy of mixing risks and returns. Greedy developers who consistently turn down good deals in a blind quest for perfection don't last long in this business."

In the third major type of transaction, a classic joint venture, the developer finances construction with a short-term bank loan, assumes all the development risk and signs an agreement with a joint venturer to purchase the property at completion. Another of HRO's downtown projects is structured this way.

To cover the $55 million development budget, HRO invested $11 million of its corporate cash and took a bank loan for the balance. The joint venture agreement, this time with Aetna Life & Casualty, called for the institution to purchase the building outright within two years after completion, the sale price to be based on the building's income performance at closing. Here we see the developer's bottom-line accountability in its purest form. Should the property lease up satisfactorily, it would bring an estimated $75 million. But a poor rental performance, which is, in effect, the owner's income stream, would bring less than the $55 million development cost. Ronson would lose money on the project.

The developer's most significant return is his gain on the sale. He earns no fees, no bonuses, and rarely even draws a salary. He risks years of his time and millions of dollars of his capital on a project that may start in the red and stay that way. Should a three-month steel strike produce costly delays, should the rental market turn flat once the building is set for leasing, should the property simply fail to attract tenants for aesthetic or competitive reasons, the developer's payment from the joint venturers may be $10 or $20 million less than his development costs. It could wipe him out.

Time is a two-faced companion that can enrich the developer or ruin him. Just why this is so relates back to the bank financing. With $100 million outstanding, every month that construction extends beyond schedule can cost the developer more than $1 million in interest charges.

"They say that in life, timing is everything, but it's never more important than in commercial development," says a New York banker active in real estate financing. "Once the developer exceeds his deadline, he's in dangerous territory. Here's where the inexperienced go under. They can't cover the incremental interest costs or they don't have enough capital to fund the job after the loan funds are exhausted. At this point the project's in jeopardy. We don't want to take over—God, no—because that puts us in the real estate business and we don't know that one too well. But if it's the only way of protecting our interests, we'll foreclose and look for a buyer."

Astute observers who have watched developers rise and fall over the years agree that timing—the ability to bring in complex commercial projects on time—is the bottom-line skill, the DNA molecule of first-rate developers. This is one of the few complex logistical problems in American business that is still not computerized. But the new breed of MBAs that are cropping up in real estate consulting firms say this is only a matter of time.

"Most of the timing and other planning activities developers have done by the seat of their pants can now be done faster and more effectively by computer," says a Jones Lang Wootton executive, whose background is primarily academic. Gently cradling a stack of printouts as if they were the Dead Sea Scrolls, he rambles endlessly about the greater glories of data processing. "We can design programs that bring some science to the developer's activities. Whether it's monitoring the various stages of a construction project or calculating the yield on a given property, the computer can serve as an invaluable management tool. One exercise, the sensitivity analysis, determines how a property's anticipated yield will be affected by construction delays, market conditions and fluctuating interest rates. Our clients are delighted to have this data."

Which clients? When told of this ode to the computer, Ronson, one of Jones Lang Wootton's most important clients, responded by snatching up a book-thick printout from his desk and casually tossing it into the wastebasket.

"Enough said."

His message is that commercial developers earn their money, not by plugging data into IBM 360s, but instead by fusing vision, determination and the profit motive into an entreprencurial force that creates, builds, and profits.

"A developer is a very nebulous thing," says Paul Mc-Donough, senior vice president of international marketing for George A. Fuller Construction Company. "A man can call himself a developer and yet when he empties his pockets, he finds he has nothing inside. The real developers, the guys who add their personalities to the skyline, have pocketfuls of skill, instinct, moxie, and backbone. Through some magic, they put together money, people and materials and make it all blend together to get things done. Putting it most bluntly, I'd say successful development is a function of intelligence and balls."

Adds the financial vice president for a major Connecticut-based insurance company, an active participant in joint venture deals with dozens of the nation's leading developers, "Big league developers are not computerizable. Their strength is the strength of great chess players. They can figure all the moves—from when to buy a vacant lot to how to finance the structure that will be built on it—ten steps ahead of the fact. And they do it better than computers because they can adapt immediately to changing circumstances.

"There is also a matter of pride and of personal philosophy. As old-school believers in the work ethic—in the do-it-yourself-or-don't-do-it-at-all philosophy—many of the titans of commercial development would likely shun full-scale computerization of their activities even if this were shown to produce vastly beneficial results. They simply don't trust what they can't hold in their hands, stare in the eyes, or relate to on the strength of a handshake."

To compensate for this lack of technical assistance, the leading developers surround themselves with a coterie of highly paid experts skilled in every facet of commercial real estate. Roughly analogous to a presidential cabinet—except that they are independent operatives paid fees rather than salaries—this circle of aides tends to day-to-day relationships with the developer's various constituencies, including zoning boards, politicians, bankers, the IRS, joint venture partners, and the building trades.

The idea—rooted in recognized principles of business management—is based on the theory that the chief executive (in real estate or, for that matter, in the White House) must be free of daily details in order to focus on his most important functions: planning the company's long-term goals and setting the course to achieve them. Because the developer is, above all else, the visionary, the deal maker, he must have the opportunity to plan, to innovate, to provide the creative input that results in the development of the right building in the right market at the right time.

Ronson, a devout believer in this management format, credits it with much of the success he has enjoyed both in

Europe and the United States. Both his eighteen-person corporate staff at HRO International and his external cabinet
of independent advisers are set up to allow him to function
as a manager of consultants.

"I have the best accountants, architects and contractors
in the business," he says, glancing disdainfully at the discarded printout, "and I ask them to work under a simple
system. I pay them premium fees and I reward them generously when they do well. When they do not, I fire them.

"My consultants manage my affairs on a daily basis
and I, in turn, manage them. I don't think this business
can be computerized but I also know that one man can't
balance all the tiny little balls himself. By putting consultants in place throughout every aspect of my operation, I
can have them tend to the thousands of details that need
attention on any given day, being assured that only the material problems—the issues of overriding importance—come
to me. The system automatically directs my efforts to those
matters that require the CEO's involvement."

Ronson's cabinet looks like this:

1. CPAs: Kenneth Leventhal & Co., an aggressive midsize
   accounting firm with a strong specialty in commercial
   real estate. Especially savvy in structuring joint venture
   financing.

2. Architects: Fox & Fowles, a young, dynamic shop whose
   principals, Robert Fox and Bruce Fowles, are earning
   critical praise for breathing life into the austere steel
   and glass towers that have become the mass-produced
   Model Ts of office building architecture.

The firm's strength is in its ability to make clear aesthetic statements within the confines of commercial acceptability. Fox & Fowles's warm brick walls and earth-tone fa-
cades have proven to be popular with corporate tenants and
correspondingly with the developers whose prosperity, or
lack of it, depends on attracting commercial tenants.

It is of the utmost importance that the developer select an architect who understands and accepts the investor/ developer objectives and criteria in the construction of the office building. The architect who is capable of designing only costly monuments is not the person to engage to design an investment grade office building in which little or no preleasing is anticipated. The architect must accept the challenge of keeping costs to a minimum consistent with the risk involved.*

"There's an accepted rule in this business that every time you begin a new development you should seek competitive bids from architects, engineers and construction companies," Ronson says, gazing pensively through the tinted windows of his eighteenth-floor office, his attention divided between the conversation at hand and the work crews banging together one of his emerging structures across the street. "But I challenge the idea that competitive bidding is always the best way to go. Granted, you may shave a fraction of a percentage point from the fees—rarely more than that because the firms tend to come in with very similar bids—but you can lose out in more important, if unmeasureable, ways. Once my team understands the way I want things done, they can apply that knowledge to every Ronson development. Sure, each project differs in some ways, but the fundamentals remain quite similar. When the same team is on board throughout, I don't have to repeat myself ad nauseam—and the participants don't have to reinvent the wheel."

The continuity factor is most important in the developer's relationship with his construction firm. Because this blue-collar member of the development team is active in the most capital intensive phases of commercial development, its performance, along with the leasing agents, can have a material effect on the development's profitability.

* John White, president of Landauer Associates, writing in *Real Estate Review*. Reprinted by permission.

Construction firms can be hired on one of two bases: as general contractors or as construction managers. The difference is one of legal liability and risk. As general contractors, the firm commits itself to build a project, according to the developer's specifications, at a guaranteed maximum price. Should the development run over budget, the general contractor absorbs the loss.

Just what degree of risk this entails depends on the point in the planning stage the general contractor is required to commit to a dollar figure. Generally speaking, the earlier the commitment, the greater the risk and the more cushion the contractor will build into his fees to protect his profit margin. To commit on the basis of partially completed plans—as he is often called on to do—the contractor will seek as his fee an amount equal to 5 to 10 percent of the building's projected cost. This percentage, or "spread," can be reduced by allowing the contractor to base his cost guarantees on final plans.

When serving as construction managers, contractors are insulated from bottom-line exposure. In return for a reduced fee—typically 2 to 3 percent of the building's budgeted cost—the construction manager simply serves as the developer's operations department, assigned with the primary responsibility of getting the building built on time and on budget. But the firm is not liable if the project exceeds its cost projections. The developer assumes the financial risks.

The George Fuller Company, which claims to have pioneered the construction management concept, defines it as "the allocation of comprehensive authority and responsibility for planning, organizing, coordinating and supervising the construction of a project to a single manager."

According to a Fuller client report, this includes:

- Consultation on construction methods during the design stage as a means of reducing the costs of the work.
- Progressive estimating as the design proceeds to guide toward economy, the selection of alternate materials and building systems and components.

- Reduction in the overall project's time span by permitting earlier commencement of the work and beginning procurement and construction during design.

- Preserving for the owner the competitive feature of a general contract by procurement of each and every subdivision of work by lump-sum bid subcontracts, lump-sum bid material and equipment purchasing.

> Until recently, general contractors, in addition to dealing with various subcontractors, have performed one or more of the trades themselves . . . This type of general contractor has been largely superseded by a 'broker' type (also called 'construction manager') that performs no trade work itself. Instead, it estimates costs by inviting all the trades to submit bids for their respective specialties. It maintains a staff of cost estimators, purchasing agents, and construction superintendents, in addition to necessary support personnel. This relative handful of personnel exerts profound influence on the efficiency of the construction process . . .*

Let's explore how the developer/construction manager relationship comes to life in an actual development—HRO's building at 175 Water Street.

"When I first saw the property, it was a Fast Park parking lot, a relatively unproductive wedge of land in the heart of the financial district," says Jack Scaldini, a Fuller project manager assigned to the Ronson account. "Howard had just hired Fuller as his construction manager and we were getting ready to draw up the preliminary plans for the building. It is our job to plot the progress of construction, to establish a schedule for starting and completing each component of the development. The preliminary plan must be completed before ground is broken."

As project manager, Scaldini is Fuller's top field commander at the Water Street site. A soft-spoken man with a thoughtful demeanor that is atypical of construction execu-

---

* John White, *Real Estate Review.* Reprinted by permission.

tives, he holds a B.S. in economics and is an adjunct faculty member at New York University's Graduate School of Business. His erudition is indication that the project manager, though based at the construction site, is a sophisticated business executive entrusted with some measure of fiscal responsibility for the development he oversees.

For the duration of the Water Street project—for as long as it takes to build the building—the property will be under Scaldini's supervision. For him, this will be a sixteen-hour-a-day mental and physical drain. This high-pressure marathon is intentional. Sophisticated developers vest responsibility in a personally accountable chain of command that shares their risks and rewards in all phases of the project from planning to leasing. In the construction phase, the buck stops at Scaldini's battered Salvation Army desk in a rented walkup that serves as his command post across the street from the building.

In a way, he serves as chief operating officer of a small construction company. A full complement of Fuller staffers—all of the components of the corporate office with the exception of legal—are represented at the Water Street site and all report to Scaldini. His key lieutenants include the mechanical coordinator, office engineer, accountant, and superintendent. All are tied to an incentive plan funded by the developer.

"Incentive-minded developers believe that putting money in someone else's pocket is the best way to put money in their own," explains William Mango, Fuller's chief executive. "They reward both construction company and its executives. In our deals with Howard Ronson we are entitled to extra compensation if the jobs come in ahead of the projected timetable. One of the jobs we're running right now is likely to be completed six months early. Because our contract calls for an extra $100,000 for every month that we beat the deadline, we'll pick up an extra $600,000. That's in addition to the bonuses our executives will earn for their contributions to the job."

Scaldini's Water Street bonus program, for example,

can substantially increase his annual salary. Should the building be ready for occupancy by National Westminster's banking staff on or before the day specified in the production schedule, he may pocket a lump sum $75,000 check. For the opportunity to earn a bonus of this magnitude, Scaldini will literally work himself to exhaustion, sacking out on his office cot a hundred times or more because he's worked too late to go home or because he's too weary to make the commute.

"I pay the salaries and the bonuses for all the people Fuller places at the site," Ronson says. "This is in addition to the construction company's basic fee for the job.

"But I don't regard the bonuses as an extra expense. I look at it as control. By controlling the purse strings, I'm in excellent position to motivate the people who can make or break my buildings. I have enormous leverage to prompt them to put out 100 percent every day I'm at risk."

Visiting Scaldini at his command post on an especially hectic day, Ronson notices a framed photograph of the project manager's family. "See that picture?" Ronson asks. "That's not here because Jack's sentimental. It's just that he goes home so infrequently he may forget what they look like."

Scaldini nods, his pained expression revealing that Ronson's quip is less of a joke than he'd like it to be.

Construction managers are pivotal to a developer's bottom-line performance because they control all of the materials and workmanship that go into his projects. Their power comes from subcontracting with independent sources to buy and install virtually every building component from top soil to ceramic tiles and then coordinating these subcontractors in accordance with the project's master plan.

"We have to see a building not only as an integrated whole but also as puzzle pieces that must be painstakingly fitted together to make that whole," Scaldini says. "It's in the preplanning process—the work we did when 175 Water Street was still a parking lot—that we identify each component part, assign it a start and a completion date, and draw up specifications so that subcontractors can bid on the job. This preliminary work—one of the key behind-the-scenes functions of the development process—exerts a pervasive influence on all that follows."

Once a rather methodical, horse-before-the-cart procedure, preplanning has been made infinitely more complex by a production technique that now requires construction managers to activate planning and building activities simultaneously. Called "fast-tracking," this increasingly popular method of construction is tied directly to the economics of development, specifically the race to reduce costly construction borrowing and to secure a more immediate return on the developer's capital.

With fast-tracking, detailed plans and specifications for every component of a building are drawn while construction is in progress. When ground is broken, for example, specifications are designed for the next stage of construction, structural steel, but not for subsequent stages such as interior lighting and sprinkler systems. Final plans for this work don't go on the drawing boards until the towering derricks are pounding the foundation into the earth, until the lumbering cement mixers are circling the site, waiting to turn their payload into concrete floors. Always the engineer and the draftsmen stay just far enough ahead of the foreman and the laborers to allow work to progress. This tightly spaced synchronization is based on a complex logistical grid that requires men and materials to converge at precise points along the production schedule. A major failure at any of the key transactions can jeopardize all that has come before, turning what was meant to be a cost-saving exercise into a cost overrun. Preventing this—assuring a smooth, uninterrupted workflow—is the project manager's responsibility. He must make certain that the interrelationships that drive a successful fast-track mesh like the coils and gears in a Swiss timepiece.

"Early into the Water Street job we were about a week ahead of schedule on steel fabrication when the erection contractor suddenly announced that they were going to

Scheduling a Project by the Fast-Track Method

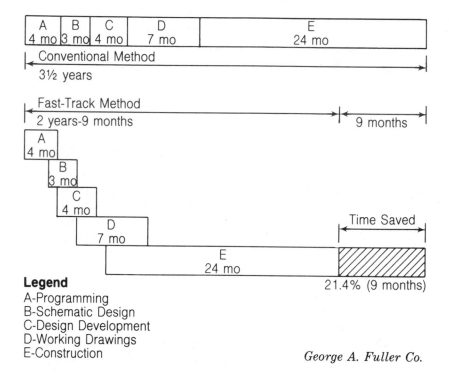

Legend
A-Programming
B-Schematic Design
C-Design Development
D-Working Drawings
E-Construction

George A. Fuller Co.

cease all overtime work," Scaldini recalls. "Why? Because the flow of steel from the fabricator had slowed down to a trickle. The erection crews feared that if they continued on overtime, they'd soon outpace the fabricator and would find themselves idled by the lack of available steel.

"Well, damn it, I wanted very much to protect that one week production lead we'd worked so hard to achieve, so I flew to Pennsylvania to meet directly with the chairman of the fabricating firm. It seemed he had too much work in his shop and wasn't able to produce quite as quickly as his contract required. But by meeting with him personally— by taking the time away from the site—I made a strong statement about the importance I attached to schedule compliance and that if he failed to perform, he'd be on our shit list—meaning no future contracts from Fuller. This clear, I was able to get the production faucet turned on again full flow. Another developer probably suffered as a result of our good fortune but that wasn't my concern.

"I rely on my personal credibility to assure that the subcontractors meet our production schedules. Typically, when a sub signs a commitment promising delivery on May 1 he makes a mental note, judging by the project manager's past performance, that he'll really have to deliver it some time beyond that date. If he knows from experience that the PM generally runs three months behind schedule, he'll think in terms of July. But should the PM surprise everyone, including himself, by actually being ready for delivery on May 1, he'll probably be out of luck. The sub may be unable to juggle his commitment in time to honor the contract.

"But it needn't be this way. The project manager who runs a tight operation and who is virtually always ready for subcontractors on the schedule dates, has trained them to think May 1 when they sign May 1. They know in advance that they'll have to honor their contract to the letter or it's the last contract they'll get from that construction firm. That's the power of credibility: it thwarts the sub's ability to weasel out of commitments."

Clearly, fast-tracking's tight schedule leaves little margin for error. Because planning and production are compressed into narrow time frames, every deadline is critical and impacts on the others. If time is lost in any major stage of construction, management must compensate for this by working around or ahead of it.

"A successful fast-tracker must keep his back pocket stuffed with any number of alternative courses of action," Scaldini explains. "The ability to switch gears and to move instantly in another direction is what keeps the development on schedule in spite of the delays and snares it's bound to encounter along the way.

"At Water Street, we ran smack into a Manhattan cement strike just as we were preparing to pour the concrete floors. You generally go to cement once the steel erectors have put up 15 or 16 stories. This is more than just a timing move: major engineering factors come into play. Concrete creates a so-called diaphragm that holds the structure together, preventing the steel frame from wobbling or losing its integrity.

"As soon as I got wind of the impending strike, I made arrangements with cement plants on Long Island to serve as back-up sources. But this proved to be a dead end when the Island guys decided to call a sympathy strike in support of their New York brethren. Suddenly I found myself without a viable source of concrete. So I had to reach into that back pocket for an alternative course of action and I found one. My decision was to proceed with the production schedule—temporarily stabilizing the building with additional cabling to retain its core integrity."

"In addition, we prepared each floor for cement so that we could pour as soon as the trucks were rolling again. When the strikers did go back to work our advance measures paid off. We poured nine fully prepared floors in ten days, about a third of the usual time. The bottom line is that what looked at first like a major delay turned out, thanks to management alternatives, to be nothing more than an inconvenience."

Fast-tracking is not without risks. The process allows for a minimum of flexibility in changing or revising building specifications. Once the foundation is poured, for example, the position of the steel columns is fixed. Because fast-tracking demands that specifications be drawn while construction is underway, the designer has little leeway to make changes at any stage in the construction process. He must work within the confines of the steel, glass, and concrete that is already in place. With traditional construction all specs are completed and approved before ground is broken. Should a change be required or an error corrected, plans can be recast from the ground up. Everything is still on paper. Fast-tracking's trade-off is that flexibility is sacrificed in exchange for speed. An error in the initial design is much harder and more costly to correct, if it can be corrected at all.

Even more worrisome, the intended economics of a fast-track can come back to haunt the developer should the schedule be so badly botched that work continues well past the projected completion date. This is substantially more expensive than closing a traditionally managed project on schedule, even if both take the same amount of time. The reason is that fast-tracking incurs higher construction costs up front. To shave six months or more from the standard timetable, the developer authorizes substantial overtime, putting most of the trades on sixty-hour weeks. Should the building open for tenants on or before the fast-track schedule, these incremental labor costs pale when compared to savings in debt service and the faster return on the developer's investment (through earlier tenant occupancy). But if construction is halted long enough to idle the trades (a strong possibility had the New York cement strike lasted months rather than weeks) the overtime paid to that point turns out to be a wasted expense.

The project manager, his bonus and his family's standard of living at stake, lives in fear of that. His healthy respect for Murphy's Law and his determination to prevent what could go wrong from seriously damaging his project, time and dollar budgets, are the developer's front-line defense against a serious reversal that can cut into his profits.

"But there are no universal truths in this business," Bill Mango warns. "Sometimes there can be too much efficiency—a fast track that's too fast.

"What do I mean by that? Well, the job can be moving along so quickly that the building's likely to be completed four, five, six months ahead of schedule. Great, you say? Maybe not. If the developer keyed his leasing campaign to the construction timetable—as he very well should—he may not be able to fill the damn place at the earlier completion date. The leasing agents haven't yet prepared for the job— they haven't assigned staff, printed brochures or written advertising copy. That's ominous—the last thing the developer wants is a finished building devoid of tenants. When that happens, the property takes on the image of a white elephant. It becomes very hard to lease. So the developer may actually want to slow things up just long enough to give his leasing people time to gear up their marketing effort.

"The lesson here is that a good construction manager has to know what can go wrong when everything seems to be going right. You have to know the full impact every unexpected development can have on the project and you have to relay that information to the developer on a timely basis. Most developers will relish having their projects completed early—especially if it's a landlord's market—but others may think it a curse. Your job is to give them the option to choose—not to inform them of a fait accompli. You have to be tough, blunt, thoroughly informed and willing to bust ass to make things go right for your developer client."

Observing Mango in action, it is clear he has a way of getting his message across. Seated at his desk shortly after returning from a business lunch, he is distracted by the piercing whine of a high-speed drill. He calls for his secretary.

"Yes, Mr. Mango."

"What the hell's going on out there."

"They're doing some repairs in the reception area. One of the men is drilling holes for door hinges."

"Tell him to stop. I can't hear myself think."

"Yes, Mr. Mango."

She tiptoes from the office.

Mango resumes his work, only to be jarred moments later by the whine of the drill. Again he calls for his secretary.

"Yes, Mr. Mango."

"Didn't I order that noise stopped?"

"I told him to stop, sir, but he insisted nothing could be done. You see, the work must be finished before five o'clock."

"Bullshit. Tell him to cut it now and to start again after five when we've all left."

"But, Mr. Mango . . ."

"Tell him!"

The door closes. Mango, distracted, struggles to maintain his composure. Minutes later the drilling resumes. Now clearly agitated, he screams for his secretary. Once again she enters the office, this time visibly shaken.

"Yes, Mr. Mango."

"What do you mean, yes, Mr. Mango? Didn't I tell you to have that drilling stopped now?"

"Yes, but the man insisted that—"

"Look! March directly to that son-of-a-bitch. Tell him this is my last warning. That if I hear that noise again, he's going out the nearest window. That I'll toss his ass onto Third Avenue."

The secretary backed out of the office. The door clicked behind her. The drilling stopped.

7

The Brothers Reichman
and the Strategy
of "More is More"

Those who built New York were not the old families
who acquired lands through colonial grants and then
waited for the unearned increment. The real empire
builder was the man who took a chance in a new section
with a new building, backing up his judgments with
his own money. The truth is that the speculative builder
is the outstanding factor in New York's growth and
supremacy.

J. P. Lohman
New York Evening Post,
1923, special issue

If Howard Ronson and his European-style modest-sized developments are at one end of New York's real estate community, another canny interloper from the British Empire is
at the other end. Actually a trio of developers, the brothers
Reichman.

Paul, Albert, and Ralph Reichman—Toronto-based developers extraordinaire who invaded New York in 1976 with
what many consider to be the most astute real estate acquisition of the century—have since become the city's most impor-

tant developers and in the process have propelled themselves to the ranks of the world's wealthiest families.

"Money! Compared to these guys, no one else has it," says a normally serene real estate consultant who has worked with the brothers on three major deals. "Save for the Saudi royal family, I'd say the Reichmans are the richest people on this planet. Their business holdings—which are privately owned—are valued at more than $12 billion. Do you know how many banks wish they had that kind of figure on their balance sheets?

"You know the song 'Only in America—Land of Opportunity'? Well, these three must hum that tune all day. But I'd like to change the lyrics to 'Only in American real estate.' That's the only place you get that rich that quick."

Born in Vienna, the Reichmans, now in their fifties, were forced to flee the Nazis while still in grade school. Father Samuel, an egg exporter in Austria, first moved the family to Paris and then to Tangier, a port city that was an active trading market for the nationals of a half dozen European countries. Blessed with an aptitude for financial transactions, Samuel became the city's leading currency trader, and the family prospered in its new home.

But after the war, the formerly safe haven of Tangier trembled with social and political undercurrents. A growing resentment against European control of the city came boiling to the surface, threatening to overthrow the commercial establishment. For a family sensitive to political turmoil, this was a clear sign to pick up stakes and move on. Toronto, already home to a small clan of affluent Jewish émigrés, became the next stop for the Reichmans. Soon after their arrival in 1956, the brothers returned to the family's commercial roots in importing and exporting, this time trading in the seemingly diverse lines of steel and tile. Naming their company Olympia, in recognition of Ralph's fascination with Greek history, they quickly built it into a highly profitable venture, one that led them, quite by accident, into real estate.

The thriving business soon needed a bigger warehouse. Fatefully, the low construction bid of $125,000 seemed too high to Paul and Ralph and they put up the warehouse themselves for $70,000.

That convinced them that they could build cheaper than anyone else. Paul, Albert, and their father went into real estate, while Ralph continued to run the tile business, as he does today. The family called their real estate company York Developments, named for the county surrounding Toronto.

From the start the Reichmans retained ownership of their properties in order to pyramid their wealth. By the mid-1960s, when the tile and real estate companies combined to form Olympia & York, Paul and Albert had dotted the Toronto suburbs with warehouses and factories. They emphasized quality: graceful landscaping instead of acres of concrete, brick in place of aluminum siding . . .

Their first big break came in 1965, when they bought a 500-acre tract of land near Toronto from the foundering Zeckendorf empire for the bargain price of $17.8 million. They recouped their investment in six months by slicing off and selling a few lots. Then they put up a cluster of office buildings on the property and have continued to build there to this day.*

The Reichman formula is at the same time strikingly similar and dissimilar to Howard Ronson's. In substance the two have much in common. All are independent, entrepreneurial risk takers guided by a contrarian view and sense of timing that has parlayed cash investments into increasingly substantial property holdings.

But in development style, they could hardly be more dissimilar. Through the family business, Olympia & York, the Reichmans shun modest buildings, preferring instead

---

* Shawn Tully, in *Fortune*, June 14, 1982, p. 89–92. Reprinted by permission.

to develop collosal projects of up to 8 million square feet with price tags of $1 billion or more.

A fundamental component of the Reichman success formula is to use the profits earned on one deal to expand their capital base and to provide the financial wherewithal for subsequent and increasingly larger developments. Fueled by the success of the Zeckendorf coup, for example, they embarked on a building spree developing office buildings in Calgary, Ottawa, Toronto, and topped by the construction of their first monster project, the seventy-two-story 3.5-million-square-foot First Canadian Place, a building that single-handedly boosted Toronto's inventory of office space by 10 percent.

At the time, this was the brothers' biggest gamble and their closest brush with disaster. The leasing stage, originally scheduled for the standard two years, took twice as long to complete.

"The mark of a top developer is the ability to hang tough when things look bleak," says a vice president of a commercial brokerage firm. "The Reichmans were under enormous pressure to reduce rents at First Canadian in order to aid the leasing effort. But they refused and, as it turns out, wisely so. I hear that the last tenants paid more than three times as much per square foot as the initial lessees. If the brothers had caved in, the building may have seemed like a loser. But they knew they had a good property and they kept their confidence in it. More important, if they felt insecure, they never showed their cards in the marketplace."

In the midst of this trying period, the gutsy brothers made their boldest move, taking a speculative flier on a New York deal that every Manhattan developer and joint venture institution had already rejected out of hand.

At the time, the National Kinney Corporation was actively peddling, for $320 million, a collection of eight Manhattan properties it had acquired through its acquisition of the Uris Building Corporation. Disappointed by the properties' high vacancy rates, Kinney was eager to unload them on a break-even basis. Kinney's management, then bearish on

New York, feared that a glut in the city's office space would keep rents low for years.

"But I felt differently and I convinced the Reichmans to buy the Uris portfolio," says O&Y executive vice president Edward Minskoff as he nibbles on triangles of breakfast toast, delivered warm and freshly buttered to his ornate conference room at the company's New York headquarters at 245 Park Avenue. A former investment banker and commercial broker, Minskoff first brought the Uris deal to the Reichman's attention. "I thought it made for a superb buy. It met the four basic tests that are fundamental to virtually all successful real estate acquisitions:

- First, we could buy the properties for one-third their replacement costs;
- Second, they were all located in Manhattan's prime business areas;
- Third, the rents were undervalued, affording plenty of upward potential;
- Fourth, the properties' mortgage financing was half the cost we would have had to pay for similar long-term loans.

"Most important, I was confident that the New York market would come out of the trough that had depressed rents in the early to mid-70s and that the building's vacant space would be quickly snapped up. Fortunately, the Reichmans came to share my optimism. We commenced negotiations on the properties in October 1976, and signed the contracts in March of the following year."

Blessed with the wisdom of hindsight, it's hard to imagine anyone having turned down the deal. Today, the Uris properties (as they are commonly known) are worth more than ten times their purchase price. Any one of the units, if sold separately, would fetch more than the Reichmans paid for the entire portfolio.

"What many people don't realize," Minskoff says, explaining O & Y's justification for the purchase in the midst of a sluggish rental market, "is that in the commercial real estate business, the wise approach is to look toward the future rather than doting on the present.

"Assume we're interested in developing a new building from the ground up. That can take three years or more from concept to leasing. So why be overly concerned with the here and now when the more legitimate concern is projecting market conditions for the time when we'll be ready to start leasing. If our studies reveal that the market will be favorable in three years, then we'll likely go ahead with the project regardless of the current rental climate.

"A similar philosophy applies to the purchase of standing structures. Granted, a high vacancy rate may not be pared down overnight, but we're not in this business for immediate results. If we can acquire a property for an exceptionally low price, knowing from our research and experience that the conditions contributing to the low price will change for the better in two, three, perhaps five years, we'll buy and wait for our investment to appreciate."

Just how well the market adapts to rent increases is the determining factor in Olympia & York's planning for new developments. The go-ahead is very much a function of projected income exceeding projected costs.

"Before flashing the green light for a new project, the developer has to tally both hard and soft costs," Minskoff explains. "The former refers to expenses incurred on the actual construction work; the latter includes design, legal and accounting fees, marketing, expenses and so forth.

"In New York today,* hard and soft costs to develop new properties range from $150 to $250 per square foot depending on the cost of the land. For argument's sake, let's figure $150 as the average cost. With financing at 15 percent, interest would be $22.50 per square foot, add another $7 per for taxes and $7 for maintenance and you have a breakeven figure of $36.50 per square foot. Projected market rent levels will have to be at a minimum $38- to $40-

---

* 1983.

per-square-foot level to make the development economically
feasible. We also figure our rent adjustments this way. They
should reflect replacement costs to develop similar buildings
in the current market.

"The same kind of thinking applies to property purchases, as well. One of the reasons we bought the Uris buildings was that calculations showed the asking price to be
about a third of replacement costs. We'd have had to spend
three times as much to build comparable properties."

Clearly, the huge asset base provided by the vastly ap-
preciated Uris properties afforded the Reichmans extraordinary borrowing power, enabling them to expand beyond their
New York–Toronto power base.

"In all, the debt against those buildings runs to some
$1 billion—less than 40 percent of their value, the conserva-
tive percentage of debt to market value that O & Y maintains
on its Canadian properties. Half the debt is being used to
finance the World Financial Center, as well as office buildings
in Los Angeles, Dallas, and Boston. That money is both
cheaper and available for longer than a construction loan
would be. The Uris loans carry a floating rate, currently
tied to Eurodollar rates and below the prime rate, and they
mature in fifteen years. Even the biggest developers pay
higher than prime on construction loans, which are due when
the building being financed is completed."*

Major O & Y projects, commenced since the conclusion
of the Uris deal, include Olympia Centre, a sixty-three-floor
office tower with more than 200 condominium units, and a
four-level 190,000-square-foot Neiman-Marcus department
store in downtown Chicago; the World Savings Center in
Los Angeles; Dallas's Arco Tower; restoration of Boston's
Exchange Place, including an additional million-square-foot
office tower; and Portland's Fountain Plaza, a multiuse urban
complex encompassing 700,000 square feet of office and retail space, a 285-room luxury hotel, seventy-three residential
units and a 1,000-seat cinema.

* Ibid.

But all pale by comparison to the company's biggest project to date, the massive World Financial Center, an 8-million-square-foot behemoth, two-thirds the size of its Manhattan neighbor, the World Trade Center. Once again the brothers Reichman are betting the company on a project so large that it literally dwarfs all that has preceded it. If successful, it promises to confirm their position as the crown princes of commercial real estate.

Just how the Reichmans came to develop the World Financial Center is indicative of their entrepreneurial flair, the instinct for deal making that is the birthmark of the great developers.

> The location had been a white elephant almost since 1968, when New York State created an agency to develop the Hudson River site partly out of landfill from the excavation for the nearby World Trade Center. Various developers had broken ground in the 1970s, but always abandoned their plans. In 1980 a competition drew proposals from twelve developers, including O & Y. When the other contenders made their sales pitch to Richard Kahan, chairman of the Battery Park City Authority, they described grandiose visions for the site. Paul Reichman simply unfolded a single piece of blue paper listing the authority's bond repayment schedule and asked softly, "If I were to guarantee the payments in that column, would I be on the right track?"
>
> "Somehow," says Kahan, "he understood that my main interest was to keep the bonds afloat."*

Positively gargantuan even by Reichman standards, the World Financial Center shoulders the Manhattan skyline from a fourteen-acre site flanking the Hudson River.

Composed of four granite and glass towers of from thirty-three to fifty-one stories each, the complex—which was designed by Caesar Pelli, dean of Yale's School of Archi-

---

* Ibid.

tecture—offers 6 million square feet of usable office space, 100,000 square feet of retail space, and 150,000 square feet of recreational, exposition and other public space.*

Rising from the water's edge, the towers and their connecting substructures resemble enormous gatehouses standing ready to process the crush of commerce and humanity that is drawn to Manhattan to buy and to sell; to speculate and to trade. In contrast to the stark, simple lines of the World Trade Center that looms in the background, the Reichmans' complex is a busy mélange of geometric designs and intricate architectural features. Its glass skin reflects the water to its face, the city to its rear, and mirrors the history and complexity of its urban setting.

When plans for the World Financial Center were unveiled, *New York Times* architecture critic Ada Louise Huxtable wrote:

> The shape of the tower comes directly from the planner's guidelines. These specified that the buildings were to be set back at the third, ninth, and twenty-fourth floors, to relate physically and symbolically to the predominant heights of lower Manhattan buildings.
>
> The three-story section parallels the area's remaining early-nineteenth-century structures, and in keeping with tradition, is treated essentially as a masonry wall. This level also provides the scale and surface experienced by the pedestrian. The ninth- and twenty-fourth-story setbacks reflect the size and style of the later downtown buildings, with more glass and less stone. The top stories, soaring to today's heights, are to be sheer, shining glass. The building's caps, or crowns, suggest the classical or art deco tower of the 1920s and '30s without nostalgia or whimsy . . .
>
> It has the urban sophistication, the architectural standards, the financial prospects and the critical mass to

---

* The balance of the space is for maintenance or design features and is not usable.

put it over the top. For those of us who see this as a landmark extension of the city's skyline drama, the prospect is exhilarating. But out of habit and inclination I am still keeping my fingers crossed.*

The Reichmans had their fingers crossed for another reason. Groundbreaking, which commenced in the fall of 1981, came at a time when most of New York's development community (save for fellow contrarian Howard Ronson) was sitting on its hands waiting for some sign that the abrupt end of a three-year spiral in Manhattan rents was not the precursor of a drastic plunge. Many also feared that a recent building binge had created an inventory of excess space that would take as long as a decade to absorb.

But the Reichmans, clearly aware that they were taking a gamble, were still willing to roll the dice. Credit their bravado to the family's registered trademarks: confidence in the market and a remarkable flair for making spectacular deals. Skeptics—and there were more than enough of them in Manhattan to hold a parade up Fifth Avenue—ridiculed the brothers for committing to an extravagant development in what appeared to be a bear market. The grapevine buzzed with gleeful rumors that the interlopers from the north were about to fall flat on their bearded faces. But these dire predictions discounted the Reichmans' marketing skills and their penchant for quick-strike offensives. In less than a year, they successfully leased 4 million square feet—more than half of the World Financial Center's available space. How they did it makes for a primer in land rush entrepreneurship and has valuable lessons for local developers struggling to lease up commercial properties anywhere in the nation.

To make the World Financial Center a success, the Reichmans returned to their roots, bringing to New York real estate the same fundamental techniques patriarch Samuel used to swap currency in Tangier. They became traders.

* Ada Louise Huxtable. *New York Times*, May 24, 1981.

O & Y moved boldly to sign tenants. Last summer real
estate broker John C. Cushman III tried to sell the company a Manhattan skyscraper owned by City Investing
for $175 million. At that price both Prudential and Equi-
table had turned it down; O & Y also said no. Cushman
suggested a deal reminiscent of trading in an old car
for a new model: O & Y would buy the building for
$175 million and City Investing would move into a tower
at Battery Park City* on a long-term lease, paying a
stream of rental income totaling $850 million over thirty-
five years. Paul agreed, reasoning that the premium
for the City Investing building was the price of landing
a prestigious tenant.**

It may have been a bargain. Just as a building slow
to rent is seen as a white elephant, those that come to market
with an impressive list of charter tenants are immediately
viewed as highly desirable properties. With the Reichmans
out to create a financial services center, enlisting a prestigious tenant the likes of City Investing would be just the
thing, they believed, to create a ground swell of interest
in the new building. If they had to buy a property to spark
the chain reaction, the brothers were prepared to make the
investment.

Sure enough, the City Investing deal led quickly to another marketing coup that virtually assured the development's success. It all started with the Reichmans' observa-
tion that many of New York's premier tenants lease a
patchwork of office space from Wall Street to upper Park
Avenue. As their businesses expand over the years, these
high-volume users of commercial space house new divisions
and acquisitions wherever sufficient space is available at the
time. Knowing that this dislocated setup is inefficient from
the standpoint of rental rates and corporate logistics, O & Y
set its sights on finding candidates likely to be interested

* Later renamed the World Financial Center.
** Shawn Tully, in *Fortune*, June 14, 1982, p. 98. Reprinted by permission.

in consolidating their operations in the World Financial Center.

The search paid off when American Express, easily one of the most glamorous and far-flung financial empires, signaled its interest in the relocation idea. But Amex chairman Sanford Weill, a noted deal maker in his own right, wanted to make a trade similar in fashion to the one struck between the Reichmans and City Investing. If O & Y would agree to purchase Amex's current headquarters building at 125 Broad Street, Weill would commit to a major lease at the brothers' downtown complex.

Once again the Reichmans agreed to a take-it-or-leave-it deal, paying American Express $240 million for the property—a cool $180 million gain for the credit card folks. But the terms were far from one-sided. In return, O & Y had its most prestigious tenant* and, as they say in the record business, a "gorilla" (blockbuster) lease guaranteeing the developers of $2 billion in rent over thirty-five years. With two bold strokes, they all but assured the success of their biggest—and potentially most rewarding—gamble.

* The fifty-one-story American Express tower, the largest building in the World Financial Center complex, is scheduled for completion and occupancy in 1985.

8

Lock Your Rolodex: In the Land of the Million-Dollar Brokers

> In the real estate brokerage business, you don't dare go to the john without locking your Rolodex. If you forget, the person at the next desk will be on the phone to half your clients before you return.
>
> *James A. Austrian*
> *Partner, Jones Lang Wootton,*
> *real estate brokers and consultants*

Credit for the Reichmans' successful marketing of the World Financial Center must be shared with the Manhattan broker who first suggested the buy/lease deal to City Investing. In turning what appeared to be an irreconcilable impasse into a highly profitable transaction, he played a role familar to many of real estate's most successful operatives. He served as a catalyst.

"The man who taught me the real estate brokerage business—a former chairman of Cushman & Wakefield—beat it into my head from the earliest days of my career that in real estate you can't sit by the phone waiting for business to develop," says Steve Siegel, C & W's current chief executive. "You have to make it develop. Brokers can earn big money year after year only if they are active proponents of the development process, only if they recognize that real estate deals have too many components, too many variables for everything to simply fall into place. They match buyers and sellers, property owners and developers, bankers and builders. By rubbing these forces together, they get sparks, energy, deals, money."

Siegel's business strategy is to father real estate developments, and then to nurture the offspring with a long list of income-producing services. By acting as a catalyst for commercial real estate developments, a brokerage firm expands the market in which it competes and simultaneously assures itself of an inside track in securing much of this incremental business.

When Jones Lang Wootton mated Howard Ronson and National Westminster Bank, the British-born realty consultants earned fees for structuring the ninety-year lease, and commissions for renting that portion of the Water Street space the bank was subleasing. Similarly, Cushman & Wakefield won an exclusive brokerage contract for its role in creating another downtown complex, Continental Center. Here we see the broker's role as land rush catalyst in its purest form.

"Like many of New York's fast-growing financial services firms, Continental Insurance was having great difficulty squeezing its expanding staff into its old and rather cramped corporate offices at 80 Maiden Lane," says C & W vice president Raymond O'Keefe. "Because Continental's management was unsure of how to handle the problem, they hired us as consultants, asking that we study the matter and come up with viable solutions. Looking back now, I believe they'd hoped we could find a way to increase the building's capacity so they could remain at the same location. But even a cursory review of the problem revealed this to be impossible. The total amount of space and the design configurations it allowed were simply inadequate for the corporation's needs."

The options, typical in a case of this sort, were to lease additional space in an existing structure, to prelease space in a spec building still under development, or to develop a new facility expressly for Continental. After weighing the variables, both in terms of costs and its client's current and future space requirements, C & W recommended a new facility.

"We favored a new development for two reasons," O'Keefe explains. "First, Continental's appetite for space was so great—600,000 square feet immediately and 1 million square feet in the near term—that the firm would have to lease the equivalent of an entire building to assure itself of ample room. Second, we knew of an available property, located on Maiden Lane and Pine Street, that would make an ideal site for Continental's new headquarters. The parcel had been assembled a decade earlier to pave way for a speculative office building. But the completion of the assemblage in the early '70s coincided with a collapse of the downtown rental market brought on by overbuilding in the late '60s. As a result, the developer never broke ground, the spec building stayed on the drawing board, and the property became a parking lot. We suggested that the time had come to take advantage of the assemblage and that Continental should purchase the property using it as their headquarters site. They liked the idea and agreed to it almost immediately.

"But the project still had to clear a few stumbling blocks. It seemed that local zoning forbade the construction of a new building on a scale large enough to satisfy Continental's needs. Luckily we were able to get around that problem by purchasing air rights from a bank of rights created by the development of a nearby historic district, the South Street Seaport. But then an additional complication surfaced when Continental announced its preference for working with a development partner to share the risks and the responsibilities of getting the tower built. This left us with the job of finding a second party willing to take an investment position in the deal. Again we were able to effect a swift solution, this time bringing in Rockefeller Center Development Corporation as Continental's joint venturer. Although Continental later bought out the Rockefeller interests, creation of the partnership proved to be the decisive factor in getting the deal off the ground."

C & W's choice of Rockefeller Center Development Corporation was not a random selection. In one of the many interconnecting relationships that wind through the real estate industry, both Cushman & Wakefield and Rockefeller Center Development Corporation are owned by the same corporate parent, Rockefeller Center, Inc. C & W's ownership changed twice in the 1970s. Originally acquired by the RCA Corporation in 1970—at a time when American corporations were haphazardly snapping up unrelated subsidiaries in a bout of conglomerate fever—the real estate brokerage firm was subsequently sold off to RCI in April of 1976. The second acquisition proved to be more enlightened.

As real estate professionals fully attuned to the importance of financial incentives, RCI awarded 20 percent of C & W's stock to the firm's top managers, many of whom are responsible for negotiating the multimillion-dollar transactions that have made C & W the nation's largest commercial broker.*

Today, there is a smell of affluence at C & W's New York headquarters. Questioned about the company's financial performance, Siegel searches for a way to reveal C & W's revenues—a figure of which he is justly proud— while still protecting his corporate rear end.

"We are a subsidiary of a private company that doesn't have to, or for that matter want to, report its income. So I'm barred from revealing C & W's commission billings. But let me put it this way: a recent newspaper article reported the figure at $100 million and they were off by only 5 percent."

A high percentage of C & W's revenues flow to an elite group of sales brokers who, after the standard 50/50 com-

---

* Although Merrill Lynch and Coldwell Banker report substantially higher revenues, they are active in both commercial and residential markets.

mission split with their firm, earn as much as $2 to $4 million annually. Of C & W's 700-odd brokers, the top twenty-five consistently earn $1 million or more, the top 500 average $200,000 and the balance, relative newcomers to the field, dot a sliding scale that drops off to zero. Because it costs management $30,000 a year to keep a broker at his desk, those who cannot cross a $75,000 gross-commission threshold are dismissed.

"Some of our people become rich selling real estate." Siegel beams and then turns self-consciously serious. "But we also have others breaking their butts only to wind up with nothing. Not a dollar. In a business with no upside limitations, there is also no downside protection. Our compensation is linked directly to our performance. In this respect we're similar to the developers we work for."

Not quite. Granted Cushman & Wakefield staffers can and often do log hundreds of hours piecing together property deals that never come to pass or that wind up going to competitors. But as licensed brokers—as middlemen in the land rush—they may serve as catalysts for development, but never as equity participants.

"Leasing agents have controllable risks," says Howard Ronson. "If the market is flat, their commission income is lower than it might be. So the worst that will happen is that they'll have some red ink. But their operations are limited to people and telephones. All they have to do is cut back on either to control costs and losses.

"But developers have buildings, which in a down period can be enormous financial burdens. Our losses are not controllable. We can bleed to death if things go wrong—if our properties don't get rented as quickly as we've projected."

The broker's risk is limited to wasting time better spent on more productive deals. Neither the firm's nor the individual's capital is at stake. Even when their client/developer's project is a total fiasco—when the property leases up a costly year behind schedule—the broker may come away with $10 million in commissions. Although brokers do play a key role in stimulating the real estate market, the picture they draw of themselves as the developers' partners is just so much salesmanship.

Broker Michael Herschfield is one of the few in his trade who'll admit to this. A pale-skinned, emaciated man, given to irreverent comments about landlords, developers, and assorted real estate moguls—traditionally the broker's sacred cows—Herschfield cuts a strange figure for the president of a New York brokerage firm. A successful entrepreneur almost in spite of himself, he backed into real estate after disastrous experiences in academia and a family business.

"My short-lived academic career started in 1973 when I was a twenty-three-year-old college grad with degrees in biology and psychology and not the slightest idea of what I wanted to make of my life. One day, having nothing better to do, I stopped by New York University's faculty offices to visit a former professor. Fortunately, or unfortunately, depending on your point of view, I happened to overhear a conversation he was having with the chairman of the biology department.

"It seemed that a grad school faculty member had left school less than a week before the new semester was to start and the department was in dire need of a replacement. Suddenly, the chairman looked at me and said, 'Hey, Herschfield has a biology degree. Why don't we offer him the job?' When I retorted that I wasn't qualified, my former professor said, 'No problem. We'll enroll you in graduate school. As long as you're working toward your doctorate, you can teach at this level.'

"As I said, I had nothing better to do so I accepted the job, which turned out to be just the kind of nonchallenge I was suited for at the time. Life couldn't have been easier. I never went to grad classes—not one. The extent of my involvement with the school was to spend a few hours on campus teaching and collecting my paychecks. The rest of the time I just loafed about. But my free ride didn't last very long. I guess the school caught on that I wasn't exactly their most inspired professor. Within six months of my starting date, they bought out my contract."

Herschfield's next stop was the medical laboratory owned and managed by his father. Presumably, the senior Herschfield took in his wayward son as an act of charity. At least the boy would eat. But even fathers have their limits.

"We didn't exactly get along," Herschfield continues. "And I guess I have to accept the blame. He'd been running the business for years but in less than a month as his apprentice, I was certain that I knew how to do it infinitely better. My conviction in that regard turned out to be a gap we couldn't bridge."

On the streets again, Herschfield decided to base his next move on a rather unscientific survey of career opportunities.

"I lived, at the time, in New York's Chelsea section, in one of those modest apartment buildings popular with young singles. When I was down to the last few dollars I'd earned working for my father—when it seemed that finding another job was going to be an absolute necessity—I approached a group of my neighbors, all about my age, and asked them what businesses they were in. As it happened, all of them worked for advertising agencies. "That sounds good," I said, 'I'll go into advertising.' To a man they advised against it. 'Big mistake. It's the pits.' 'Okay,' I said. 'Let me rephrase the question. If you had to do it all over again, what business would you choose?' They responded like a well-coached chorus. 'Real estate.' "

In what was easily the most decisive action of his young life, Herschfield decided to launch his third career.

"I didn't know anyone in real estate—I didn't even know what real estate people do—so I just checked the *Times'* help wanted ads with the determination to take the first offer I could get. Sure enough, someone was advertising for a real estate job. It was one of those bullshit come-on ads. You know, the make-a-million-dollars-no-experience-needed variety. But what the hell, I didn't know any better so I went for an interview.

"The place turned out to be one of those old, schlock brokerage firms that take any kind of business that comes their way, be it residential, commercial, whatever. A sign in the window—a second-floor walkup on East Fifty-second Street—read Garrick & Co. I was met at the top of the stairs by a disheveled fellow who seemed to be either terminally ill or terminally tired. Anyway, interviewing me, if you can call it that, was obviously a great strain on his system. He wanted to dispense with it quickly. 'Want to work in the store leasing department?' he asked. 'I don't know anything about leasing stores,' I answered. 'I'll repeat,' he said impatiently. 'Want to work in the store leasing department?' 'Sure,' I said, sensing, perhaps for the first time in my life, when to keep my mouth shut. 'Okay,' he sighed, clearly relieved at having completed his recruiting assignment. 'From now on you're the store leasing department.'"

An inauspicious introduction to real estate, to be sure, but Herschfield, undaunted as always, accepted the offer and proceeded to make something out of nothing. In a repeat performance of his brief stint in his father's business, he informed Garrick's owner, after only a month of employment at the firm, that he could vastly improve the business were he free to run it. This time, he made arrangements to do just that.

"I bought the business for the princely sum of $3,800 cash. Why? Because in my sudden emergence as a budding capitalist, I saw an excellent opportunity to make money by transforming a losing business into a profitable one.

"The key revelation that this could be done came to me within weeks of going to work for Garrick. I realized that of the city's hundreds of real estate brokers, not a single firm focused on the retail market. Clearly, this was a void begging to be filled. The established brokers, the Cushman & Wakefields, looked down on retail brokerage. Your typical C & W guy considered it beneath his station to dicker around with nervous and demanding merchants whose deals, for all the aggravation they brought, were rather small compared to those negotiated with office building tenants. But from my perspective as a guy looking for a way to get a foot in the real estate door, this represented an untapped market. One with the promise of substantial profits for the broker who could claim a major stake in it."

In New York's brokerage caste system, commercial brokers are the Brahmins, residential brokers are lower forms of civilized life, and the retail agents are untouchables. Partly because he was offended by this and partly because it represented virgin sales potential, Herschfield set out to establish his fledgling company as the city's only brokerage firm dealing exclusively with retail accounts. Adding to the novelty, he decided to reverse standard brokerage practice by representing tenants rather than store owners.

"Everyone said I couldn't do that because it's the owners who give brokers their listings. But they were only half right. True, the owners give the listings but it takes two parties to strike a deal. If I could get the tenants to come to me, to trust me, then I believed I could control the market."

This time Herschfield was taking on a formidable challenge. As a group, Manhattan merchants are suspicious, arrogant, distrustful, two-faced, deceitful, pugnacious, bellicose—and that's their good side. Tell them that an object in your hand is black and they'll think you're lying, it's really white, but you've figured out some way to make it look black. Most are survivors of depressions and assorted business disasters, conditioned by collective experiences and genetic imprinting to believe that bankruptcy is always a week, maybe a month, away. And they are convinced that everyone who tries to sell them something—save perhaps for their accountants—is trying to profit at their expense. To rob them blind.

It was on this hardboiled group that Herschfield was pinning his hopes. His decision to go this route was partly a psychological/emotional outlet. As a self-described "totally immature twenty-three-year-old," he enjoyed tilting at real estate's windmills, and relished the idea of showing Cross & Brown, Cushman & Wakefield, and other brokerage leaders that there was money to be made serving a market they'd long ignored. But, in all fairness, it must be said that Hirschfield was guided by entrepreneurial instinct as well as youthful antagonism. He eventually profited from the land rush because he was blessed with the sixth sense that distinguishes successful investors, developers and brokers.

"I knew full well that I couldn't win over the merchants simply by posting a sign on my door, RETAILERS WELCOME, or by taking out an ad of this sort in the *Times*. I knew that gaining their loyalty would be a slow build and that it would work only if I did more for them than anyone had done before.

"My starting point was to *represent* retailers rather than simply sending them leases to sign. Traditionally, an office building broker working on a retail deal would call the merchant and say 'There's a nice store over on Thirty-fourth Street, go look at it and see me when you get back.' God forbid the merchant asked about the volume of pedestrian traffic. 'How the hell do I know,' the broker would snap. 'Go stand in front of the store and count heads.'

"I decided to replace that kind of nastiness with a service firm concept. To provide merchants with marketing information including accurate traffic counts, local demographics and space utilization studies. I wanted them to view my firm, my brokers, as consultants as well as sales people and I intended to back this up with meaningful services rather than the usual hype."

Slowly, Herschfield's strategy started paying dividends. Word spread through the merchant grapevine that Garrick was a source of reliable information, an ally in store planning and a friendly force in tenant/owner negotiations.

"Typically, when the parties to a retail lease sit down to hammer out a deal, the brokers line up with the hand that feeds them, the store owners, helping them shove every kind of horrendous lease provision down the merchant's throats. I challenged the status quo, and shocked everyone at the table, first by showing up in jeans (I didn't own a suit) and second by cursing and raving and catapulting myself on the owner's desk in an effort to get the merchant a fair deal."

A vice president at a leading brokerage firm remembers it well.

"Herschfield's reputation became that of a meshugana—a crazy man. He did things that at our firm you got fired for. But the merchants evidently liked his style. I think they came to see in him a certain kinship, a quality that inspired confidence and trust. He was more like them than the *normal* brokers they'd been forced to deal with in the past."

With merchants calling Garrick when they needed space, the brokerage firm expanded from a staff of five to fifteen and started gaining control of a growing sector of the retail market. It was at this point that Herschfield—driven by the thrill of his new-found success and mellowed by the rites of passage of his twenty-fifth birthday—recognized that his firm could become a dominant force only by building bridges to retail store owners as well as tenants.

"That's when I decided to buy a suit and to go into partnership with Charlie Aug, a commercial broker with an active store department. Because his ties were with the owners, the union of our businesses made for a perfect fit. Corporate synergy at its most fundamental level."

Herschfield decided to position the newly christened Garrick-Aug as the property owner's advisor as well as his broker. Borrowing a page from his successful campaign to win over the merchant community, he set out to prove to developers that he could fill a void in their business operations.

"Typically, office building developers are very savvy guys when it comes to marketing the space in the structures they create, with one glaring exception, the ground floor retail area. Surprisingly, they've never learned to master this space in spite of the fact that as the most visible part of the building, it comes to a tenant's attention first and can influence his opinion of the entire property. In addition to generating extra income, a well-planned retail space can have great leverage in successfully leasing the bulk of the building's space.

"Because developers don't know how to make this work—because they know amazingly little about stores and merchants—I knew I had an excellent opportunity to service them in one important but often overlooked aspect of the development process. Not as a partner, a right-hand man or any of that nonsense, but simply as a professional, capable of teaching them how to extract incremental profit from a building through more effective utilization of generally neglected space."

To promote his new service, for which he expected to collect consulting fees as well as commissions, Herschfield hired public relations agencies to place stories in real estate journals touting Garrick-Aug's capabilities as development consultants.

"I've always relied more on PR than advertising because in the real estate business people tend to put more faith in news articles than in ad copy. When I write an article praising my firm, the PR people get it placed in real estate trade magazines where it appears under an editor's by-line. Readers, who have no idea that I'm the source of all these wonderful comments about Garrick-Aug, think it's the gospel. The mechanism is so powerful it scares me.

"In the late '70s, we started billing ourselves in those trade articles—with a bit of poetic license—as the city's largest brokerage firm dealing only in retail space. Soon after the stories appeared, new clients started calling to say they wanted to work with us for that reason. But what they didn't know was that we were the *only* firm dealing exclusively in retail brokerage. We could have said that we were the smallest ones doing it on an exclusive basis and that would have been equally correct."

Herschfield's rickety appearance, his nervous mannerisms, camouflage the savvy entrepreneur behind the gentle façade. A plaque on his desk, CUTE BUT RUTHLESS, is more revealing than first-time visitors might suspect. A telling example of how the man's mind figures the angles is evident by his manipulation of public-relations activities.

"I hire two PR agencies even though our company's

workload doesn't warrant that. I do it because it keeps the firms on their toes. They're both so terribly frightened of losing out to the other that they give Garrick-Aug more attention than accounts ten times our size. I love it."

But Herschfield owes his success to more than clever image-making. Bringing to negotiations his own patented blend of *chutzpah* and moxie, he has a way of coaxing merchants to operate in a manner that supports the developer's underlying objectives while simultaneously creating an environment that serves the store owners as well. His basic thrust is: 1. to help developers capitalize on the retail portion of multiuse buildings; 2. to plan the retail aesthetics so that they enhance rather than detract from the property's appeal; 3. to extend the developer's control directly into the stores, giving them prerogatives ordinarily considered within the merchant's domain.

"All of this is increasingly important to developers because city governments are now offering them zoning benefits as incentives for creating retail space," Herschfield notes. "Urban planners—obsessed with the idea of having public access areas in city centers—are encouraging developers to incorporate pedestrian concourses and atriums, usually with retail shops, into their building designs. Those who comply are often allowed to add bonus stories to their buildings—perhaps four floors of rentable space beyond the limit ordinarily allowed by local zoning. Hearing this, developers get on the hotline with their architects, ordering them to make provisions for public space.

"But in many cases, the space they create is not properly planned and turns out to be in violation of the city's codes. Result: bonus denied. One developer buried the retail space so deeply into the building's bowels that visitors could enter the lobby, take an elevator to the corporate offices and never see a store. That kind of setup doesn't do anything for pedestrians, it doesn't win development incentives and equally important, it doesn't generate high retail rentals. Landlords and their tenants suffer."

When Herschfield's client, Madison Equities, put up a

670,000-square-foot mixed-use building at 875 Third Avenue, Garrick-Aug structured the 30,000 square feet of retail space so that pedestrians using the building's concourse as little more than a weather shield were forced to pass by no less than half of the stores in the retail complex. To assure a uniformly attractive look and to protect the developer (as well as the bulk of the merchants) from the tawdry effects of hand-scrawled merchandising signs and sloppy door-front sales bins, retailers at 875 Third Avenue and other Herschfield-managed properties are required to provide thorough specifications, including color schemes and display materials, detailing how their stores will look from end to end.

"If the tenant is new to us, if we haven't dealt with him before or we have reason to distrust him, we'll attach a copy of these specifications to the lease," Herschfield says. "Should he subsequently make any changes that violate our aesthetic concepts, we'll declare him in default. Good-bye, tenant.

"I recommend to my clients that they extend their right to veto displays, signs and the like three feet into the store. The property owner's rights usually end at the glass line but I don't think that goes far enough."

The lease agreement for 875 Third Avenue reads as follows:

Storefront Criteria:

1. *Retail Control Zone (RCZ):*
   Landlord has established a Retail Control Zone pursuant to Section 8.1AA of the Lease in all retail units, which extends 3'0" into each store from both the interior (on the CPS) and exterior (on street) storefronts. Within this area, Landlord reserves absolute and continuous control of all aspects of Tenant design and presentation including, without limitation, signage, lighting and convector enclosure. This control by Landlord shall remain in effect throughout the entire term of the Lease plus any renewals and extensions.

"You can't have some swami merchant shlock up the aesthetics of a $100 million building by displaying a giant Buddha that glows in the dark. And let me tell you, putting a stop to this sort of thing benefits most of the merchants as well as the developer. Those store owners who work hard to maintain a first-class, sophisticated look don't want some oddball tampering with that. Aesthetic control brings maximum traffic—that's good for the developer and his tenants."

Just how good is evidenced by the high retail rents Herschfield's buildings command. Manhattan's prime retail space ranges from $40 to $500 per square foot, with the top end generally limited to the most fashionable blocks along upper Fifth Avenue from Fiftieth to Fifty-seventh Streets. At midtown and Third, in the vicinity of Madison Equities' property, street store rentals average $40 to $60 per square foot. But the Herschfield-designed space at 875 Third claims rentals of up to 50 percent above the going rate. Manhattan merchants, impressed as they are with the well-planned retail environment and the forced flow of traffic, are willing to pay the premium.

The net effect is that Madison Equities has a more profitable and productive building, and Garrick-Aug, as the broker-catalyst, bolsters its reputation and gains the rights to represent the space and to earn commissions as retail tenants come and go throughout the building's life. Much like Holmes & Kennedy, catalysts for development on the residential side, Herschfield creates opportunities, plants his flag on ever larger sectors of the market and reaps the rewards for years to come.

This astute and aggressive game plan has helped the erstwhile biology professor to build his firm into an increasingly important participant in New York's land rush, employing forty brokers with average earnings of $200,000. Consulting services provide Garrick-Aug with the prestige and the entrée into development projects, leasing space accounts for most of the dollars.

For all their differences, this revenue mix is similar to that of the office building brokers. Cushman & Wakefield, which like Garrick-Aug offers its clients a laundry list of development services from site analysis to the selection of general contractors, earns 75 to 80 percent of its revenues from leasing space. But C & W's Siegel nurtures and promotes consulting services for much the same reasons that Herschfield authors trade magazine pieces on the subject.

"Our development consulting and building management divisions—through which we manage 70 million square feet of space—are vitally important because they afford us a measure of market control," Siegel explains, illustrating how the full-service broker's marketing grid absorbs new business and feeds it into the company's related services. "Consulting, because it is a catalyst for development—as in the Continental Center deal—creates leasing opportunities. Building management, because it tends to be a long-term appointment, retains those opportunities."

Siegel's comments reflect the classic chronology of a broker/developer relationship. Typically, brokers get their hooks into a building when the construction phase is nearing completion and the developer's thoughts—preoccupied to this point with brick and mortar and production schedules—turn to generating income from the property by leasing it or selling part of his equity to a joint venture partner. Because the sales price is based on the property's rental income, the broker's performance can have a multimillion-dollar impact on the developer's capital gain.

The commission-based compensation system under which brokers operate assures that they share the developers enthusiasm for renting every square foot. The vision of a steel and concrete shell rising from Manhattan's gray-brown earth to join the crowded skyline makes a broker's heart flutter. All that virgin space! The possibilities race to mind. Xerox would love the top two floors for their newly expanded in-house legal staff. Price Waterhouse is rumored to be in search of a new home for its fast-growing consulting practice. Ogilvy & Mather has run out of space for its media buying department. If only a small percentage of the combinations click, the brokers will profit handsomely. For a

500,000-square-foot building commanding an average rent of $50 per square foot, the first round of leases (at ten year terms) will produce commissions of $7.5 million.*

The average commission rate varies from market to market and is always subject to negotiation. In New York, the accepted and customary range of commissions on a 10-year lease is 28–32 percent of the first year's rent. This can be less when the developer encourages open competition among the brokers and makes it clear that he will award the assignment solely on the basis of price. The bitchy competitiveness that reduces the relationships among the leading brokers to a mud-slinging contest prompts them to occasionally make and accept low-ball bids just to keep the business away from the competition.

In their role as leasing agents, brokers can serve developers on an exclusive basis, as "agencies," or as one of many firms competing to lease space in a given property. Agency status is a sought-after plum because, much like being named a Sotheby's affiliate on the residential side, it assures the broker of a fee.

"When we have an agency, we have a contractual commitment to perform for that owner, to work to market his space and to report on our performance," says C & W's Raymond O'Keefe. "This obligates us to invest in advertising, personnel, and related expenses whatever it takes to lease up the building. But the owner also has a responsibility, a financial one, and that's what enables us to assign a sales team specifically to his account. He is obligated to pay us a full commission on every lease we negotiate and an override, equal to half the full commission, for every lease negotiated by another broker. We will never reduce our standard commission rate to secure an agency but we will take less of an override if we think that's what it will take to sew up the deal."

The following agency listings from New York brokerage firm Cross & Brown's marketing brochure of February 10, 1982, are circulated to prospective tenants and to the broker-

---

* Based on 30 percent of the first year's rent for a 10-year lease.

age community. Because of the override provision, Cross & Brown is secure in sharing the information with competitors.

CROSS & BROWN COMPANY
Exclusive Agency Listings

BUILDING BROKER TELEPHONE	SPACE	AREA	RENTAL PER SQUARE FOOT	POSS	TERM
MANHATTAN					
12 Barclay St	Ent 2nd	2,500	13.00	Imm	Arr
Seekamp/	Ent 3rd	2,500	13.00	Imm	Arr
Tratten	Ent 4th	2,500	13.00	Imm	Arr
(212) 943-0543	Ent 5th	2,500	13.00	Imm	Arr
	Bsmt"A"	2,500	Upon Request	Imm	Arr
	Sub-bsmt "B"	2,500	Upon Request	Imm	Arr
253 Broadway	Pt Grd	2,274	30.00	Imm	Arr
Hollenbeck/	Bsmt	7,000	15.00	Imm	Arr
Buttenmuller					
(212) 943-0543					
19 Park Place					
Seekamp	Ent 2nd	3,500	Upon Request	Imm	Arr
(212) 943-0543	Ent 3rd	3,500	"as is"	Imm	Arr
2 Hammarskjold Plaza					
(866 Second Ave)					
Seeler/	Pt 4th	1,434	34.00	2/1/82	5 yrs
Goddess	Pt 6th	1,200	32.00	5/1/82	Deal Pending
(212) 840-3200	Ent 7th	6,000	35.00	8/1/82	5 yrs
630 Third Ave	Pt 21st	3,600	31.00	Imm	Lease Pending
Nager		approx.			
(212) 840-3200					
800 Third Ave	Pt 36th	2,905	48.00	3/9/82	6/30/86
Hoffman/	Pt 36th*	2,760	48.00	7/1/82	6/30/86
Sealy	Pt 36th	1,111	48.00	7/1/82	6/30/86
(212) 840-3200					

*This unit may be available as early as 4/1/82

Many prominent owners, Olympia & York among them, maintain friendly relationships with the brokerage community in spite of their refusal to award agencies.

"We have a professional in-house leasing department

that we think gives us the best, most cost-efficient system for renting our properties," says O & Y's Ed Minskoff. "But we invite brokers in to see our buildings, we hold previews for them, and we cheerfully pay commissions when they bring us tenants. We just prefer not to give out agencies."

O & Y's stance, while it does not please brokers, is considered acceptable. Any damage to their pride is soothed by the balm of the multimillion-dollar commissions O & Y pays out in the course of a year. "In most cases, those who refuse to grant agencies don't do so because of the override," Siegel says. "Instead, it's because they believe the other brokers in town will not be motivated to give the property their best shot. The overrides really don't amount to much when you realize that the cost of carrying a million-square-foot building for a month or two is greater than the amount you'd have to pay out in overrides."

John White, chairman of Landauer Associates, makes these instructive comments about broker selection and compensation:

> The exclusive renting agent or consultant is an important member of the development team. His leasing skills and knowledge of tenant prospects are critical to the project's success. Most developers select an agency or consulting firm to be responsible for rentals, although some developers believe in direct employment of renting personnel. Developers considering agencies or consulting companies find it easy to identify those with a proven record of success. It is also easy to discover which agencies have the depth of staff that is essential to success. All too frequently, the powerful personality of the agency head is not sufficiently backed up by a proficient staff. Thus, the wise developer interviews all those who will be involved in the rental effort. Another factor that the developer must consider when rating candidates for rental agent is the number of competitive buildings that an agency may be simultaneously renting. Problems of overextension of staff and conflicts of interest must be

avoided. It is sometimes rewarding to select a younger or lesser known agency that will exert an extra effort and that has no conflicts. However, such an agency is likely to have fewer high-level tenant contacts than an experienced agency. The choice is never an easy one.

An exclusive rental agency agreement can specify that commissions will be paid on one of two bases:

- The rental agent may merely be authorized to split commissions with an outside broker who concludes a lease transaction.
- If an outside broker negotiates the lease, that broker receives a full commission on the transaction, while the rental agent receives an override commission (usually one-half of the full commission). This arrangement is much to be preferred in a competitive market. It gives extra motivation to brokers and enhances the project's rental prospects.*

"Experienced developers award agencies only to those brokers who view their contractual guarantee as the basis for a total commitment to the marketing effort," Steve Siegel says. "When developers name us as their agency, they don't want to hear excuses about market conditions or any such thing. They've hired us to lease all the space in that building and they expect us to get it done.

"That's where the broker pays his dues for gaining the agency. Should a downturn in the economy or a sudden glut of space jeopardize the leasing effort, even the most successful developers can come apart at the seams. They are bundles of nervous energy—as anyone would be with millions of dollars riding on every project. Should they have reason to fear, or even suspect that they have reason to fear, they bring their anxieties to their brokers. I can tell you that's very trying.

"Because agencies are so taxing, well-managed broker-

* "How to Plan and Build a Major Office Building," in *Real Estate Review*, Spring 1980. Reprinted by permission.

age firms put a limit on the number of exclusives they'll pursue. I say this as someone who had to learn this the hard way. Early in my career, when I was working in the field as a Cushman & Wakefield branch manager, I competed very aggressively for agencies, using the guaranteed business they brought to substantially increase my office's commissions. But this growth-at-any-price policy can lead to trouble. For each agency you land, you need a competent executive to be in charge, to serve as a liaison with the developer.

"Should you be too successful in locking up agencies— should your level of business commitments extend beyond your internal organizational capabilities—you can have more agencies than your office can manage effectively. When I found myself personally responsible for six or eight agencies, I had to admit that I was spending too much time fielding frantic phone calls. There weren't enough hours in the day for policy making, for my branch management duties. So I decided, whenever we were in danger of getting ahead of ourselves, to call for a moratorium on new agencies until we expanded our staff to the point that responsible executives were available to share the workload."

Siegel's picture of the hand-wringing developer obsessed with his property's leasing performance is an accurate portrayal. Developers are mildly schizoid. One personality component, that of the visionary entrepreneur, is balanced by a Dickensian detail man who appears blind to the massive tower that rises from the ground in his name. Convinced that prospective tenants judge the building's surface appointments rather than its superstructure, he fusses endlessly on the choice of carpeting, interior color schemes, and lighting fixtures.

Accompanying Howard Ronson on a tour of Tower 56 during its midconstruction phase, a visitor is taken by the developer's lack of interest in the structure itself—in the grand fusion of men and materials that shapes his urban Sphinx. Instead, he fiddles with the individual control units on a fifth-floor air-conditioner.

"I think corporate executives will like this touch, don't you?"

His visitor seems unimpressed.

"You don't? Come now. Each executive will be able to set the temperature in his office at any time of the day. He won't be subject to a central control. I wish I could show you how it works but unfortunately there's no electrical current here yet . . ."

"Let's move on, Howard."

Ronson crouches to the damp concrete floor, still fussing with the dials.

"I think this will be a super selling point. Now that I've explained how it works, don't you agree? I have to remember to discuss this again with the boys at Jones Lang. I want to be absolutely certain that this is stressed in the leasing promotion."

Clearly, Ronson has strong ideas about what will make his building attractive to tenants. That's until the space proves slow to rent. And he recognizes that a new approach is in order. The broker will hear from his agency client far more often than he would like. It goes with the turf.

Well-managed brokers aim for a mix of clients that includes development companies (i.e., Olympia & York), corporate tenants, and independent developers. This balanced roster multiplies the marketing opportunities, smooths the cyclical patterns that can make real estate brokerage a precarious business, and complements the broker's role as a real estate catalyst. By actively pursuing developers, landlords, attorneys, bankers, and tenants for sales leads, the broker picks up bits and pieces of information on available properties, corporate space requirements, urban renewal plans, zoning changes, and assemblages that, in the right hands, become the seeds of development deals. The broker who speaks to more people and speaks to them first stands the best chance of preempting his competitors in the marketplace—of selling a sought-after lot on Columbus Avenue or leasing a newly vacated floor in the Sears Tower.

Even the most astute brokers will admit that success in the business is partly a matter of being in the right place at the right time. But they will add, and rightly so, that persistence and hard work vastly improve the broker's chances of claiming the post position when opportunities materialize. Put simply, good brokerage, on the individual level, is a matter of covering the bases sixteen hours a day for six, sometimes seven days a week. For most of this time, the broker is hooked up to his life support system: a four-button touch-tone telephone complete with WATS lines, MCI lines, and automatic redialing.

The pressure is excruciating. As the electronic call tone beep, beeps through the receiver, as the connection is made, and the line rings at Donald Trump's office, the C & W broker wonders nervously if the broker at the next desk or one across town at competitors Edward S. Gordon, Cross & Brown or Jones Lang Wootton hadn't called Trump hours before. Minutes before. Hadn't sewn up the deal while he was exploring a dead end with American Express. For a moment he considers hanging up and dialing a more promising prospect—Prudential's Gordon Clagett—before the others touch bases there too.

But wait. Perhaps the others called Clagett first, thinking it was too late to do business with Trump. The call to Trump, now ringing at the other end, may beat out a Cross & Brown broker on the phone with Clagett. This second-guessing, this knowledge that for every good deal there are a thousand hungry brokers in pursuit, takes its toll. Barry Rollins,* a thirty-seven-year-old Cornell MBA, squints against the daylight that angles through the half-closed Levelors in his cubbyhole office. Chain-smoking Marlboros, lighting up each time the butt in his hand turns to ash, he starts his 8:30 A.M. to 9:30 P.M. workday with an instant breakfast of Tab, the *Wall Street Journal*, and an hour of hot-line calls. Checking in with the administrative partner of a tax law firm rumored to be in search of 50,000 square feet of midtown office space, he senses within a few minutes of idle conversation that the tip is erroneous. Haunted by

* Fictitious name for a practicing New York broker.

the fear that his competitors are making inroads with more promising prospects, he struggles to politely conclude the call.

"When do you think you'll have a clear picture of your needs?" he asks, his left index finger tracing a page-one *Journal* story on a newly released Conference Board survey.

"Good, good. I'll make a note to check with you then." He inches the phone from his ear, only to find that the lawyer is in a talking mood.

"The state of the market? Wish I knew. Real estate's so unpredictable."

Clearly, the lawyer thinks differently.

"That's very interesting," Rollins lies, rolling his bloodshot eyes. "I never thought of tying occupancy projections to Dun & Bradstreet failure reports. You may have something there. Okay, as I said, I'll put a tickler in my calendar to call you, shall we say August first? . . . Fine, fine. It's a date."

Stabbing a call button, he clears a line and dials the next number on his list.

"The phone is a lifeline," Siegel says. "Brokers have to use it to keep in touch with current clients and equally important, to cultivate new relationships. Cold canvassing is a distasteful but terribly important part of the job. In this business more than any other, you can't simply stay in place. Unless you consciously work to move ahead, to gain new clients, you'll fall hopelessly behind.

"You lose clients by attrition, competition, personality conflicts, any number of things you can and sometimes cannot control. Because good brokers are acutely aware of this, they're always forcing themselves to make new contacts.

"It works like this: When I was a branch manager, I'd call a major corporation and ask the receptionist or the personnel office for the name of the executive in charge of real estate. If I was lucky, I'd get the right name and my call would be switched to the appropriate vice president's office. I'd ask his secretary if I could kindly speak with his eminence. Without exaggeration, 99.9 percent of the time she'd say that he was in a meeting. Of course I knew from experience that this was corporate gamesmanship—that the guy was probably in. But who was I to protest. I'd play along, following up the call with a letter officially introducing myself and requesting a meeting to discuss his real estate needs.

"The response? 99.9 percent of the time there'd be no response at all. No return letter. No acknowledgment of any kind. But was I fazed? Not at all. Good brokers can't give up that easily. I'd call again, hoping the letter and the first call had paved the way for a face to face meeting with the VP. So I ask again, 'May I speak with the vice president now?' "

"99.9 percent of the time the smug little secretary coolly responds, 'No, you may not.' But this isn't reason to be discouraged because in real estate brokerage it's not the 99.9 percent that matters. No. It's that one-tenth of a percent of the time when you do get through that is everything. Suddenly, after a zillion calls, the vice president, or the developer or some other sought-after prospect gets on the phone, says, 'Let's make an appointment,' and in an instant that persistence—God bless that persistence—pays off."

Adds Barry Rollins: "For every hundred deals you labor over, you pour your guts into, perhaps one comes to pass— one puts money in your pocket. But it's that one in a hundred that keeps you tethered to the phone for every hour of the day that you know there'll be someone on the other end to answer it.

"This business is not at all like your typical sales job. I know because I've done that kind of work too. Immediately after leaving school, I landed a position selling medical equipment. I stayed with it for five years because it was a good job, because I experienced rapid professional and financial growth and because I closed sales virtually every day. So I always had the satisfaction and the security of a steady income stream.

"The problem is, I soon reached an earnings plateau.

In a good year I could make, at the most, $75,000 and the top guy in the office—the company superstar who was there so long he was part of the furniture—made $110,000. I wasn't satisfied with that kind of ceiling so I turned to brokerage where I'd heard there was absolutely no limit on income potential.

"What happened? In my first three years of leasing space I made less than I'd earned selling microscopes to doctors. One hell of a lot less. Every time I was certain that I had a leasing deal in my grasp, it fell apart or was snapped up by a competitor. In my darkest hour, near the end of my third year, I was days away from closing a 70,000-square-foot lease when the landlord died of a massive stroke and his widow called off the deal. No reason given. Up to that point, I'd made a princely $11,000 for the first nine months of the year. That one big deal would have put me over the top—would have made up for the three dry years I'd put into the business—but it wasn't to be. I thanked God my wife was a practicing attorney. We didn't need the money to eat.

"Still, the disappointment over the one that got away and the growing sense of frustration with my pitiful earnings led me to consider dropping out of the business. After a good deal of soul searching—much of it quite painful, I might add—I decided to give it one more try, setting February as the deadline to make it or bail out. An ulterior motive for staying on board was that the company paid a $1,000 Christmas bonus at the end of January and I wanted to collect that before moving on.

"But thank God, thank God, I didn't need it. Two weeks after the widow axed my big deal, her husband's executor rescinded her order and agreed to the lease. I had my first big commission check coming my way and, even more important, I was on a roll. Within three months, a steady volume of business started coming my way. It seemed that the executor wanted to lease up all the commercial properties in the deceased's estate, rejuvenate their income stream, and sell them off to the highest bidders.

"Partly because he liked the way I worked and partly, I think, because he didn't know anyone else in real estate, he threw all the business my way. In the year I was supposed to be back in the medical supply business, I generated $2.1 million in commissions for myself. That was my record year. I have since broken the million-and-a-half mark twice, and have never dropped below a million.

"Establishing a key contact moves things off center. If you're lucky, the connection leads to a few big deals which in turn gets momentum going in your favor. Your name gets around, you make the real estate columns, you're sought after by the people who, because of their property holdings or their bucks, control major chunks of the market-place. But even with this spontaneous combustion, 90 percent of the deals you work on still evaporate at some point in the negotiations. In one of my million-plus years, I didn't earn a dollar in commissions until after Labor Day. Because you have to make your living on the strength of a couple of big deals, you have to keep working for them nonstop, keep extending your network of contacts. New clients mean new opportunities. Get cocky in this business and you'll go a year or more without making any money.

"When you leave my office, take a look at the fifty or so brokers out there on the main selling floor. I'd say ten will end the year making less than the porters who sweep up the place when they leave. It's the fear that this catastro-phe could befall any one of us, coupled with the positive reinforcement that if things go well we can buy another townhouse or a silver-gray Porsche, that keeps us dialing the numbers, making the calls, pushing, driving, staying up so late and rising so early that it's often a waste of effort to go to bed."

Says Richard Seeler, president of Cross & Brown: "Some property owners and developers take a certain pleasure in complaining about how much money brokers make. But deep within, they know that our success serves their interests as well. The very prospect of earning a substantial sum of

money is what keeps our people working on client assignments when they could be sleeping or sunning somewhere
in the Caribbean.

"We always see an upswing in the use of in-house leasing efforts in strong sellers' markets when every square
foot of space is gobbled up as soon as it is available. But
when the advantage shifts to the buyers, when you have
to go out and comb the market for tenants, many of these
same do-it-themselfers embrace the brokers. They know
there's no more powerful sales force than highly trained
real estate professionals driven by the opportunity to earn
big commissions."

Seeler hardly looks the part of an aggressive sales manager thirsting for ever-greater commissions in the laissez-
faire world of Manhattan brokerage. Rather, his low-key
demeanor more closely resembles that of a precinct desk
captain for the city's police department. His honest, straightforward style differs markedly from his counterparts at
other leading brokerage firms. The man positively refuses
to engage in the competitive carping that sours relationships
between the city's brokers. Although other brokerage CEOs
also claim a profound distaste for petty put-downs, all make
the boilerplate statements about goodwill and professional
integrity and then proceed to take pot shots at their competitors. It goes something like this:

"I don't want to detract from Cross & Brown in any
way, but you're talking about a mediocre firm that is about
as effective in leasing buildings as my eight-year-old son. I
mean, if the kid got on the phone with a thousand prospects,
sooner or later, he'd make a few deals—just by the law of
averages. But he wouldn't be fast, he wouldn't be impressive,
and I think that's a fair characterization of Cross & Brown.

"But as I said, I don't want to say anything bad about
my competitors. If someone wants to work with them, that's
their problem. Some people fly on DC-10s too."

Informed of these barbs, Seeler remains unfazed.

"New York has an inventory of 300 million square feet
of office space to rent plus an additional 100 million in the

immediate suburbs. If I can't make money serving a market of that size, and doing it without putting down others, then I don't belong in this business."

Cross & Brown, one of the nation's largest independent brokers, is a street-smart New York outfit with six offices in the metropolitan area and boutique branches in Connecticut and Florida. Founded in 1910, the firm's long list of interesting deals dates back to 1911 when it leased to Henry Ford a storefront at 1733 Broadway for the city's first automobile dealership.

Today, Cross & Brown's 100-odd brokers handle property sales of $100 million and leases totaling $600 million annually. A fully integrated shop, C & B (like Cushman & Wakefield and Garrick-Aug) nudges its clients into service grids designed to generate additional sources of income and to keep the accounts from establishing ties with competitive brokerage firms. C & B's divisions include property sales and leasing (residential and commercial), building management, construction, insurance, and even office cleaning. Should a C & B client seek the broker's services in acquiring an office building for its investment portfolio, Seeler's associates can structure the deal, manage the property, handle the leasing, alter the space to fit tenant requirements, do maintenance and repairs, and even empty the waste baskets when the staff goes home for the night.

Chief among C & B's auxilliary services is its building management division. In this capacity, the brokerage firm runs clients' buildings in a quasi-ownership capacity, collecting rents, hiring and firing staff, leasing space, tending to maintenance, and maintaining controls on building services.

"When we manage a building, the only thing the owner has to do is deposit his checks—and we give him a check once a week," Seeler says.

Fees for management services average 10 cents per square foot. For a 500,000-square-foot building, the broker (as building manager) collects $50,000 and, equally important, controls the space for sales and leasing. Although the management fee pales in comparison to brokerage commissions, the aggregate fee for a multibuilding contract can climb to more than a half million dollars. This represents bankable revenues that flow to the corporate treasury year after year, thus providing the integrated brokerage firm with a source of steady income to smooth out leasing's cyclical patterns and to provide the capital along with commissions for establishing a corporate infrastructure. This translates into money for computers, staff accountants, engineers and a branch office network.

The latter is of increasing importance. Much like their residential colleagues (Sotheby's, Previews, Merrill Lynch) commercial brokers are moving to replace interstate referrals—the traditional basis for servicing clients nationally—with central marketing organizations. Here the industry giants have a decided advantage. Cash-rich and backed by the Rockefeller resources, C & W has invested millions in building its own branch organization. When a New York–based C & W client needs more clerical staff space for its west coast integrated circuits division, C & W can assign the search to its Los Angeles office, thus keeping the business in-house. But Cross & Brown, basically a New York firm, must refer the search to a Los Angeles broker, hoping to share in the commissions should a deal be made.

C & B's approach is weak on several counts. First, it allows the client to slip out of the broker's grip. Although C & B, as the listing broker, may claim a commission, it has failed to keep the account within its in-house marketing grid. Also, owners and developers are recognizing that a property's market extends beyond its physical setting. A sixty-story office complex on New York's Avenue of the Americas may attract corporate, legal, and accounting tenants from Chicago, Houston, Dallas, San Francisco, and Atlanta. The brokerage firm with an established sales organization in these target markets is most likely to be appointed agency for the property. Previews' founding concept of "the broader the exposure, the easier the sale" is gaining unanimous acceptance in commercial as well as residential real estate.

Aware of its competitive shortcomings as a local broker, Cross & Brown has tried to shore up its position vis-à-vis the nationals by creating a quasi-network of its own, the American Realty Services Group (ARS). This affiliation of twenty-odd brokers services the nation's top commercial markets.

"Because all of the members are leading brokerage firms in their home towns they can send referrals to one another with absolute confidence that clients will be served well anywhere in the U.S.," Seeler says, underlying the organization's founding concept.

"Just this morning I had breakfast with a client whose firm needs additional office space in Dallas. No problem. I'll send him to our ARS affiliate, the Henry S. Miller Company, Dallas's biggest and best commercial broker. This is not, as some may suggest, a makeshift solution. New York brokers with branch offices in Dallas could not hope to serve my client nearly as well as he'll be served by Henry S. Miller. That's because branch offices are not native to the markets they serve. Many are run by transplanted New Yorkers who are still relative neophytes in Dallas, Chicago, or what have you. Not so with the American Realty Services Group. That's why our service is actually superior to that of a centrally owned branch network."

There is a germ of truth to this. Even Steve Siegel admits that a broker's skills are not entirely transferable from one market to another and that it takes three to five years for newly opened branch offices to become proficient in the local community. But it's worth the wait. The control and marketing clout of a branch network far outweigh its failings. One suspects that Seeler is acutely aware of this. As resolutely as he defends ARS, it is all too similar to its residential cousin, the Confederation of International Real Estate. By creating a national organization, ARS members can claim to be on an equal footing with a Cushman & Wakefield. This, it is hoped, will keep the major agencies—those that require a national marketing campaign—from slipping away to the big, multibranch competitors.

But the strategy is not likely to work. Real estate operatives are too shrewd to be hypnotized by an illusion. To continue to compete for national accounts, local brokers will have to make the substantial investment required to open, staff, and promote their own branch offices. But there is an enormous risk here: to justify the investment, the firms must generate a huge volume of incremental business. This is a risk Seeler seems reluctant to take.

Clearly uncomfortable with the subject of national marketing organizations, he shifts the conversation back to his favorite theme of broker incentives.

"Good brokerage, you know, is a matter of securing the top people in the business and giving them unlimited opportunity to make deals and to earn commissions. That's the only way a real estate sales force can function effectively and it's also the only way clients can be properly serviced. Who happens to own the office is not important."

9

The British Invasion:
Jones Lang Wootton
and the Fine Art of Assemblages

When most people hear talk of the "British invasion"
they think of the war of independence or the Beatles.
But I think of something far more important to real
estate brokers—the coming of Jones Lang Wootton.

The executive vice-president
of a Manhattan brokerage firm

Until 1975, Seeler's comments on incentives and commissions were virtually unchallenged throughout the brokerage community. But in May of that year, an iconoclastic force burst on the New York real estate scene, bringing with it a vastly different philosophy of broker performance and rewards. Jones Lang Wootton, Britain's most prestigious real estate consultants, had invaded the States.

Established in 1837, JLW traced its roots to "the profession of the land," a loose-knit fraternity of realty experts assigned to manage the property interests of Britain's landed gentry much as chartered accountants looked after their books. Throughout the nineteenth century, the profession developed a body of rules and accepted procedures culminating in its upgraded status to a certified position, the

"chartered surveyor." The designation, granted by the Royal
Institution of Chartered Surveyors, is defined as one whose
basic expertise is "the assessment of what an interest in
property is worth at a particular time. This may be in connection with the purchase, sale, letting, investment, rating, insurance, compensation, or taxation. He may also be involved
with Estate Agency—the negotiation for sale or purchase,
leasing, or auction of all types of property—and Estate Management—the management and maintenance of residential,
commercial, and industrial property acting on behalf of both
landlord and tenant."

Although the nature of property holdings has changed
dramatically over the years, chartered surveyors have retained their position as the preeminent managers of real
estate in the United Kingdom. From their origins in service
to royalty to their current assignments on behalf of English
developers and investors, they have remained influential and
indispensable guardians of British real estate interests.
JLW, a firm of chartered surveyors,* describes the profession's evolution this way:

> Reward through the grant of lands brought riches, privi-
> lege, and power to those in the service of former mon-
> archs. The great urban estates arose from the fields
> and forests and around growing towns—fields, forests,
> and towns alike owned often by only one family on whom
> whole populations depended for their livelihoods and
> prosperity. The estates were extensive and, although
> many remained rural and virtually unexploited, others
> were developed to meet the demands of the day—some-
> times for those only slightly less privileged and powerful
> than the landowners themselves; sometimes for the arti-
> sans and laborers who worked the mills and factories
> established in those areas rich in natural resources.

> The Church and the monasteries had held land and
> power on a massive scale. Equally, during the industrial
> revolution, the mill and mine owners built not only facto-

* This designation is limited to JLW's UK partners.

ries but also the streets of small, cramped homes to
house their workers attracted from the farms and vil-
lages. Rent and rich barons became pantomime jokes—
and the myth of the grasping, evil landlord has, in its
way, affected the course of political history.

But whoever the owners were—the dukes, the mill owners, the Church—their lands and buildings had to be
managed and maintained, the extent of their holdings
set on plans, new buildings erected, estate workers employed and paid. And so surveyors, concerned with good
husbandry of property whether urban or rural, developed skills in the service of the great estates.

Surveyors still offer that service even though society
has changed and, although the fabric of many of the
great estates remains, ownership has passed in many
cases to the state, to local authorities and to the major
financial institutions such as pension funds and insurance companies.*

In flanking British property interests as they marched
across the globe, Jones Lang experienced dramatic growth,
establishing a presence in Dublin, Brussels, Antwerp, Paris,
Amsterdam, Rotterdam, Frankfurt, Hamburg, Sydney, Can-
berra City, Melbourne, Perth, Hong Kong, Singapore, and
Kuala Lumpur. But its most astounding success came nearly
a century and a half after its founding, with the opening
of its Manhattan office, launched in recognition of New
York's emergence as the world financial center.

"In 1974, Jones Lang Wootton's London headquarters
dispatched a young partner to survey the American market,
with an eye toward determining if a chartered surveyor
would be accepted here," says James Austrian. "Upon his
return, he wrote a bullish report, recommending that management should indeed open a New York office. Soon after,
I was recruited from Landauer Associates to start up the

* "Progress in Property," Jones Lang Wootton, May 1979. Reprinted
by permission.

new venture. Partly because of timing and partly because we were offering something different, we grew rapidly from two professionals and a secretary, to more than 140 people."

JLW differs most dramatically from native New York brokers in that it brings to Manhattan real estate a proper British respect for tradition and a more pristine definition of professionalism. As the man in charge, Jim Austrian is the personification of the JLW style. A slightly built fellow given to nondescript gray wool suits and wire-rim glasses, he appears to be genuinely proud not only of his company's explosive growth but equally of the methods it has employed to achieve it.

"We are the only major brokerage firm in the city that does not pay its employees brokerage commissions. Every single person in this firm, yours truly included, is compensated on a salary basis. That factor alone is why we believe that hiring Jones Lang Wootton is a more propitious decision than hiring one of our competitors.

"Why, you may ask, should clients care how we pay our people? How does this affect the leasing of buildings, the sale of properties? Although there are a number of complex issues involved here—including questions of human behavior and professional conduct—for the sake of simplicity we can say that it boils down to the difference between working with a team and working with individuals."

Austrian's contention is that by compensating Jones Lang staffers on a salaried basis rather than as commissioned sales people,* he replaces the "lock your Rolodex" syndrome that is endemic at standard brokerage firms with an atmosphere of staff cooperation and teamwork. To Austrian's way of thinking, standard brokers are not business firms in the traditional sense but rather collections of sales people assembled under one roof to do similar work often with conflicting personal objectives.

"The commission system is onerous and counterproduc-

---

* Although JLW earns commissions on property sales, the broker responsible for the transaction does not earn a piece of the deal. The revenues are shared by the partners in salary, bonuses and profit-sharing.

tive to the client's best interests because it forces the brokerage firm's sales associates to compete with one another
rather than to pool their talents and experience in pursuit
of common goals.

"At our firm, when a person has to go to the bathroom,
he tells, I repeat, he *tells* his colleagues where to find the
Rolodex. If a client calls in his absence, the JLW executive
wants his associates to have access to all the information
they'll need to properly help that client. When there's no
fear of losing a commission to the person at the next desk,
the staff's energies are directed at servicing the account
in the most professional manner rather than at protecting
themselves from each other. Each client gains the experience
and the perspective of numerous experts rather than the
jealously guarded advice of a single salesman."

Talk like this makes Austrian's competitors seethe.
Much the way native New York developers resent Howard
Ronson's successful foray into what they percieve as their
protectorate, local brokers are teed off that this other British
interloper has stolen some of their thunder.

"Look, this professional surveyor crap is just so much
nonsense, English style," snaps Steve Siegel. "We're all professionals—successful brokers have to be professionals in
every sense of the word. That means knowing your market,
knowing your clients, knowing a hell of a lot about property
values and financing. But we don't think that knowledge
alone is enough. After all, this isn't academia and brokers
aren't in business to collect doctorates. Our objective, every
broker's objective, is to lease up buildings on schedule, to
find tenants even when the market's saturated with new
construction, to ferret out buyers when everyone seems to
want only to sell. Well, let me tell you, that takes incentive
as well as know-how and paying healthy commissions is the
only way to get the kind of incentive that keeps people working nonstop on dozens of deals until their objectives are
secured. Jones Lang Wootton's concept makes for nice advertising copy but it doesn't work. Granted they've been
party to some substantial transactions but they owe that

to their parent company's connections with British banks and pension funds. The New York operation has managed to get a lot of undeserved press attention simply by inheriting business that's already in the family and therefore unavailable to other brokers.

"Let me add that their one-time grip on Ronson's properties has been loosened. We've now gained some of the agencies—including the building at 45 Broadway Atrium—that at one time would have gone automatically to them."

JLW's competitors carp that the firm's salary levels—$40,000 to $60,000 for young associates and $100,000 to $200,000 for partners—are low compared to the earnings of commissioned brokers of equal experience and stature. This, they say, prompts the heavy hitter producers to abandon JLW's conviviality for the crass commercialism of a commission house.

"The best people in this business can work wherever they choose," Siegel adds. "Everyone competes for their services. So why would a superachiever accept an artifical cap on his earnings when he could cross the street to Cushman & Wakefield and virtually write his own check? I don't care what business you're in: the universal rule is that the best people want—let me say demand—the best compensation. This is especially true in real estate."

Yes and no. Although JLW's salaried-teamwork system seems to run counter to real estate's entrepreneurial spirit, the difference is that brokers are not in the real estate business. Like the lawyers that argue zoning appeals and the CPAs that structure cash flow statements, brokers provide services to real estate's genuine articles, the landlords and developers. Those brokers imbued with a sense of professionalism are not driven to careen from firm to firm in search of the biggest pay-off. This in spite of the fact that they do their jobs as well as or better than those tied to six-figure commissions.

Jim Austrian is the pluperfect example. Were he self-employed, were he entitled to share in the deals he engineers, his income would grow exponentially. But the man thor-

oughly enjoys his role as a real estate professional carrying
on the traditions of a venerable firm. Interviews with JLW
clients, with New York bankers, and with institutional joint
venturers who have dealt with Austrian indicate that he is
widely respected as a savvy deal maker and a tenacious
guardian of his clients' interests.

"While others in his capacity cruise around town in Mercedes limousines, usually arriving on the scene of a lucrative
deal the day after the best opportunity has come and gone,
Austrian just seems to materialize when the buyer or seller
is most vulnerable to accepting his clients' terms," says a
bank vice president who asked to remain anonymous because
"In this business, you can get in hot water for revealing
whom you admire as well as whom you detest. I must say
that Austrian, in his own understated way, accomplishes
more than any other real estate adviser I've ever worked
with."

Austrian's prominence is due, in equal measure, to his
successful introduction of JLW's teamwork approach in the
United States and to his personal skills as a real estate catalyst. Specifically, he is a leading practitioner of assemblages,
an arcane real estate procedure that is at the very heart
of commercial development. Put simply, assemblers piece
together—often at enormous cost—the dozens of pre-exist-
ing property rights developers must acquire before com-
mencing construction on a parcel of land. In a mature real
estate market, where virtually every site is encumbered with
a maze of ownership interests—developers cannot proceed
without the assembler's services.

Should Olympia & York decide that a corner at midtown
and Third Avenue is ideal for a speculative office building,
their first prerequisite is to buy the property. The problem
is, on any segment of a typical New York block there is
likely to be a hodgepodge of standing structures—say, two
coffee shops, an apartment house, a brownstone, a sushi
bar, and a prewar six-story office building—each owned by
a landlord (corporate or individual) whose title to the property (the so-called "fee interest") must be purchased. Sur-

prisingly, were this the only obstacle, the assembler's job would be relatively easy. Real estate brokers and consultants experienced at this Byzantine process claim that land owners are generally reasonable, business-minded real estate professionals. Make them an offer that reflects current market values and a fair return on their invested capital and, with a bit of bargaining, they'll often accept the deal without questioning the buyer's motives.

But even if every owner at midtown and Third falls easily in line, agreeing to sell his property rights for a fair price, O & Y is still enjoined from building on the site. That's because for every fee interest they acquire, there may be ten, twenty, or perhaps one hundred tenants holding valid leases granting them the right to live or conduct business in the apartment house, the coffee shop, or the sushi bar the owner is willing to sell.

Before the developer can break ground, he must acquire these so-called "leasehold interests." Should he fail to accomplish this—should a tenant refuse to budge at any price— he would be forced to abandon his plans for the site. The assembler—whose ultimate responsibility it is to prevent this—may have to resort to bribery, threats, cajolery, bluffs, intimidation, and, if all else fails, total capitulation to the tenants's demands.

"An assemblage is very much like a jigsaw puzzle, not only because of the obvious parallel of fitting together intricate elements, but also because the finished picture only emerges fully when the last piece is put in place," Austrian explains. "To carry the metaphor even further out, I have an image of a puzzle of the Mona Lisa with the key piece missing right from the middle of that famous enigmatic smile. That's certainly no work of art—but put in the missing piece and you've really got something."

Austrian's puzzle analogy refers to the fact that a partially completed assemblage—even if the missing sliver of property accounts for less than one percent of the desired building site—may be useless to the developer and may represent millions of dollars of partially unrecoverable acquisition costs. In this case, the assembler has failed on two levels: in his attempt to achieve the immediate objective and in his role as a catalyst for the real estate development.

That commercial tenants are often to blame for this failure is attributable to greed and to the free market mechanism of supply and demand. Should a merchant discover that a store he leases is square in the middle of a building sought after as part of a major assemblage, he learns—or is so advised by his attorney—that he is in the driver's seat, blessed by timing and coincidence with the chance to make a killing. The way to do that becomes clear: to hold out. To refuse to make a deal until the assembler—acting for the developer—comes up with an offer (some call it a bribe) big enough to make the tenant rich for life and thus to clear the way for the sixty-three-story steel and glass behemoth that will rise from the ground where his newsstand barely eeked out a profit for the preceding decade.

This scenario, damaging as it may be to the developer's preliminary budget, is still considered a successful assemblage. The real nightmare is when a diehard holdout defies the collective wisdom that "everyone has his price," and refuses—for business or personal reasons—to budge from the site for as much as a blank check. Experienced developers anticipate this threat and try to minimize its impact by designing a dozen or more architectural configurations on the proposed site, some accounting for a totally successful assemblage, others reducing the size of the building in the event that an outlying parcel cannot be acquired.

Armed with these blueprints, the assembler can develop intelligent strategies for dealing with holdouts because he knows the minimum tract of property that will allow for a feasible development and which parcels can be sacrificied while still permitting a scaled-down design. But he is powerless when an immovable force occupies a strategic position—one integral to all of the various architectural configurations. This intransigence may be enough to kill the deal.

Austrian ran smack into a roadblock of this sort in the course of his ill-fated assemblage for the bluest of New

York's blue chip banks, Morgan Guaranty. The case is interesting in that a world-class financial institution committed to spending $40 million to assemble a desired parcel was brought to its knees by a lone holdout. But the real shocker is that the cantankerous party turned out to be the City of New York. The rewards of assemblage brinksmanship are so great that even bureaucrats are tempted to play the game. In this case, everyone lost. The story begins with Morgan's plans to consolidate its New York employees in a proposed $250 million skyscraper on a two-acre site near the New York Stock Exchange. Austrian, hired to conduct the assemblage, immediately established a hit list of six major buildings which, were they not acquired, could jeopardize the entire project. The challenge was complicated by the fact that three of the buildings were owned by some of Manhattan's shrewdest real estate operatives: Sol Goldman, one-time owner of New York's Chrysler Building; Joseph Wohl, a major collector of apartment buildings; Harry Helmsley and Lawrence Wein, partners in the Empire State Building (Helmsley is now best known to the public for the hotel group his second wife runs under the family banner).

But Austrian found that luck was on his side as he set out to negotiate for the fee interests. The timing of the assemblage dovetailed with the recession that had plagued lower Manhattan properties since the early 1970s. When Austrian set out to make his purchases (in 1979), building owners were delighted to find that buyers were back in the market.

> Within two weeks, Austrian had a contract to buy the Wohl building for $6.8 million. Wohl, who died a few months later, apparently thought the purchaser wanted to move into a big chunk of space about to be vacated by a law firm. The negotiations with Goldman were handled over the phone in less than two weeks, concluding in a sale price of $2.7 million. Goldman, pleased with the deal, never even asked the broker to identify the buyer.

Striking the deal with Helmsley and with Wein proved stickier. The biggest tenant, Paine Webber, had been planning to break its lease and move to the World Trade Center in 1981. Suddenly, in the midst of Helmsley's negotiations with Austrian's man, the World Trade Center deal fell through and Paine Webber asked Helmsley for a new, long-term lease that would have cost Austrian millions extra to buy out, and might have wrecked the assemblage. Shrewdly using the Paine Webber offer to put the pressure on, Helmsley called one afternoon to say, "I'm meeting with Paine Webber at three. Do we have a deal?" Austrian sent his broker over to Helmsley's office with a letter offering $19 million. Helmsley shook the broker's hand on the deal, then said no to Paine Webber.

The contract with Helmsley and Wein still had to be submitted for approval to 350 limited partners. Austrian suffered through what he describes as "two months of sweat." If Goldman or Wohl happened to be among the partners, a distinct possibility in the intertwined world of Manhattan real estate, they would obviously realize that an assemblage was in process. To Austrian's relief, neither man was part of the Helmsley group, and the contract was ratified.*

But a hitch developed with the Goldman property. Because he owed $1.7 million in back taxes, the city had taken title to the building through a so-called "in rem" proceeding. This was not the first time a Goldman property was foreclosed in this way. In the past, the owner could redeem his holdings simply by paying the back taxes. But this time City Hall refused to capitulate. Using the Goldman case as a warning to other delinquent taxpayers, the city foreclosed on the property permanently. Suddenly, a new owner was in the picture—a municipal government—and this presented

* Shawn Tully, in *Fortune* magazine, "The Block That Got Away," July 13, 1981, pg. 45.

a far more difficult challenge than Austrian could have imagined.

Thinking that the mayor's office would be delighted to have a new office complex generating $15 million a year in tax revenues, Austrian decided to level with city officials, revealing that the property was sought as part of an assemblage. Soon after, a Morgan executive sat down to negotiate directly with the city's General Services Department, offering $2 million for the former Goldman property.

The question was: would civil servants (read "rubes") take the measly offer, a full $700,000 less than the Goldman deal? Not exactly. Using a crafty negotiating ploy of its own, the city indicated that the property was ideal for government offices and threatened to use it for that purpose unless, of course, Morgan would pay the new asking price: $17 million. Austrian and his banker clients were stunned. What they failed to anticipate was the Koch administration's determination to end the two-centuries-old practice of making sweetheart real estate deals for political purposes and to begin using the city's most valuable asset (real estate) to help speed its financial recovery. In a speech to Columbia University's Law School commencement of 1981, Koch told the story of an abandoned public school the city had put on the market for sale to private buyers. When a religious group offered several hundred thousand dollars, Koch politely indicated that he was no fool and hung up the phone. Minutes later the religious leader called back, this time boosting his offer to several million dollars.

Koch's message was clear: give notice that the city refuses to be a pushover for special interests and petty offers will swiftly mushroom into respectable sums. The tough offense appeared to work. After a few months of bitching and moaning about the city's asking price, Morgan came back with a nonbinding bid of $11,750,000. But the deal fell apart shortly thereafter. Morgan, having second thoughts, withdrew its offer, informing Austrian that the assemblage was not to be. Acting for the bank, Jones Lang Wootton sold the two buildings acquired at the outset of the assemblage to Olympia & York and collected $2 million in fees for their sales, acquisitions and management services. A respectable paycheck, to be sure, but nothing compared to the sum JLW would have earned had a completed assemblage served as a catalyst for a major building to be leased and managed for years.*

The lesson to be learned from the Morgan fiasco is to keep assemblages secret for as long as possible, thereby reducing the threat of holdouts and slashing to one-tenth the amount of money assemblers must expend to acquire fee and tenant interests.

To keep their missions under wraps, assemblers often pose as garden-variety brokers, casually interested in acquiring property rights for third-party occupants. Denied the tempting specter of a cash-rich corporation turning out its pockets to complete an assemblage, owners and tenants are more reasonable in their demands.

"One of the proven tactics of the assembler is to treat each transaction separately, going to great extremes to disguise from each seller (or tenant) the fact that the buyer, in each case, is indeed the assembler himself," Austrian explains. "This is much easier than it may seem at first, but like everything else in assemblage, it does require careful planning."

In dealing with the initial owners in the Morgan assemblage, Austrian explains, "three distinct corporate identities were created, each with different officers, expressed purposes, identities, addresses, lawyers, and agents. In one case, the stationery read 'Robnuncyn Land Co., Inc. . . . Diversified Investments for the Housing and Hospitality Industries' . . . to support the notion that the company wished to acquire the obsolete office property for possible conversion to condominium housing and a ground-floor restaurant. It also permitted easy written communications with the only remaining tenants: both restaurants . . .

* The city subsequently auctioned the property in 1983 for $13.15 million—a record price for a New York parcel sold at public auction. The buyer was Trans World Equities, a real estate concern.

"The easiest situation would involve a single owner/ occupant or at least a single-user building. In putting together the site that now houses the AT&T World headquarters on Madison Avenue, I confronted a small building occupied entirely by an upmarket ladies' wear designer. We sent a broker confidant to see the local agent for the property with the advice that the assembler (a consultant) had clients from Europe and he—the agent—had a feeling the ultimate occupier was a French coutourier starting out in the U.S. Coincidentally, an item reporting just such a thing appeared in a local gossip column at the time purchase negotiations were heating up." The biggest risk of assemblage—the ransom that must often be paid when an owner or tenant sniffs out what is really happening—is balanced by what are affectionately known as the windfalls. "Windfalls are those deals that simply fall into your lap," Austrian continues. "Many windfalls cannot be predicted but others can. I am referring to certain classes of seller or tenant whose interests almost by definition can be acquired at a perfectly reasonable price. In these cases, the tenant, or owner, either has no idea of the value of his interests to you, or as in the case of a tenant, his leasehold is not his most valuable asset. Often, tenants are ready to retire, really want to relocate (sometimes they are even in the process of relocating) or simply recognize they are not in the business of selling leaseholds.

"A good example of the latter circumstances occurred on East Forty-eighth Street with a national chain shoe store. I went directly to the president of the company in Massachusetts, told him exactly what I wanted to do, promised we would pay him all of a completely fair consideration, and promised that if he figured all of his out-of-pocket expenses for relocating to comparable space, we would simply pay it without haggling. He did, we did, and to this day I am confident it was a fair and acceptable deal for both parties.

"A windfall situation can often be created by purchasing the business. The lease just comes along as part of the assets. This may take a bit of role-playing but the rewards can be great. It helps to have many personal friends in disparate businesses who enjoy the occasional theatrics of an assemblage. So far, my friends and I have run restaurants, saloons, hardware and leather-goods stores, a messenger service, and a photostat business.

"In each of those cases, the cost of the entire business, including operating losses, was substantially less than the likely cost of buying up the leasehold. Again, deals of this sort are only feasible in those halcyon days of an assemblage when you can luxuriate in secrecy. Once the news gets out, the strategy takes a dramatic turn.

"My last restaurant fling worked out exceptionally well, and with an ironic twist which, I think, carries with it some message about fair dealing. On a Fifty-second Street assemblage, the existing coffee shop operator assigned his lease to two young Greek entrepreneurs, just starting out, who naively overlooked a demolition/termination clause in their lease. They no sooner got their restaurant in gear when the owner, a contract vendor to us, delivered the sixty-day termination notice. The new owners were horrified. They learned of the pending sale and came to us hat in hand to see if they could stay open long enough to stay alive while they looked for another location.

"Luck was with all of us because I had just begun an assemblage across from Saks Fifth Avenue and needed to acquire the Kenby Coffee Shop which was sitting in the middle of the site with a lease running until May 31, 1990. Also, we felt genuine sympathy for the plight of the assignees.

"Basically what we were able to do, in effect, was to arrange for the misfortunate young fellows from Fifty-second Street to buy the Kenby business and immediately operate it profitably for the six or eight months remaining while we completed the assemblage. They made a strong profit without any real investment: the seller of Kenby got a fair price for his business and we bought the ten-year lease for a song."

But the real beauty of the business/purchase ploy is that "By keeping Kenby open under new management, we carried on for months the illusion that no assemblage or demolition plan could possibly be underway. We saved a million dollars on the cost of the Forty-eighth Street assemblage through this combination of circumstances."

Austrian flashes the sly, toothy grin of a schoolboy who has managed to pirate a copy of the final exam and to score an A on the test. He clearly delights in outfoxing the marketplace. But he is also quick to point out that for all of their cloak-and-dagger techniques, their theatrical trappings, assemblages are carefully engineered business strategies.

Although the process gets most attention in the major metropolitan cities where the size and the complexity of the deals make them more interesting, the ability to conduct successful assemblages is crucial to developers and brokers (acting as real estate catalysts) in towns where the tallest structure tops out at three stories. Acquiring a used-car lot and a general store from a site designated for a new grain elevator demands much the same principles as ousting two dozen tenants from a prewar building on Chicago's Loop. Austrian's techniques can be applied to virtually all assemblages. Consider his advice:

The order in which to attack the fee and leasehold rights is as follows:

1. Tie up the land parcels with the longest reasonable contract terms;
2. Negotiate with the potential spoilers and windfalls;
3. Negotiate lease terminations with the longest-term tenants;
4. And then grind it out with all the rest.

When grinding it out, approach each tenant offering to relocate him (without revealing that an assemblage is in progress) according to the following terms:

- Indemnification of any out-of-pocket expenses created by the relocation;

- Relocation to better accommodations than he is leaving;
- Help in making it a hassle-free and painless relocation;
- The promise that there will be some real money in his pocket at the end of the day.

The major items to be calculated carefully and realistically (better to be on the side of generosity) are:

1. Rent differential: compare the tenant's current monthly rental with market rentals for similar or even better space of at least the same area—or slightly larger—available in the marketplace.

   Multiply the differential by the number of months remaining on the existing lease, starting with the first realistic date the tenant could occupy the new space.

   The arithmetic in a typical realistic situation might look like this:

   - New rent, monthly, for 4,000 square feet of office space at $27 per square foot per annum. This equals $9,000 (monthly figure).
   - Existing rent: 3,800 square feet at $7 per square foot per annum, given monthly: $2217.
   - Monthly rent differential equals ($9000 − $2217 =) $6783.
   - Number of months, say, 17.
   - Rent differential: $6783 × 17 = $115,311.

2. The budget for improving new space is a function of the business being relocated at the standard acceptable to the specific tenant. For this exercise, let's establish that number at $35 per square foot, or $140,000 total.

3. An experienced removal company is a good friend in this business. In exchange for loyalty, they make prompt, accurate estimates and provide excellent service. Assuming this hypothetical tenant runs an uncomplicated business which requires the relocation of basic furniture, decor, files, office machines and the like, we may get an estimate of, say, $4,000.

4. Do not overlook elaborate safes, alarm systems, computer equipment, photo editing gear, and recording equipment. These can present highly specialized, expensive moves involving highly technical rigging and installation. In the subject case, assume this tenant, an advertising agency, uses one very sophisticated and delicate videotape editor/ splicer. Shutting that down, dismantling it, moving it, reassembling it, aligning it, fine-tuning it, testing it, and finally putting it back in service could be an extra $5,000 bill.

5. Ancillary business expenses encompass such items as reprinting all stationery and business forms, sending out removal notices to customers, relocating the telephones, legal fees and all the little extras that no one thinks of in advance. Let's use $6,000 for these extra items.

6. Often I will intentionally omit any consideration of business losses in preparing a budget because a very well planned and coordinated relocation should obviate the risk. However, especially in the case of a retail business, some losses may reasonably be contemplated—and those must be entered into the equation. (Caution: agree to a loss of net profit, not of gross sales).

7. The "pocket money" estimate should bear some relationship to the sum of the actual reimbursables, so let's add those together to see where we stand in this example:

Rent differential	$115,311
Leasehold improvements	140,000
Removal	4,000
Special removal	5,000
Ancillary business expenses	6,000
Business loss	0
Total of reimbursable expenses	$270,311

"I would say the first stab at a total budget to induce this ad agency to give up their lease a year and a half early, under prevailing market conditions, should be $370,000 or $100,000 over the actual expenses that may be faced by the tenant."

A deal? Not necessarily. As we have seen, the rub in assembling is that a perfectly fair settlement may not motivate a tenant to move. As clear and rational as Austrian's budgetary exercise may be, it carries no legal weight, no power to force the party to relocate. The essential fact of every assemblage is that the tenants are being asked to move against their will. Even if they know nothing of the art of assemblages, they may know much about the meaning of raw power. Austrian has seen it many times.

"Often, after going through the entire analysis with a tenant, in great detail, he will turn to me and say, 'That $370,000 sounds real great at first blush, Jim, but I am lucky enough to be holding all the cards in this game; I was planning to stay here for the rest of my business life. I like it here and I've been associated with this spot for twenty-seven years. I see you'll pay the seventeen-month rent difference but what happens in the eighteenth month and forever after?'

" 'No thanks Jim, much as I respect and admire your straightforward approach and your client's limited resources, I'll just stay right here for another year and a half. That is, unless you will just put a million tax-free dollars in my pocket right now—in which case I'll be out of here and you'll have the keys by the weekend.' "

End of discussions? Again, not necessarily. The assembler/broker, in his role as real estate catalyst, is driven to consummate a deal. He must rationalize payment of the bribe, finding some way to convince the developer to put up the money. The problem here, Austrian admits, is not as much economics as the very psychology of the land rush.

"My experience has proved repeatedly that office developments in my marketplace can always afford to come up with the bit extra necessary to pay that outrageous, despicable, greedy demand of the heartless holdout who would dare to leave his grubby little saloon smack in the middle of your gorgeous plaza fountain display. What the developers really regret is not the audacity of the holdout, as much as the fact that they themselves weren't so lucky as to hold a ten-year lease on the most essential square foot of land in the middle of someone else's assemblage."

10

The Building That Saved
an Airline

Ninety percent of all millionaires became so through
owning real estate. More money has been made in real
estate than in all industrial investments combined.

Andrew Carnegie

Tales of million-dollar holdouts—of billion-dollar blocks—reduces real estate to a string of zeros across the face of a
Texas Instruments calculator. But this can be misleading,
for real estate—unlike paper assets that ebb and flow with
every change in the Dow Jones Averages—is a physical asset
of enduring value. But how do we put that value in perspective? How do we take the full measure of its worth? How
do we grasp the magnitude of the land rush? How do we
give meaning to the string of zeros?

One approach is to relate the numbers to something
tangible. For starters, imagine, if you will, Pan American
World Airways. Flag carrier of the United States.

Nonstop flights from 48 U.S. cities to 66 cities in 50 countries spanning the globe. 143 jetliners, 27,600 employees, and a world famous corporate headquarters, the Pan Am Building on New York's Park Avenue.

On the face of it, Pan Am appears to be a thriving multinational corporation rich in reputation, experience, and corporate assets. But this exotic image—the product of a Mary Wells–inspired advertising campaign that recreates the airline's former glories—conceals the fact that this is one wounded bird. Among the worst performers in the lackluster U.S. airline industry, Pan Am has suffered through nearly a decade of fiscal turbulence, brought on by soaring debt service (incurred to purchase a new generation of planes), OPEC-driven fuel costs, and destructive fare wars. The subject of numerous bankruptcy rumors that swirl, several times a year, through Wall Street's investment banking firms, Pan Am has managed to avert its closest brushes with disaster by selling off its most valuable assets. Not the prized routes, the offices in London or Copenhagen. To survive—to come through its bleakest hours—Pan Am has sold real estate.

It had no other choice. When everything else went sour the value of the Pan Am Building—the company's major real estate holding—exceeded the sum total of the corporation's shares on the New York Stock Exchange. To the world, Pan Am was an airline with a side interest in real estate. To its top management—and to a small circle of financial analysts—the reverse was true.

"In the mid to late 70s, Pan Am's senior executives found themselves faced with a tight cash squeeze and pessimistic near-term revenue projections," says a Wall Street analyst and long-time Pan Am watcher who asked that his identity be concealed. "They didn't have to be Bernard Baruchs to know the implications of that. Either Pan Am took some drastic actions to pump cash into the corporate cockpit or its days as an airline were numbered. It was then that they decided to play their only card: to sell the Pan Am Building."

When Pan Am's board of directors—faced as it was
with few options—voted its approval, Jim Maloon, the airline's executive vice president and chief financial officer,
hired Landauer Associates to handle the sale. A real estate
consulting firm, Landauer is more or less a home-grown
version of Jones Lang Wootton. Much as JLW has prospered
in service to Britain's blue-chip institutions, Landauer has
cultivated an unchallenged position as the premier real estate adviser to America's corporate elite. The firm's client
list—including Pan Am, GM, CBS, and Coca-Cola—reads like
a condensed version of the Fortune 500. Also like JLW, Landauer shuns hard-sell tactics. The mood in its whisper-quiet
offices (located coincidentally in the Pan Am Building) is
reminiscent of a distinguished law firm. John White—a polished gentleman inclined to dark wool suits and sober silk
ties—could easily pass for a former Supreme Court justice
winding up his career as a senior partner at Millbank, Tweed,
Hadley & McCloy.

"We don't just buy and sell properties like ordinary brokers," White declares, with the haughtiness of John Hous-
man's professor Kingsfield. "You might say we are a real
estate version of the investment banker but on a private
basis. Our sales of large properties are accomplished as private transactions with large institutions such as life insurance companies or pension funds and with the major investors, real estate investment and development companies.
And unlike brokerage firms, we are always assured a minimum fee for accepting the engagement and a performance
fee if we succeed. For every placement, we study, we research, we advise. Then if a sale is in order, we agree to
conduct it. But only if it is in order."

That was the question facing White when Pan Am first
brought its corporate crisis to his doorstep in 1977. At the
time, Pan Am owned (through its corporate lessee Grand
Central Building, Inc., GCB) 55 percent of the building that
bore its name. After an initial review of the property and
the current real estate market—"to determine if a sale was
in order"—White and Landauer Senior Vice President Grant

Green informed Maloon of their belief that the airline could earn an enormous gain on its investment in the building—enough to temporarily resuscitate the carrier's flagging finances—providing Pan Am agreed to buy out the building's 45 percent minority leasehold and the underlying land (then leased from the Penn Central Railroad). Deferring to Landauer's expertise in property marketing, Pan Am quickly agreed to proceed on this basis. But there were obstacles ahead.

"The Pan Am Building's future was cloudy at best," Green notes. "The owners, other than Pan Am, were the estate of Erwin Wolfson, which owned 40 percent of the leasehold, and William Zimmerman, Wolfson's attorney prior to his death, who owned 5 percent. Several lawsuits were pending among GCB's shareholders. In one, two minority shareholders had sued GCB and Pan Am because the GCB board, 50 percent of which was controlled by Pan Am, did not choose to pay any dividend. Instead it held back these funds for anticipated capital expenditures. . . ."*

Green knew that these conflicts would obfuscate Pan Am's attempts to secure 100 percent ownership of the property. Compounding this was a difficulty in determining the property's value.

"Most of the original twenty-to-thirty-year leases in the building had been made in 1963," Green continues. "Although lease clauses required tenants to reimburse the owners for increases in real estate taxes and operating expenses, the clauses also imposed varying ceilings on these escalators. Neither the building's owners nor the tenants had anticipated serious and substantial inflation in the relative economic tranquility of the early 1960s. No one could then have foreseen the devastation that the escalation ceilings contained in the original leases could produce, once inflation began to move sharply upward in 1966. In essence, they fixed rents, while building expenses mounted rapidly."**

* *Real Estate Review.* pg. 24, Summer 1982.
** Ibid.

Because the old leases would be expiring over a number of years—and would then be replaced by higher rental agreements—it was difficult to project the building's future revenues and net operating income. But Landauer knew fully well that the property's marketability—as well as the price it could fetch—could not be determined until meaningful projections reflecting these increases were developed. With this in mind, Green and White assigned a team of outside software consultants to write a custom computer program to calculate all the variables on the property's financial performance.

"The program automatically inserted estimated new market rents as leases expired, deleted the old limited expense escalation reimbursements, substituted a new base year beyond which the tenant pays its full share of all future expense increases, and assured a new formula for operating expense reimbursements," Green notes. "The results were very revealing. It was apparent that the real estate would show only very modest net income until 1983–84, when 1,150,000 square feet of leases expired. Together with Pan Am's 350,000 square feet,* this 1.5 million total square feet of released space represented 67 percent of the 2.25 million rentable square feet in the building. The real estate market in the meanwhile was undergoing a substantial recovery. Thus while the return until 1983–84 was meager, there was every prospect of significant rent increases and dramatically improved net operating income thereafter. If the minority interests in the leasehold were to be acquired, it was critical to do so as quickly as possible."

White moved with dispatch, first approaching the minority lessees who, it was rumored, had been offered a deal for their interests by Harry Helmsley. Because Helmsley was notorious for insisting on seller financing, White believed he could snatch the deal away by offering the lessees cash. The ploy worked.

---

* The amount of space Pan Am occupied.

"I felt that an all-cash offer would be attractive to the seller and we managed to conclude a transaction for the 45 percent interest for under $10 million," White recalls. "As a condition of the sale, all suits between the shareholders were dropped. Looking back at the $10 million 1979 price, it seems incredibly cheap in light of the ensuing inflation in rents and values."

With surprising ease, Landauer successfully negotiated what had appeared to be its most difficult hurdle. In short order, Pan Am owned all the shares in the GCB and completely controlled the leasehold. But a sticky problem remained. Penn Central, then bogged down in bankruptcy proceedings, had title to the land under the building. Any offer Pan Am might make for the land would require the approval of the Bankruptcy Court, which could take months. Even more troublesome, Pan Am's public offer for the property could start a bidding war. Under the bankruptcy laws, another party making a high bid could seize the land out from under Pan Am.

But White, cagy deal maker that he is, came up with a ploy to diffuse this threat. After intense negotiations with Victor Palmieri Associates, the turnaround consultants representing Penn Central's trustees, he decided to make an offer to purchase the 150,000-square-foot parcel for $25 million. The modest price of $167 per square foot was possible because the land was tied to a lease, the rents for which were then very low. To protect the deal from the pitfalls of court proceedings, White delayed the "closing of the land purchase until the emergence from bankruptcy of the renamed Penn Central Corporation, thus avoiding the need for formal court approval of the transaction. The seller's emergence from bankruptcy eliminated the possibility of the intervention of a last-minute high bid . . . Now Pan Am, through GCB, was the 100 percent owner of the land, building and all improvements. The land purchase provided, of course, that continued use of the subsurface for Conrail and Amtrak rail service under long-standing agreements could continue. At this point, inclusive of the first mortgage, Pan Am had an investment before depreciation of about $105 million in the property."*

Shortly after the land sale was consummated, another timing factor came into play—one for which White, for all his talent as a real estate mover and shaker, could not take credit. The Manhattan rental market soared skyward, well in advance of Landauer's earlier projections, catapulting rents in all the major commercial districts to new highs. Convinced that this was the time to sell (January 1980), Maloon instructed Green to calculate a new set of income projections—to reflect the spiraling rents—and to prepare an offering statement for the property on this basis.

Landauer's revised calculations took the shape of a sixteen-year cash flow projection, designed to reveal the impact of renegotiating expired leases at substantially higher rentals.

"The allure of the building was in the knowledge that 67 percent of the leases, inclusive of Pan Am's take-back lease, would expire by 1984," Green explains. "The average rent level at the time of sale, even with Pan's office space at the market, was only about $13 a square foot. Fifty percent of the leased space was due for renewal in 1983 to 1984, and was renting at an average under $10 a rentable square foot whereas the rent matrix projected the renewal value at about $35 per average rentable square foot."**

Based on this, White believed, at first, that the building could fetch $325 million. Upon further study, however, he upped his estimate to $350 million, then $375 million and finally $400 million. This bold projection took Pan Am's senior executives by surprise; few, if any, had believed the building could command so high a price. But White was convinced that a sophisticated buyer would perceive the full value of future rent increases, thus finding the $400 million an appropriate sum.

When the final go-ahead to sell was given in April 1980,

* Ibid.
** Ibid.

Landauer immediately set its sites on major U.S. and European pension funds, both of which were moving more aggressively toward real estate investments.

"I also believed that major life insurance companies might be interested despite the disintermediation they had sustained in the high interest environment from increased policy loans and loss of guaranteed income contract business," White says. "I thought they might form a small consortium among themselves to buy."

Independent investors and developers were all but eliminated from consideration, dependent as they were on commercial bank financing. With the prime hovering at the forbidden altitude of 20 percent, staggering debt service would eat into their profit potential.

His target market narrowed primarily to the big financial institutions, White decided to conduct a limited marketing campaign aimed at a select group of prominent pension funds and insurance companies. This less-is-more approach was also born from his concern that an indiscriminate sales effort might create an image of weakness, prompting speculation that Pan Am was pressed to unload a problem property. It was no secret that the building had been laboring under the dual burdens of rising costs and restrictive leases.

To counter any notion of a fire sale, White took the offensive, presenting the property on the basis of its strong income projections rather than its past performance. His air of confidence—based partly on a talent for market preparation that distinguishes top brokers—made it seem as if he were selling Central Park for $100 an acre.

To further bolster the image of strength, prospective buyers were not asked to bid,—they were *permitted* to bid, providing they first qualified for the honor. As a prerequisite for receiving his offering statement, White demanded that would-be bidders prove they could afford the purchase, that they sign a confidentiality agreement not to divulge the offering material to outsiders, that they obtain Landauer's approval to give the documents to possible joint venturers, and that they agree to idemnify Pan Am and Landauer from any commission liability to a broker or other third parties. Incredibly, thirty-five financial institutions—all of those on Landauer's hit list—agreed to the terms; and phase one of the sale was underway.

Keenly aware that the broker's presentation can color the market's perception of a property, White structured an integrated campaign designed to convey the impression of a premium building. If the medium is the message, the message here was that the successful bidder would have to dig deep into its corporate purse to walk away with the prize.

"Several large transactions during the prior two years had been concluded at prices that were larger than the original asking price," Green explains. "This was anomalous because the term 'asking price' implies that it is the value ceiling that the buyer should approach. White hit on a substitute term, the 'most probable selling price.' This term avoided the implication that the price was a ceiling. It was the most likely price and buyers could pay more if they desired."*

With the elaborate offering brochures and an accompanying fifteen-minute audio-visual presentation cleared by Pan Am, White dispatched a high-level Landauer team to meet with target prospects in Europe and the United States. Quickly, it became apparent that at least ten offers could be forthcoming. To make the most of this, and to keep the parties competing against each other for a protracted period of time, White asked each interested buyer to submit an initial offer by July 9, 1980. Landauer agreed to respond to each by July 16. Then a second round of offers could be made and submitted by July 23, culminating in Pan Am's announcement of the highest bidder by noon of July 28.

The two-phased offering procedure, keyed to a set time schedule, prevented the possibility of a preemptive bid that might prematurely halt the bidding process, artificially limiting the sales price. Again, White was acting contrary to

* Ibid.

standard brokerage practice. Typically a preemptive bid is sought after because it is a guaranteed sale at substantial terms. But the downside is often overlooked.

In the rush to accept the preemptive bid, the seller eliminates other prospects that may, given the time and the opportunity, come forth with even more generous offers. No one knows this better than the preemptive bidder himself. Typically, he uses the quick strike tactic to weaken insecure sellers, boldly cutting off competitors before they have the opportunity to eliminate him. He uses time, not money, as his most potent weapon. But by carefully structuring the bidding process—by forcing all prospects to comply with a published timetable—the broker controls the clock and, in his own way, manipulates the bidding.

More of White's brilliantly conceived strategy was unveiled in the July 16–23 period. Landauer executives met with each of the major players, not to thank them for their bids, but to suggest ways of improving them. Again White kept all the parties in the dark. No one was told how much the others had bid nor by how much they would have to improve their offers to stay in the running. The only message was to aim higher, higher, higher—without limit.

By noon of July 23, Landauer had four substantially improved offers, two of which immediately surfaced as the top contenders. One was superior in price; the other on terms. After two more days of deliberation, Pan Am announced its decision. On Friday, January 25, the airline's chief executive, William Seawell, telephoned Robert Schwartz, vice chairman and chief financial officer of Metropolitan Life, to reveal that the insurance company was the prospective new owner of the Pan Am Building. The price . . . $400 million. The flag carrier's gain on the real estate sale, roughly $270 million, was more than it had earned in the previous ten years of flying airplanes.

"The sale of the Pan Am Building and the subsequent sale of the airline's Intercontinental Hotel division for $500 million—another real estate deal—were crucial to the corpo-

ration's survival," says an airline analyst for Shearson/
American Express. "Both came at the time when Pan Am
was in desperate need of cash."

Pan Am had clearly joined the land rush. The fever
was spreading.

Says Landauer's Green:

> The sale undoubtedly heightened interest in the sale
> and lease-back of headquarters and regional office build-
> ings of major corporations. It represents a new method
> of financing in which cash can be raised and capital
> gains of an unusual amount realized. The sale lease-
> back can be an effective alternate to more conventional
> financing methods as commercial banks, bond issues or
> use of internally generated monies. . . .*

Adds Landauer's Executive Vice President John Bailey:

> Corporate real estate managers are beginning to use
> real estate as a profit center. They are recognizing that
> their real estate assets have, in some cases, far more
> value than the figures listed at cost on their books.

> If properties are converted to dollars, that money can
> be plowed back into the company's principal business—
> and the company can make more money than by simply
> owning and occupying real estate, or by occupying real
> estate inefficiently . . .

> Pan Am was sitting on a very valuable asset, but the
> dollars were more valuable to the firm in the operation
> of its business . . . As long as there is a cash squeeze
> and high interest rates, corporate finance people should
> look at their facilities to see whether or not they can
> sell or lease a property, move to a less expensive facility,
> and reemploy the capital more profitably in the business
> operation.**

---

* Ibid.
** Ann Nydele, *Facilities & Design Management*, June 1982.

This cashing in on real assets is not limited to potential bankruptcy candidates. Its appetite whetted by Pan Am's success, General Motors—the airline's neighbor on Manhattan's East Side—decided to put its fifty-story, marble-faced New York headquarters on the market for $500 million. Hungry for cash to fuel a $40 billion crash modernization campaign required to produce competitive cars for the eighties, the auto giant had tripled its long-term debt from $880 million to $2.5 billion. Selling the office tower for half a billion would provide substantially more capital without the heavy interest costs of additional borrowing.

With its reputation—thanks in part to the Pan Am coup—approaching that of a real estate miracle worker, Landauer was hired to perform similar magic for GM. But by the time the behemoth from Detroit brought its tower to market in April 1981, New York rents had flattened again— buyers were fewer and more squeamish—and GM's price tag of $500 million was considered too big—for an outright purchase, that is.

But prime real estate's great advantage as a corporate asset is its adaptability to a wide range of financing schemes. If the value is there, creative strategists will find a way to extract it. Stymied in their attempt to conduct a traditional sale, White and GM's treasurer Robert O'Connell made an end run around the market, striking an interesting deal with Corporate Property Investors, a real estate investment outfit owned in part by major pension funds. The terms provided GM with its $500 million but in the form of a low-interest loan. Basically, the deal called for GM to pay CPI 10 percent interest on a ten-year loan, rather than the 15 percent it would have had to pay in the money markets.

The savings—which GM owed to its real estate holdings—came to a cool $250 million. As a sweetener, by structuring the transaction in the form of a loan, GM did not have to pay capital gains taxes on the difference between the building's $100 million cost and its proposed sale price.

But what was in it for CPI? Why lend $500 million at five points below the going rate of return? The deal gave CPI the option to buy the GM building in 1991 for $500 million. (Until then, GM owned the building.) In accepting the terms of the equity loan, CPI was betting that in an inflationary decade the property would appreciate substantially beyond the striking price.

Reading between the lines, we see that GM effectively used real estate to finance the production of Cadillacs, Oldsmobiles, Pontiacs, Buicks, and Chevies.

Shortly after the transaction was completed, a New York brokerage executive summed it up this way:

"Airlines come and go; automakers roar and putter out; boom times turn to recessions and come full cycle again. Through it all real estate survives. *Only real estate.*"

Index